Northumberland County, Virginia

DEEDS, WILLS, INVENTORIES, ETC.

1737-1743

Mary Marshall Brewer

HERITAGE BOOKS
2019

HERITAGE BOOKS
AN IMPRINT OF HERITAGE BOOKS, INC.

Books, CDs, and more—Worldwide

For our listing of thousands of titles see our website
at
www.HeritageBooks.com

Published 2019 by
HERITAGE BOOKS, INC.
Publishing Division
5810 Ruatan Street
Berwyn Heights, Md. 20740

International Standard Book Number
Paperbound: 978-1-68034-827-9

NORTHUMBERLAND COUNTY, VIRGINIA
DEEDS, WILLS, INVENTORIES, ETC.
1737-1743

Will. Grace Span of Northumberland Co. 16 Feb 1737. To my brother
Cuthbert Spann all my estate. 10 Apr 1738 this nuncupative will of Grace Spann
decd was presented in Northumberland Co Court by Cuthbert Spann adminr
which is admitted to record. Attest: James Fontaine clerk. (Pg 1)

Will. Edward Turner of St. Stephens Parish, Northumberland Co. 22 Feb 1737.
... [faded] ... to sons William Turner & Edwin Turner my land ... to dau Mary?
Turner my best bed with bedstead ... my will is that my estate be divided
between my five children that is Wm, Edwin, Mary, John & Elizabeth ... 80 lbs
of tobacco in John Jones' hands ... [faded] .... Wit: John Turner, Rebecca
Garner. Proved 10 Apr 1738 by the wits & Fielding Turner adminr with the will
annexed made oath thereto & on his motion the same is admitted to record.
Attest: James Fontaine clerk. (Pg 1)

In obedience to an order of Northumberland Co Court dated 14 Mar 1737 we
John Coles, Richard Smith & Wm Downing appraisers did meet at the house of
Israel Fogg & being first sworn by Capt John S[?] have appraised the estate of
Thos Foulson decd: pewter, candle box, cows & calves, beds, bedsteads,
pillows, rugs, blankets, books, table, lumber, glass bottles, 1 bull, 13 hogs, 7
pigs, 1 old spinning wheel, trunk, old chest, iron pott, pot hooks, etc. [Not
totaled] Abner Neale & James Fignor adminrs. Israel Fogg, Leah Fogg. This
appraisement of the estate of Thos Folson decd was presented into court 10 Apr
1738 by Abner Neale & James Fignor adminrs & admitted to record. (Pg 2)

In obedience to an order of court held 13 Mar 1737/8 John Foushee, Robt Clark
& John Lewis appraisers have met at the house of John Lancaster decd &
appraised all & singular the estate of the afsd John Lancaster as was presented to
our view: 1 horse, 1 mare, 4 cows, 1 cow & calf, 2 young steers, 1 heifer, 5
barrels of Indian corn, flock bed & stead, feather bed, trunnel bed, sheets,
blankets, ruggs, pillow, all his wearing apparrell, table cloth, 1 book, etc.
Negroes: man named Tom, woman named Vilet, woman named Winney, man
boy named Will. [Not totaled]. Presented in court by Wm Boaz exor 10 ---
1738 by admitted to record. Attest: James Fontaine clerk. (Pg 4)

9 Jan 1737. Deed of Lease. Thomas Everit of Great Wiccomoco Parish,
Northumberland Co for 5 sl leased unto John Nutt of same place a tr of land in
the sd parish it being pt/o the tr of land the sd Thos Everit now doth live on
containing [?] bounded by Feoging Swamp ... for 6 months ... . Wit: Aaron

2

Taylor, John Taylor, Thos Short. Ackn 10 Apr 1738 by Thos Everit & Hannah Everit (the sd Hannah being first privily examined by Mathew Quill & Mathew Kenner gent & at the motion of the sd John Nutt admitted to record. Attest: James Fontaine clerk.

9 Jan 1737/8. Bond. I Thomas Everitt of Great Wiccocomoco Parish, Northumberland Co am firmly bound unto John Nutt of same place for 100 pd ... the condition of this obligation is such if the sd Thomas Everitt shall well & truly perform & fulfill the covenants, grants & articles on his part mentioned in the [above] deed then this obligation to be void ... . Wit: Aaron Taylor, John Taylor, Thos Short. Ackn 30 Apr 1738 & admitted to record. Attest; James Fontaine clerk.

8 Apr 1738. Deed of Lease. Edward Lawrance of St. Stephens Parish, Northumberland Co planter for 5 sl leased unto Rodham Kenner of same place a 268 a. tr of land which was granted to the sd Lawrence by patent dated 22 Apr 1731 bounded by the land formerly of Richard Thompson (Tomson), the land formerly of Henry Massey now of John Lewis & Claughtons Cr ... during the term of 6 months ... . Wit: John Lewis, James Shaughan, Michael Ryan. Ackn 18 Apr 1738 by Edward Lawrence & Sarah Lawrence (Sarah being first privately examined by John Waughop & Mathew Quill & admitted to record. Attest: James Fontaine clerk.

10 Apr 1738. Deed of Release. Edward Lawrence of St. Stephens Parish, Northumberland Co planter for 300 pd sold & released unto Rodham Kenner of same place gent a 268 a. tr of land ... [same as above] ... . Wit: John Lewis, James Shaughan, Michael Ryan. Ackn 10 Apr 1738 by Edward Lawrence & Sarah Lawrence (the sd Sarah being first privily examined by John Waughop & Mathew Quill gent & admitted to record. Attest: James Fontaine clerk.

10 Apr 1738. Bond. I Edward Lawrance of St. Stephens Parish, Northumberland Co am firmly bound unto Rodham Kenner for 600 pd ... the condition of this obligation is such that whereas the afsd Edward Lawrence hath by deeds of lease & release [see above] sold unto the sd Rodham Kenner a tr of land, if the sd Edward Lawrance does well & truly perform, fulfill & accomplish all ye articles, clauses & covenants mentioned in the sd deeds of lease & release then this obligation to be void ... . Wit: John Lewis, James Shaughan, Michael Ryan. Ackn by Edward Lawrance 10 Apr 1738 & admitted to record. Attest: James Fontaine clerk.

10 Apr 1738. Deed. Thos Berry of Wiccocomoco Parish, Northumberland Co for 80 pd sold to John Stott Junr of St. Mary's White Chappel, Lancaster Co a 200 a. tr of land in Wiccocomoco Parish bounded by Wm Barrett, Nuleans Cr &

David Lattimore, by certain bounds proposed to Flaxpon Cove, it being pt/o a patent formerly granted to Henry Wicker decd dated 29 Nov 1652 ... & the sd Thos Berry doth hereby covenant & agree together with his now wife Patience to acknowledge this deed in court upon demand .... Wit: John Berry, Partin James. Ackn 10 Apr 1738 & admitted to record. Attest: James Fontaine clerk.

Will. John Shurley. 17 Jan 1737/8. To my son John Shurley my home plantation. To my son Danll Shurley my lands at the Coach Road adj to the lands of my brother Richard Shurley decd. To my afsd son John one feather bed & furniture. To my son Danll one feather bed & furniture. To my son Argaland Shurley one feather bed & furniture. To my son Joseph Shurley one feather bed & furniture. To my dau Grace one feather bed & furniture. I give to my dau Elizabeth one feather bed & furniture. I give to my afsd children all the rest of my estate to be divided amongst them. I appoint my son John Shurley my executor. Wit: John Foushee. Proved 10 Apr 1738 & admitted to record. Attest: John Fontaine clerk.

8 Apr 1738. In obedience to an order of court dated 14 Mar 1737/8 John Coles, Richard Smith & Wm Downing did meet at the house of Israel Fogg & did appraise the estate of Thos Foulson decd in money & did possess the sd Israel Fogg & Leah his wife with 1/3 pt/o the sd decd's estate according to our division. This report was returned 15 Apr 1738 & recorded. Attest: James Fontaine clerk.

10 Dec 1737. Deed. Edwin Fielding of Great Wiccocomocco Parish, Northumberland Co for 1600 lbs of lawfull tobacco sold to Thomas Davis of same place a 40 a. parcel of land in the sd parish bounded by the land of the sd Edwin Fielding, Reedy Br, Esqr Robert Carter, Joseph Heales & Ambrose Fielding .... Wit: Aaron Taylor, George Smith. Ackn 2 May 1738 by Edwin Fielding & Judith his wife (she being first privily examined by John Waugh & Matthew Quill gent) & admitted to record. Attest: James Fontaine clerk.

4 May 1738. Deed. William Wildy of St. Stephens Parish, Northumberland Co for 1,660 lbs of lawfull tobacco & three pistoles sold to Ellis Gill of same parish a 15 ½ a. parcel of land in the sd parish bounded by a br that leads up to Motley's old field, land formerly of William Hobson & the main road that leads from the Church to Motley's old field .... Wit: Tho Gill, George Berry, John Resterson. Ackn 8 May 1738 by Wm Wildy & Winifred his wife (she being first privily examined by John Waugh & Mathew Quill gent) & admitted to record. Attest: James Fontaine clerk.

4 May 1738. Bond. I William Wildy of St. Stephens Parish, Northumberland Co am firmly bound unto Ellis Gill of same place in the penal sum of 3,320 lbs

of lawful tobacco in casks ... the condition of this obligation is such that if the afsd Wm Wildy do & shall well & truly observe, perform, fulfill, accomplish & keep the covenants, articles, clauses, conditions & agreements mentioned in the [above] deed then this obligation to be void ... . Wit: Thos Gill, George Berry, John Resterson. Ackn 8 May 1738 & admitted to record. Attest: James Fontaine clerk.

6 May 1738. Deed of Lease. Between Wm Mash of Wiccocomon Parish, Northumberland Co & Samll Webb of St. Stephens Parish, same co, wit that the afsd Wm Mash for divers good causes considerations him thereunto moving but more especially for & in consideration that the sd Samuel Webb is to maintain the sd William Mash in good & sufficient diet, cloaths & lodging whereof the sd William Mash doth hereby ackn himself fully satisfied & contented doth grant, bargain & lett unto Samll Webb a 40 a. parcel of land in Wiccomomon Parish during the term of the sd Samuel Webb & his now wife Mary Webb's life ... . Wit: Will Webb, James Mash, James Webb. Ackn 8 May 1738 & admitted to record. Attest: James Fontaine clerk.

6 May 1738. Bond. William Mash of Wiccomomon Parish, Northumberland Co am firmly bound unto Samll Webb of St. Stephens Parish, same co for 12,000 lbs of good sound tobacco in cask ... the condition of this obligation is such that if the sd Wm Mash shall fulfill & keep all covenants & conditions in the [above] deed then this obligation to be void ... . Wit: Will Webb, James Mash, James Webb. Ackn 8 May 1738 & admitted to record. Attest: James Fontaine clerk.

18 May 1738. Deed of Lease. Bridgar Haynie of St. Stephens Parish, Northumberland Co for 1,000 lbs of tobacco leased to Thomas Dameron a 50 a. parcel of land called the Narrow Neck & being pt/o the land that was given to him by his father Col Richard Haynie in St. Stephens Parish ... during the term of 16 years ... [faded] ... . Wit: Thos Pew, Samll Downing, Richard Haynie. Ackn 12 Jun 1738 & recorded. Attest: James Fontaine clerk.

18 May 1738. Bond. I Bridgar Haynie of St. Stephens Parish, Northumberland Co am firmly bound unto Thomas Dameron of same parish for [?] thousand lbs of tobacco ... the condition of this obligation is such that if the afsd Bridgar Haynie shall observe, perform, fulfill & keep the articles & covenants in the [above] deed of lease then this obligation to be void ... . Wit: Thos Pew, Samll Downing, Richard Haynie. Ackn 12 Jun 1738 & recorded. Attest: James Fontaine clerk.

28 Apr 1738. Deed of Lease. John Neale of St. Stephens Parish, Northumberland Co planter for [?] leased to Elias Edmonds of same parish ... [faded] ... bought by Hannah Neale widow & relict of Christopher Neale decd

from Thos Macclane decd ... . Wit: James Pen, Peter Barcroft, Michl Ryan. Ackn 12 Jun 1738 & recorded. Attest: James Fontaine clerk.

29 Apr 1738. Deed of Release. John Neale of St. Stephens Parish, Northumberland Co planter for 150 pd sold & released to Elias Edmonds of same place planter a 200 a. tr of land in St. Stephens Parish adj a tr of land formerly granted to Hugh Ley & the brs of Coan River, less 140 a., pt/o the pattent formerly granted to Matthew Rodham by [?] to Michael Vanlandingham? & by sd Vanlandingham sold to Christopher Neale decd ... [faded] ... & bought by Hannah Neale widow & relict of Christopher Neale decd from Thomas Mcclane ... . Wit: James Pen, Peter Barcroft, Michl Ryan. Ackn 12 Jun 1738 & recorded. Attest: James Fontaine clerk.

29 Apr 1738. Bond. I John Neale of St. Stephens Parish, Northumberland Co planter am firmly bound unto Elias Edmonds of same place for 300 pd ... the condition of this obligation is such that if the sd John Neale shall well & truly perform, fulfill & accomplish the clauses, covenants & agreements in the [above] deeds then this obligation to be void ... . Wit: James Pen, Peter Barcroft, Michl Ryan. Ackn 12 Jun 1738 & recorded. Attest: James Fontaine clerk.

3 Jun 1738. Deed. John Algood & Mary his wife of St. Stephens Parish, Northumberland Co for 2,000 lbs of tobacco sold to Peter Presly of same parish a tr of land (being the dower of the sd Mary as relict of Clement Corbett decd) formerly was 227 a. & by the will of the sd Clement Corbett devised to the sd Peter Presley ... adj William Haynie ... . Wit: Charles [?], Robt Davis?, Silvester Welsh, Thomas Stegman?. Ackn 12 Jun 1738 & recorded. Attest: James Fontaine clerk.

-- Jun 1738. Deed. John West of Northumberland Co for 50 pd sold to John Kennedy a 37 a. tr of land being in Cherry Point adj the land of James Turnstal & Allen [?], which being the land where John Jones did formerly dwell on ... . Wit: Lindsey Opie, James Strangham. Ackn 13 Jun 1738 & recorded. Attest: James Fontaine clerk.

[Will faded] 12 Jun 1738 this will was proved in Northumberland Co Court as the will of John Watts decd on the oaths of Wm Taylor & Jams Brennan wits thereto & Ellinor A[?] adminr with the will annexed & recorded. Attest: James Fontaine clerk.

Power of Attorney. William Craig, William Hervart & Richard Hark of Glasgow, North Britain merchants whereas Wm Craig ... [faded & blurred] ... . Wit: John Graham, Wm McCaull, Archibald Gillchrist notary publick. This power of atty from William Craig, William Hervart & Richd Hark to William Dunlop was proved in Northumberland Co Court by ye oaths of John Graham & Wm McCaull wits thereto & admitted to record. Attest: James Fontaine clerk.

Will.   Thomas Brown of St. Stephens Parish, Northumberland Co.   22 Apr 1736.   To my son Thos Brown the tr of land which I now live on & if the sd Thomas Brown should die without heirs, then I give it to my son Footman Brown.   The rest of my estate I do desire may be divided between my wife & children after funeral charges & debts paid.   I ordain my wife & William Taylor executors.   My lands by her my sd wife freely to be possessed of until my children should come of age to take their parts.   Wit: John Lewis, Parish Garner. Proved 10 Jun 1738 & admitted to record.   Attest: James Fontaine clerk.

Will.   Mary Young of Cherry Point.   17 Apr 1738.   To Ann Taite my spinning wheel & boards.   To Ann Taite six yards of siersucker?.   To Frances Garner my side saddles & bridles.   To Hannah Garner my horses.   To Ann Taite & Frances Garner a peel of lace & edging.   To Susanna Blinco? 3 yards of blew [?] & 4 yards of blew & white [?].   To Mary Jones my black apron & fann & white necklace.   To Elizabeth Johnston my clock & linnen pettycoat & huckaback jacket & one plad pettycoat.   To Mr. Taite's house wench Nan one brown linnen pettycoat & one brown linnen jacket.   To Parish Garner my biggest chest.   To Thomas Stanley my smallest chest.   My pewter & potts to be divided between Ann Metcalf & Elizabeth Metcalf & Hannah Garner & Spelman Garner.   To Frances Garner one [?] & pigen & my earthen ware.   To Parish Garner what corn I have & to lueving? William Taite & Parish Garner my whole estate.   Wit: Parish Garner, Thos Stanley.   Proved 12 Jun 1738 & admitted to record.   Attest: James Fontaine clerk.

In obedience to an order of Northumberland Co Court dated 8 May 1738 we John Claughton, Richard Claughton & Geo Larnkin appraisers met at the house of Edward Turner decd & settled the acct in tobacco & money & paid Henry Metcalf decd's estate out of Edward Turner's according to ye motion of Fielding Turner adminr: Bed & furniture, 4 bushells & 3 pecks of Indian corn, 2 cows & calves, 6 hogs, 3 piggs, 1 pot & hooks, frying pan, 1 sheep, 4 earthen pans, 2 earthen potts, pewter, 1 chest, 3 hoes, 1 old pail.   John Turner the children's part: 2 beds, bedsteds & furniture, 1 old chest, 1 old box, some carpenters tools, 2 guns, some salt, pair of cash scales, 1 warming pann, peel of tar'd leather, 1 gun, etc. [Not totaled] This account of the division of the estate of Henry Metcalf decd & the estate of Edward Turner decd was returned 12 Jun 1738 by Fielding Turner adminr of Edward Turner decd & admitted to record.   Attest: James Fontaine clerk.

1738.   The estate of Edward Turner decd to? Fielding Turner ... [illegible] ...

decd's estate. Sums paid to Josias Clonere, Priscila Turner the decd's widow, a coffin on burying of Wm Jones, John Jones, Joseph Garner, John Turner, William Calley, Maj Turbervile, Richard Jackson merchant, Thos Jones. 1879 [tobacco?]. Sums received of crop of tobacco, George Rigens, John Letham. 1859 [tobacco?]. Errors excepted 10 Jun 1738 per Fielding Turner adminr. This account of Fielding Turner's agt the estate of Edward Turner decd was exhibited into Northumberland Co Court by the sd Fielding Turner & admitted to record. Attest: James Fontaine clerk.

10 Jul 1738. An additional inventory of pt/o the estate of John Gains decd. To debts recd 1,425 lbs of tobacco. George Ball Junr. This additional inventory of the estate of John Gains decd was presented into Northumberland Co Court by George Ball Junr executor of the sd decd & admitted to record. Attest: James Fontaine clerk.

In obedience to an order of court dated 12 Jun 1738 we Griffin Fauntleroy Junr, John Cralle & Bennit Boggess met at the house of William Taite & have appraised the estate of Mary Young decd that was brought to our view in money. Parcel of earthenware, 1 horse, 1 woman's side saddle & 2 saddle cloths, 1 bridle, 20 lb pewter & 2 brass candlesticks, 6 yards seersuccor, 1 old meal bag, 1 pewter tankard, pewter spoons, 1 brass spoon, 2 iron potts, 1 narrow ax, an old hoe, 2 old frying pans, an old skillet, 1 chest, etc. 11 pd 6 sl 5 pn. Wm Taite executor. This inventory of the estate of Mary Young decd was presented into Northumberland Co court 10 Jul 1738 by Wm Taite executor of the sd decd & admitted to record. Attest: James Fontain clerk.

In obedience to an order of Northumberland Co Court dated 12 Jan 1738 we James Farned, John Lewis & Ormsby Haynes appraisers being first sworn before Mathew Quill gent met at the house of the decd Thos Brown & appraised the estate in money. 5 cows & calves, 3 heifers, 16 sheep, 4 hogs, 1 mare & horse colt, 1 horse, beds & furniture, oval table, small chest, spinning wheel, cut saw, file, 1 old large chest, 12 flag chairs, 1 brass candlestick, a peel of books, 1 gun, old violin, 33 ½ lbs of pewter, 2 iron skillets, a parcel of wooden ware, etc. To the whole crop of tobacco & debts 2714. William Taylor, Ellinor Brown executors. This appraisement of the estate of Thomas Brown decd was exhibited 10 Jul 1738 in Northumberland Co Court & admitted to record. Attest: James Fontaine clerk.

Will. Sarah Bowley (Bowly) of St. Stephens Parish, Northumberland Co. 17 Jan 1737/8. To my dau Judith Read one feather bed & furniture & bedstead. To my dau Sarah Smith one feather bed & furniture & high bedstead. To my granddau Sarah Ann Bowly one new feather bed & furniture & one trundle bedstead, one 2 year old heiffer, two dishes, five plates one flowered tankard, one salt cellar & one poason? with cremer to it, one gold ring & silver [?], one chest, one box iron & heaters & one pot & hooks, 10 yards of Brembages. To my dau Judith Read my horse & saddle. To my dau Sarah Smith one great pot. To all three of my daus Mary, Judith & Sarah my wearing cloaths. All the rest of my estate amongst my five children William Bowley, Simon Bowly & my three daus to be equally divided. My desire is that my son Wm Bowly & my son Simon Bowley be my executors. Wit: Alexander Moorehead, William Nelson. Proved 10 Jul 1738 & admitted to record. Attest: James Fontaine clerk.

11 Jul 1738. Agreeable to an order of Northumberland Co Court dated 8 Aug 1737 we George Ball & Will Eustace met on the lands in dispute between the churchwardens of St. Stephens Parish & Howson Kenner & viewed the lines which the Rev. Francis Part & the afsd Kenner refused to have processioned for a division between the Glebe Land & Howson Kenner & having heard the partys & examined evidences we do order & determine that the dividing line between the afsd [lands?] to be adj Cherry Point Road proved to be a corner tree to Glebe Land by the deaths of James Farned & Benjamin Bustle as by a juries report dated 6 May 1735, the course mentioned in an escheat deed granted to Wm Dare from the proprietors office dated 5 Nov 1715 & by the sd Dare assigned to Francis Kenner & the Rappahannock Road as set forth in the afsd escheat deed .... . This report of the dividing line between the Glebe Land & St. Stephens Parish & Howson Kenner was returned 11 Jul 1738 & recorded. Attest: James Fontaine clerk.

7 Jul 1738. According to the direction of an order of Northumberland Co Court dated 13 Apr 1738 we George Ball & Thos Berry did on 28th day of the sd month meet at the plantation of William Lance he being absent (as it was sd had left the co by Martha his wife) being first sworn gave an acct of what estate Abraham Ingram was possessed with at the time of his death & according to the sd acct have estimated to 60 pd 19 sl 9 pn & according to the direction of the order of sd court dated 12 Jun 1738 we have delivered unto Samll Ingram 29 pd 4 sl 6 pn it being his pt/o his decd father Abraham Ingram's estate after funeral expenses deducted. This report of the division of Abraham Ingram's estate was returned 10 Jul 1738 & recorded. Attest: James Fontaine clerk.

22 May 1738. Deed of Lease. Joseph Millard & Jane (Jean) his wife of Methaponia in St. Stephens Parish, Northumberland Co planter for 5 sl leased to Wm Gill of Cherry Point in same parish planter a 174 a. tr of land in Cherry Point in St. Stephens Parish whereon the sd Wm Gill now lives formerly granted by patent to John Roche & by him sold to Thomas Millard decd bounded by John Opie, Wm Gardner & Capt Opie's landing ... during the term of 6 months .... . Wit: Thomas Myears, Thomas Taylor, Michael Ryan. Ackn -- Jul 1738 & admitted to record. Attest: James Fontaine clerk.

23 May 1738. Deed of Release. Joseph Millard & Jane (Jean) his wife of Methaponia in St. Stephens Parish, Northumberland Co planter for [?] thousand lbs of tobacco released unto William Gill of Cherry Point in sd parish a 174 a. tr of land ... [same as above] ... . Wit: Thomas Myears, Thomas Taylor, Michael Ryan. Ackn -- Jul 1738 & recorded. Attest: James Fontaine clerk.

23 May 1738. Bond. I Joseph Millard of St. Stephens Parish, Northumberland Co am firmly bound unto Wm Gill of parish afsd in the penal sum of 12,000 lbs of tobacco ...the condition of this obligation is such that whereas the afsd Joseph Millard hath by indenture of lease & release sold unto the afsd William Gill his right to a tr of land in the sd parish, if the sd Joseph Millard do well truly perform & fulfill the articles, clauses, grants & agreements contained in the sd deeds then this obligation to be void ... . [Signed by] Joseph Millard & Jane Millard. Wit: Thomas Myears, Thomas Taylor, Michael Ryan. Ackn 10 Jul 1738 & recorded. Attest: James Fontaine clerk.

10 Jul 1738. Deed. Allen Hunter of Northumberland Co for 40 pd sold to John Kennedy of St. Marys Co, MD a [?] a. tr of land adj John Kennedy's land that he bought of John West, Matt Zeislth's? land & [?] Newton's land ... . Wit: [?], Thos Taylor, Danll Duggins. Ackn 10 Jul 1738 & recorded. Attest: James Fontaine clerk.

10 Apr 1738. Deed. William Hughlet of St. Stephens Parish, Northumberland Co for 2,490 lbs of tobacco sold to Thos Wornum planter of sd co a parcel of land in sd parish upon Great Wiccocomoco River bounded by the sd Thomas Wornum... . Wit: Thos Wornum, Samll Wornum, Wm Smith. Ackn 10 Jul 1738 by Wm Hughlet & Mary his wife (she relinquished all her right of dower in the land) & recorded. Attest: James Fontaine clerk.

13 Mar 1737. Deed. Billington McCarty of North Farnham Parish, Richmond Co for 6,000 lbs of lawfull tobacco sold to James Blackerby of same parish bounded by ... [faded] ... . [Signed by] Billington McCarty, Ann McCarty. Wit: Wm Davenport, John Tilley, Danl Spurlock. Ackn 19 Aug 1738 & recorded. Attest: James Fontaine clerk.

20 Jul 1738. Deed. Thomas Dameron Junr of St. Stephens Parish, Northumberland Co for 12,600 lbs of tobacco sold to Yarrat Hughlet, John Christopher, John Rice & Wm Greenstreet of parish afsd a 564 a. tr of land in the sd parish being a patent granted to Adam Yarrett & the sd Adam gave the sd land to his son William Yarrett by will which sd land being sold at public outcry ... . Wit: Ezekiel Hill, Enock Rice.

26 Jul 1738. Memorandum of Agreement between Yarrat Hughlet, John

Christopher, John Rice & Wm Greenstreet that William Yarrat in his will did leave to the sd Yarrat Hughlet, John Christopher, John Rice & Wm Greenstreet being the sd William Yarrat's God children the use of the sd William Yarrat's land & the sd land being sold at public outcry according to the tennor of the sd Wm Yarrat's will & the sd Yarrat Hughlet, John Christopher, John Rice & Wm Greenstreet being the purchasers of the sd land have made agreeable division & bounds between us … . Wit: Alexander Moorehead, Thomas Dameron. This division of the land of Wm Yarrat decd was presented 14 Aug 1738 & admitted to record. Attest: James Fontaine clerk.

26 Jul 1738. Bond. Yarrat Hughlet, John Christopher, John Rice & Wm Greenstreet of St. Stephens Parish, Northumberland Co are firmly bound each to the other in the penal sum of 100 pd … the condition of this obligation is such that if the sd Yarrat Hughlet, John Christopher, John Rice & Wm Greenstreet bear an equal pt/o all damages, costs or any other charges that shall [?] ye sd land by any other of his God children & our parts so kept & performed specify'd in one Article of Agreement of division [see above] then this obligation to be void … . Wit: Alexander Morehead, Thomas Dameron. Ackn 14 Aug 1738 & admitted to record. Attest: James Fontaine clerk.

An inventory of the estate of Sarah Bowly decd taken 10 Aug 1738: 1 bed & furniture, 1 cow & heifer, 2 iron potts, 3 cyder cask, 5 geese, table & trunk, 1 dish, 1 tankard, 1 looking glass, 1 towell, 2 cups, 1 plate, 1 blanket, 3 napkins, 2 chears, 1 bag, 1 bushell of meal, 1 raw hide, 1 side of leather, 1 knife & fork, 1 hammer, 4 yards of linnen, 1 pottle bottle, 1 pottle molasses, 1 cow, 1 stear, 1 spinning wheal, 1 spit, 1 hoe, iron spit, 2 earthen potts, etc. Taken by Simon Boley. Inventory presented 14 Aug 1738 & admitted to record. Attest: James Fontaine clerk.

19 Jun 1738. In obedience to an order of court dated 18 Jun 1738 we Wm Hobson, Abram Neale & Wm Wildy met at the house of Wm Johnston & being first sworn before Thos Gill having found no acct to audit & settle have appraised all the estate of the sd Wm Johnston which was brought to our view by Thos Hall & Thos Myars securitys of the estate in money: 1 cow & yearling, 2 cows & calves, 1 young bull, bed, boulster, blanket, 1 ax & 2 hoes, 1 table, 1 spinning wheel, 3 cards, leather, cord & hide, 1 earthen pot, 1 chest, 1 old box, some salt, 1 large pott & hook, etc. 29 pd 1 sl 9 pn. This appraisement of the estate of Wm Johnston decd was presented 14 Aug 1738 by Thos Hall & Thos Myars securities for the estate of Cole's orphans & ordered to be recorded. Attest: James Fontaine clerk.

In obedience to an order of court dated 13 Jun 1738 we W. Betts, Robert Davis & Silvester Welsh being first sworn before Col Presly did meet to appraise the

11

estate of John Watts decd. 1 horse, new sadle, old sadle & bridle. [Not totaled]
This appraisement of the estate of John Watts decd was presented 14 Aug 1738
by Elinor Alvinson exor of the sd decd & admitted to record. Attest: James
Fontaine clerk.

In obedience to an order of court dated 15 Jun 1738 we John Claughton, Richard
Claughton, George [?] & John [?] did meet at the house of Robert Hutson &
settled the acct in tobacco & paid the petitioner David Williams as followed:
292#. 1 cow, 1 bed, bedstead, paid Eliza Fignor a legacy by will, 1 cow & calf,
1 mare, 1 colt, sheep, 1 gun, 1 iron skillet. [Not totaled] This appraisement was
presented -- Sep 1738 & admitted to record. Attest: James Fontaine clerk.

11 Sep ----. Deed. William Eustace executor of the will of Richard Lee gent
decd of Wiccomocco Parish, Northumberland Co for 60 pd sold to Francis
Timerlake of same parish a 200 a. parcel of land belonging to Christopher
Gratington decd & Hancock Lee gent decd devised to his son Richard Lee gent
decd who in his will gave authority to William Eustace his acting executor to
dispose thereof bounded by ... [faded] ... . Wit: Benja Olliver. Memorandum
that quiet & peaceable possession of the land was given & delivered by the sd
William Eustace gent to the sd Francis Timberlake. Wit: William Garlington,
Benja Olliver, Ambrose Jones. Ackn 11 Sep 1738 & admitted to record. Attest:
James Fontaine clerk. (Pg 24)

11 Sep 1738. Bond. I William Eustace gent of Wiccomico Parish,
Northumberland Co am firmly bound unto Francis Timberlake of parish afsd for
120 pd ... the condition of this obligation is such that if the sd William Eustace
gent shall well & truly perform, fulfill & accomplish all the conditions, articles
& clauses in one deed [see above] then this obligation to be void ... . Wit:
William Garlington, Ambrose Jones, Benja Olliver. Ackn 11 Sep 1738 &
admitted to record. Attest: James Fontaine clerk. (Pg 24)

5 Aug 1738. Deed of Gift. George Ball of Wiccomico Parish, Northumberland
Co for natural love & affection gave to my son George Ball all the land in the
parish afsd that I bought of the several persons ... [?] ... of John Bledvan? by
deed dated -- May 1719, of John Nickleson by deed dated 20 Sep 1720, of
Thomas D[?] by deed dated -- Apr 17--, of William Bently by deed dated 20 Jan
1720 & also one other deed of William Bently dated 17 May 1730 containing
137 a. of land ... . Wit: Jas Ball Junr, Bertd Ewell. Ackn -- Sep 1738 &
admitted to record. Attest: James Fontaine clerk. (Pg 24)

In obedience to an order of court dated -- Aug 1738 & according to the direction
of the sd order & [?] of George Ball & William Eustace gent dated 14 Jul 1738 I
surveyed the line that divides the land lately of Howson Kennard from the Glebe

Land ... . 21 Aug 1738 John Shapleigh. This report of the survey was returned 11 Sep 1738 & recorded. Attest: James Fontaine clerk.

At Northumberland Co Court 11 Sep 1738 it was ordered that we Isaac Basey, Thos Peterson? & Richd Denne meet before next court to divide the lands, houses & plantation of Richard Marsh decd & allot the widow her thirds of the same. 9 Oct 1738 this report was returned & recorded. Attest: James Fontaine clerk.

28 Apr 1738. A division is made between James Tomson & Mathew Kenner Senr adj the upper pt/o the bridge, Richd Tomson Senr, Mathew Aldridge & John Lewis ... . Wit: John Lewis, Danl Duggins, Richd Claughton. This agreement was presented 9 Oct 1738 & admitted to record. Attest: James Fontaine clerk.

11 Sep 1738. In obedience to an order of court dated 10 Aug we John Dougherty, John [?] & Danl Clark having met & being first sworn have appraised the estate of Wm Norman as followeth: 1 heifer, 1 cow, 1 frying pan, 1 mare & colt, small hide, some leather, 1 pot, 10 spoons, some butter, 1 old tub, 1 corn barrel, some corn, etc. [Not totaled] This appraisement was returned 9 Oct 1738 & admitted to record. Attest: James Fontaine clerk.

14 Aug 1738. Deed of Lease. William Gill of St. Stephen Parish, Northumberland Co planter for 5 sl leased to Richard Stuckey of parish afsd taylor a 100 a. parcel of land in the sd parish it being pt/o a tr of land purch by Thomas Bearcroft of Samll Churchill & sold by the sd Bearcroft decd to John Trussell decd 20 Dec 1711 & by the sd John Trussell bequeathed to Matthew Trussell & by him sold to William Gill 17 Dec 1735 adj the land late of Anthony Linton decd, a br of Broad Cr & land of William Hill ... for the term of 6 months ... . Wit: Thomas Priest, Thomas Taylor, Michael Ryan. Ackn 12 --- 1738 & admitted to record. Attest: James Fontaine clerk. (Pg 26)

15 Aug 1738. Deed of Release. William Gill of St. Stephen Parish, Northumberland Co planter for released to Richard Stuckey a 100 a. tr of land ... [same as above] ... . [Signed by] William Gill, Winiford Gill. Wit: Thomas Priest, Thos Taylor, Michael Ryan. Ackn --- 1738 & admitted to record. Attest: James Fontaine clerk. (Pg 26)

15 Aug 1738. Bond. I William Gill of St. Stephen Parish, Northumberland Co am firmly bound unto Richd Stuckey of sd parish for 10,000 lbs of tobacco ... the condition of this obligation is such that whereas the afsd William Gill hath by indenture of lease & release [see above] sold unto the afsd Richard Stuckey a tr of land, & if the sd William Gill does well & truly perform, fulfill &

13

accomplish all the articles, clauses, covenants & agreements contained & mentioned in the sd deeds then this obligation to be void … . [Signed by] William Gill, Winford Gill. Wit: Thomas Priest, Thomas Taylor, Michael Ryan. Ackn 12 --- 1738 & admitted to record. Attest: James Fontaine clerk. (Pg 27)

23 Jan 1737. Power of Attorney. Before me Thomas Bocking notary publick dwelling in London appeared Thos Matthew of Sherbow Lane, London gent (the surviving executor of the will of Thomas Matthew heretofore of Cherry Point upon Potomack River in VA merchant decd) & John Matthew of London merchant & Anna his wife which Anna was the only dau of the sd Thos Matthew decd who declared that whereas the sd Thomas Matthew decd being possessed of a plantation in Stafford Co for a term of 999 years by his will dated 6 May 1703 devised all his estate in Stafford Co to his three children John, Thomas & Anna Matthew & appointed the sd John & Thomas executors, the sd Anna intermarried with the afsd John Matthew & that John Matthew the other executor died intestate in Oct 1738 … [faded] … the sd appearers Thomas Matthew & John Matthew adminr of John Matthew & the sd Anna by & with the consent & approbation of her husband have constituted Thomas Compton of [?] MD merchant to be their atty to sell the sd plantation … . Wit: Thos Cartwright, James Genn. Proved 8 Jan 1738 & admitted to record. Attest: James Fontaine clerk. (Pg 27)

In obedience to an order of court dated 9 --- 1738 we James Daughity, John Corbell & Abner Neale have met at ye house of Daniel Clark & being first sworn by John Shapleigh gent have appraised & divided the estate of William Berry decd in ye hands of Daniel Clark & allotted James [?] his wifes pt/o ye same & likewise have divided the sd Berry's land by a line adj the Herring Cr & Peter Haile … . This division of ye estate of William Berry decd was returned 8 Jan 1738 & recorded. Attest: James Fontaine clerk. (Pg 28)

Will. Ann Kilpatrick. 12 Jun 1733. To my sons John Kilpatrick a young heifer & her increase. To my dau Anne [?] a chest. To my dau Sarah Curtis a young breeding heifer. To my dau Elizabeth Kilpatrick all the rest of my estate both reall & personall. I appoint my dau Elizabeth Kilpatrick executrix. Wit: Thos Harcum, Elizabeth Harcum. Proved 8 Jan 1738 & Elizabeth Kilpatrick now w/o John Swift executrix with John Swift made oath thereof & on their motion the same is admitted to record. Attest: James Fontaine clerk.

In obedience to an order of court dated 10 Apr 1738 we John Claughton, George Lankin & Richard Claughton being first sworn before Mathew Quill justice met at ye house of Edward Turner decd & did appraise the sd estate & inventoried the same. Beds, bedsteads & furniture, old chest, 2 guns, cooper & carpenter tools, some wearing cloaths, 2 basons, 2 wedges, 1 looking glass, parcel of old books, 2 old tables, 2 pair fire tongs, parcel of bottles, frying pan, cows, calves, bull, an old cart & wheels, etc. [Not totaled] This inventory was returned by Fielding Turner adminr & is admitted to record. James Fontaine clerk. (Pg 29)

4 May 1738. Pursuant to an order of court granted to John Hurley gent executor of the will of John Hurley (Shurley?) decd we James Farned, Edward Barnes, Robt Clark Junr being first sworn before Matthew Quill justice have appraised the decd's estate. Beds, bedsteads & furniture, 1 chest of drawers, 2 boxes, 1 trunk, 1 table & bench, table & 8 old chairs, 1 gun, parcel of books, 1 looking glass, 1 chest, 1 spinning wheel, parcel of earthen ware, 26 qt bottles, 31 ½ lbs good pewter, 14 ½ lbs of old pewter, 1 pair fire tongs, 2 iron wedges, carpenter tools, etc. [Not totaled] This inventory of the estate of John Hurley decd was returned 8 May 1738 by John Hurley Junr executor & admitted to record. Attest: James Fontaine clerk. (Pg 29)

In obedience to an order of court dated 19 Apr 1738 we Wm Garner, Wm Holt? & Richd Claughton have appraised the estate of Thos Hall Junr. 1 old book, 1 old cider cask, 30 gall of cider, 1 bag, 3 pair old shoes, 1 fiddle, 1 horse, 1 gold ring, beds & furniture, 1 chest of drawers, 1 table, a Negro woman, a Negro boy, 8 hogs, 1 cow & calf, etc. [Not totaled] This inventory was returned 8 May 1738 & admitted to record. Attest: James Fontaine clerk. (Pg 30)

Pursuant to an order of court dated 13 Mar 1737/8 we Thomas Winter, Roger Winter & John Kent being first sworn by Capt Eustace did meet & appraise the estate of the decd Wm Brent. Negroes: Man named Tom, lad named George, man named Samll, woman named Silla, woman named Nan & her child, boy named Sam. Beds, boulsters, pillows, quilts, blankets, sheets, curtains, hides, 6 old leather chairs, 3 old towels, 3 cotton napkins, table, trunk, 1 old brass candlestick, books belonging to Major Lee's estate, etc. 2610 lbs tobacco. This inventory was exhibited 12 Jun 1738 & admitted to record. Attest: James Fontaine clerk. (Pg 30)

In obedience to an order of court held 10 Apr 1738 we John Foushee, Robt Clarke & John Lewis mett at ye house of John Lancaster decd & have let a pt/o [?] John Boor his wife's pt/o ye decd's estate according to will. 6 bushells of corn, 14 lbs of hog meat, 4 ¼ lbs beef, 1 cow, 1 heifer, 1 old mare, ½ bushell salt, 7 old chairs, 1 large old table, 1 old sadle & bridle, 1 tub, 2 cider casks, 1 parcell of earthen ware, 1 old belt & wrap, 1 hide of leather, 1 bed & furniture, etc. [Not totaled] For the land: 550. The above articles is due John Boor his wife's pt/o her father's lease land that John Lancaster decd had of John Foushee. This report & division was returned 10 Aug 1738 & recorded. Attest: James Fontaine clerk. (Pg 30)

15

Will. Elizabeth Schriver (Shrever) of Northumberland Co. 17 Jul 1738. All my proveable estate of what nature or kind to be divided between my Aunt Mary Gaskins, my Uncle Richard Hull & my cousins Elizabeth Thomas, Edwin, Jurakann, Ann & John Jenkins children of my Uncle Thomas Gaskins decd to be delivered to my sd cousins as they shall attain to age or day of marriage. I appoint my trusty & good friend Col Edwin Conway, my Aunt Mary Gaskins & my Uncle Richard Hull my executors. Wit: Moses James, Elizabeth Hunt? & George Ball gent. Proved 11 7br 1738 & admitted to record. Attest: James Fontaine clerk. (Pg 31)

3 Aug MDCCXXXVIII. Deed. Richard Kenner of Saint Stephens Parish, Northumberland Co gent for 91 pd 7 sl sold to Thomas Edwards of Christ Church Parish, Lancaster Co gent a 261 a. parcel of land in Brereton's Neck adj the sd Thomas Edwards, Col Presly, Benjamin Toulson & Elias Martin, which land is pt/o a greater tr given & bequeathed to the sd Richard Kenner by the will of his grandmother Elizabeth Winder dated 14 Apr 1730 .... Wit: John Shapleigh, Benjamin George June, Lawrance Parrot. Ackn 12 Mar 1738 & recorded. Attest: James Fontaine clerk. (Pg 31)

3 Aug MDCCXXXVIII. Deed of Covenant. Richard Kenner of Saint Stephens Parish, Northumberland Co gent for settling the tr of land whereon he now lives upon Thomas Edwards in case the sd 261 a. of land pt/o 900 a. should hereafter be recovered & for 91 pd 7 sl in hand paid release to Thomas Edwards gent of Christ Church Parish, Lancaster Co gent the tr of land ... whereas Elizabeth Winder late of Saint Stephens Parish widow grandmother of the sd Richard Kenner was in her lifetime seized in a tr or neck of land called Breretons Neck containing 4,600 a. & being so seized by her will dated 14 Apr MDCCIXXX devised to the sd Richard Kenner pt/o the sd tr to wit 1,600 a. & the sd Elizabeth Winder on 14 May 1730 by her deed of gift did give to the sd Richard Kenner 700 a. of land in her sd will to him bequeathed & whereas the sd Richard Kenner is now vested in 900 a. of the land & the remainder viz his dwelling plantation with the lands being computed to contain 250 a. & bounded by Taskmenders Cr, the bay, the herring pond & Col Presly's land & whereas the sd Richard Kenner by his deed [see above] hath conveyed 261 a. of the 900 a. to the sd Thomas Edwards, & whereas the sd Richard Kenner is willing so far as in him lyeth to secure the peaceable possession & enjoyment of the 250 a. of land unto the sd Thomas Edwards .... Wit: John Shapleigh, Benjamin George Junr, Lawrance Parrot. Proved 12 Mar 1738/9 & on the motion of Joseph Ball esqr atty of the sd Edwards was admitted to record. Attest: James Fontaine clerk. (Pg 32)

Will. William Tolson of Northumberland Co planter. 22 Sep 1738. To my only son John Tolson my plantation where I now dwell. To my only dau Winifride Wornam the bed, beding & furniture to it belonging as it now stands in the plank house. To my son in law Thomas Wornam a full trim'd suit of duray? cloths with the stockings & my whitney riding cote. To my grandson Thomas Wornam my largest gun. To my son John Tolson all my wareing cloths linen & woollen (not before given). To my son John Tolson all my Smith tools & my short gun I give to my grandson William Tolson the son of the afsd John Tolson. To my granddaus Winifride & Elizabeth Tolson daus of my son John Tolson to each of them a heifer. To William Porter (who lives with me) a suit of cloaths & a small chest upstairs. To my son in law Thomas Wornam that hogshead of tobacco I have his bill for. To my beloved wife Mary Tolson the use of all the rest of my personal estate (quick & dead) during her widowhodd & afterwards to be divided between my son John Tolson & my dau Winifride Wornam. I order my estate not to be appraised. I appoint my wife Mary Tolson & my son John Tolson executors. Wit: J. Coulton, Lawrance Parrot, Charles Reason. Proved 12 Mar 1738/9 & admitted to record. Attest: James Fontaine clerk. (Pg 33)

Will. John Rider of Northumberland Co. 17 Nov 1738. To my dau Winifrid all my land on the n side of Wiccomoco River & my Negro boy named James & the first child that my Negro girl Lucy has if ever that comes to the age of 10 years old. To my dau Sarah my Negro girl named Lucy. To my wife & my two daus Winifred & Sarah all my estate that I have not already given to be equally divided. My will & desire is that my friend Charles Craven & my wife should be my executors. Wit: Argail Taylor, John Taylor, Mary Lewis. Proved 12 Mar 1738/9 & Eliz Rider executrix made oath to the sd will & on her motion ye same is admitted to record. Attest: James Fontaine clerk. (Pg 34)

In obedience to an order of court dated 8 Jan 1738/9 we John Coles, Richard Smith & William Downing did meet at the house of John Swift & being first sworn before Thomas Gill justice did appraise ye estate of Anne Kilpatrick decd in money. 1 young horse, 1 cow, 1 sow & piggs, beds, rugs, blankits, boulsters, 3 low chairs, a persel of earthen ware & lumber, a persel of glass bottles & lumber, a persel of old barrills, an old trunk, old chest, 15 ¼ of puter, iron pot. [Not totaled] These things were not appraised viz 1 dish, 2 plates, 6 spoons, 1 puter flagon, 1 old Bible, an old chest, an old spinning wheel, an old grindstone, an iron kettle, books, 1 iron spit, 1 iron pestle, 1 old table, 1 old box. This inventory was presented 12 Mar 1738/9 by John Swift & Elizabeth Swift executors & on their motion is admitted to record. Attest: James Fontaine clerk. (Pg 34)

Here followed an inventory of the estate of James Walkden decd taken by Margret Walkden adminr of the sd decd 3 Feb 1738/9. 4 cows, 3 yearlings, 2 calves, 3 sheep, 4 sows, 18 piggs, 1 grey horse, 1 horse colt, 3 beds, bedsteads & furniture, 150 lbs of beef, 70 lbs of pork, 13 lbs of tallow, 30 lbs of lard, 1 pair of Hilliards, 1 tub, a bushel of pease, 1 broad ax, 1 tub, 8 bushells of pease, 1 bag of wheat, 1 old saddle, 1 old case of bottles, 1 lanthorn, 3 dishes & 18 plates, 3 basons, 1 fine hat, hat box, wigg box, 2 wiggs, 1 new sadle, 1 curry comb & brush, 5 shirts, 1 great coat, 2 close coats, 2 jackcoats, 2 pair of breechers, 4 pair of stockins, 2 tubs, some old iron, 1 spinning wheel & cars, iron pot rack, etc. This inventory was presented 12 Mar 1738/9 & admitted to record. Attest: James Fontaine clerk. (Pg 35)

14 Feb 1738/9. Bond. I Rodham Kenner of Saint Stehens Parish, Northumberland Co gent am firmly bound unto Edward Lawrence (Lawrance) of Prince William Co in the penal sum of 70 pd ... the condition of this obligation is such that whereas the afsd Rodham Kenner hath purch of the afsd Edward Lawrence 268 a. of land by deed of lease & release dated 8 & 10 Apr 1738, now sence afsd purchase one John Evins & John Davis having intermarried with two of the daus & coheirs of John Hartly decd hath laid claim to 50 a. of the afsd land & by forceable entrée hath possest themselves of it, the sd Rodham Kenner for 30 pd 20 whereof is to be paid ready down & 10 more in Jul 1740 & the building a dwelling house 20' long & 16' wide & the clearing of 20,000 plants is willing & doth hereby oblige himself to stand all damages & doth quit the sd Edward Lawrence from his bond & warranty in relation to the afsd 50 a. of land. If the afsd Rodham Kenner doth comply with the above articles then this obligation to be void ... . Wit: Robert Clark Junr, George Johnston, Archibald Johnston. Ackn 13 Mar 1738 & admitted to record. Attest: James Fontaine clerk. (Pg 35)

8 Feb 1738/9. In obedience to an order of court dated 9 8br we Samll Blackwell & Joseph Wildey having met have layd off 1 a. of John Rider decd's land convenient for a mill & we value sd a. of land to 10 sl. The above report was returned 13 Mar 1738 by Samll Downing & on his motion ordered to be recorded. Attest: James Fontaine clerk. (Pg 36)

Pursuant to an order of court dated 8 Jan 1738 we Thomas Berry, Benjamin Waddy & Thos Winter have met at ye house of Samll Garlington decd & divided the estate according to ye direction of the sd order with the consent of both partys. This report was returned 13 Mar 1738 by Thos Burn & on his motion ordered to be recorded. Attest: James Fontaine clerk. (Pg 36)

18 Jun 1735. Bond. Leonard Howson, Richard Kenner, Howson Kenner & Thomas Edwards of Northumberland Co are firmly bound to our Sovereign Lord King George ye Second in ye penal sum of 1,000 pd ... the condition of this obligation is such that whereas the afsd Leonard Howson is appointed sheriff of Northumberland Co by ye Honble William Gooch esqr Lieut Governor of VA, now if ye sd Leonard Howson shall render unto ye Receiver Generall a particular perfect & full acct of all his Majestys Revenues & dues in this co & shall due payment make of all such publick dues as shall be levied for ye afsd co

unto ye severall person that shall be appointed to receive ye same & full performance make of all things belonging to the office of sheriff then this obligation to be void ... . Signed, sealed & delivered in the presence of ye justices & ackn in Northumberland Co Court. (Pg 36)

13 Jun 1737. Bond. John Hack, Spencer Ball & Cuthbert Spann gent of Northumberland Co are justly indebted to our Sovereign Lord King George the Second in the penal sum of 1,000 pd ... the condition of this obligation is such that whereas ye afsd John Hack is appointed sheriff of Northumberland Co by his Honble Wm Gooch esqr Lieut Governor of VA, now if the sd John Hack shall render unto the auditor a particular perfect & full acct of all his Majestys revenues & dues for this co during the time of his sheriffalty & shall due payment make of all such publick dues as shall be levied for sd co unto ye severall persons that shall be appointed to receive the same & full performance make of all things relating to office of sheriff then this obligation to be void ... . Signed, sealed & delivered in the presence of ye justices & ackn in Northumberland Co Court. (Pg 36)

21 Mar 1738. Received of William Haynie adminr of John Haynie decd full sattisfaction for the land sold by sd John Haynie decd in Essex Co & we do hereby discharge the sd William Haynie & every of the heirs of sd John Haynie decd for ever hereafter from ye claim of any person which shall or may lay any claim, right or title to ye sd land. [Signed by] Bridgar Haynie & Mary Haynie his wife. Wit: Thos Machen, Henry Webster, William Bickren. Proved 9 Apr 1739 & recorded. Attest: James Fontaine clerk. (Pg 36)

In obedience to an order of court dated 12 Jul 1737 we Saml Blackwell, John Downing & Joseph Wildey being first sworn have met & valued the estate of Richard Nelson decd in money. 1 cow & calf, 3 young steers, 3 good cider casks, 1 spinning wheel, 1 pare old cards, 1 old plow, 1 broad ax, 1 box iron & heaters, 1 old frying pan, 1 drawing knife, feather beds, bedsteads, rugs, blankets, 2 porringers, 1 pot, 10 spoons, pot iron, 1 pot rack, 1 old gun, old cupboard, 1 spit, old lumber, earthen ware, 1 water pail, 1 bucket, 1 old chest, 5 chairs, etc. [Not totaled]   This inventory was returned 12 7ber 1737 & by Saml Kelins? Junr adminr & recorded. Attest: James Fontaine clerk. (Pg 37)

In obedience to an order of court on Monday 8 Jan 1738 we Christopher Garlington, Christopher Dameron & Thos Winter have met to appraise the estate of Elizabeth Schriver decd in money. 1 old cupboard, 1 old chest, 1 old chair, 1 old couch, 2 narrow hows, 1 stear, 4 cows, 1 heiffer, 1 bull, 3 sows, 6 large pigs, 6 small pigs, 3 cider casks, 1 iron bound chest, 1 old box iron & heaters, 2 old bedsteads, 1 old bread hows, 8 narrow hows, 3 old axes, 1 iron pot rack, 1 pair steelyards, 1 old close stool, 1 flesh fork, beds, bolsters, sheets, cords, mats, blankets, 1 old can & bucket, 1 old spinning wheel, etc. [Not totaled]   The inventory was returned 10 Apr 1739 by Mary Gaskins & Richard Hull executors & on their motion admitted to record.   Attest: James Fontaine clerk.   (Pg 37)

A true inventory of the estate of William Tolson decd.   3 cows & yearlings, cow & calf, 1 bull, 1 old stear, 2 large hogs, 3 young hogs, 10 shoats, 2 horses, 1 young mare with foal, 1 std horse cart & harness, 6 gees, 1 good fish gig, 7 old cider casks, fether beds, bedsteads, rugs, blankets, sheets, bolsters & pillows with furniture, 1 old sadle, 3 bridles, 1 old side sadle & bridle, 18 glas bottles, 7 wood bowls, 4 other wooden ware, a parcel of pails, etc.   This inventory was presented 7 Apr 1739 by Mary Toulson & John Toulson executors & on their motion is admitted to record.   Attest: James Fontaine clerk.   (Pg 37)

 In obedience to an order of court dated 12 Mar 1738 we Matthew Zuill, Traves Colston & Wm Faybe? met at ye house of James Straughan & having percured the inventory of Samll Bonum decd's estate & papers relating thereunto did divide & allot to ye sd Straughan for his wifes part the Negroes, viz, Derby old man, Abil, Dinah & Sam, we likewise find the estate of Samll Bonum indebted to the sd Straughan 816 lbs of tobacco to be payed out of the estate of the orphans Samll & Thomas Bonum. We likewise find the sd Straughan indebted to ye sd orphan Thomas Bonum 8 pd 13 sl 8 pn. We also did allot to Thomas Bonum the Negroes Jamie, Samsom, Winie, Nann, Little Sam & Little Wine. We likewise find the orphan Thomas Bonum is intitled to 40 sl to be paid out of the estate of his brother Samuel Bonum to make the sd Thomas's Negroes equal to ye other parts. This report of division was returned by James Straughan & on his motion admitted to record. Attest: James Fontaine clerk. (Pg 38)

20 Mar 1738/9. In obedience to an order of court dated 12 Mar 1738 obtained by Mary Gaskins for the dividing & proportioning Elizabeth Schriver's personall estate according to her will we Wm Eustace, John Shapleigh & Matthew Quill did (the same time that we divided & allotted to her the sd Mary Gaskins & Richard Hull & his wife their pts/o Thomas Gaskins's estate) pay & allot to ye sd Mary Gaskins & Richard Hull & his wife in stocks of cattle, hogs, sheep, horses, household goods & furniture to ye sum & value of 16 pd 3 sl 6 pn each being their proportionable pt/o all ye estate of ye afsd Elizabeth Schriver then inventoried & appraised. This division was returned 10 Apr 1739 by ye auditors & on the motion of Mary Gaskins & Richd Hull was admitted to record. Attest: James Fontaine clerk. (Pg 38)

21 Mar 1738/9. In obedience to an order of court dated 12 Mar 1738 granted to Mary Gaskins executor of Thomas Gaskins decd appointing us, Wm Eustace, John Shapleigh & Matthew Quill, to proportion & allot to ye sd Mary Gaskins her pt/o her decd husband's estate given to her by his will according to ye

directions of the afsd order we did meet at ye house of the afsd Mary Gaskins 19th instant & did proportion & allot to her ye following Negroes, viz, Hafford, Judy, Lucy, Danl, Tom, Lucy & Solomon & in household goods & furniture, stocks of cattle, horses, hogs, sheep &c to ye sum & value of 50 pd 14 sl 4 pn at ye same prices mentioned for (late) Thos Gaskins inventory & for as much as the afsd seven Negroes allotted to the afsd Mary Gaskins is 1 pd 18 sl 4 pn more than her just proportion we therefore determine that she pay among the rest of the children ye afsd sum in cash. This report & division of ye Negroes & estate of Thos Gaskins decd to Richard Hull we returned in court by the auditors & on ye motion of Richard Hull was admitted to record. Attest: James Fontaine clerk. (Pg 38)

20 Mar 1738/9. In obedience to an order of court 12 Mar 1738 granted to Richard Hull for his wife's filial pt/o her father's estate in ye hands of Mary Gaskins extrx of (her father) Thomas Gaskins decd appointed us Wm Eustace, John Shapleigh & Matthew Quill to proportion & allot to ye sd Richard Hull his wife's pt/o her father's estate given to her by his will, we did meet at ye house of the afsd Mary Gaskins on 19th instant & did proportion & allot to him ye following Negroes, viz, Peg, Letty, Dick, Kit, Bess & Billy & in household goods & furniture, stocks of cattle, horses, hogs, sheep &c to ye sum & value of 50 pd 14 sl 4 pn as mentioned in (late) Thomas Gaskins his inventory & forasmuch as the afsd six Negroes allotted to the afsd Richd Hull is 1 pd 18 sl 4 pn more then his wife's just part we therefore determine that he pay to ye rest of ye children the afsd sum in cash. This report & division of ye Negroes & estate of Thos Gaskins decd to Richard Hull was returned 10 Apr 1739 & on the motion of Richard Hull admitted to record. Attest: James Fontaine clerk. (Pg 38)

8 Apr 1738. Power of Attorney. I Thomas Lutwidge of Whitehaven in Cumberland Co merchant have appointed James Paton of Whitehaven ship master my atty to ask, demand, sue for, require, recover & receive all such sums of money as shall be due to me from any person in VA or MD whatsoever ... . Wit: John Freeman, Alexander Good. Proved 9 Apr 1739 & admitted to record. Attest: James Fontaine clerk. (Pg 39)

3 Apr 1739. Deed. Bartholomew Richard Dodson of Wicocomoco Parish, Northumberland Co sold to Saml Lunsford of sd parish the following goods & chattels, viz, a feather bed & furniture, 7 head of cattle, 7 hogs, 50 weight of puter, 2 chests, 1 trunk, 1 box, 1 case of botles, 2 guns, 4 iron pots, 10 barrels of corn, 1 iron spitt, 1 box iron, 1 looking glass, together with all such things as shall be known to be mine ... . Wit: George Mills, Edmond Conway, Winiford Crafford. Proved 10 Apr 1739 & admitted to record. Attest: James Fontaine clerk. (Pg 39)

At a court held in Nov 1738 & ordered us, Yarret Hughlet & Ezekiel Hill, to allot an a. of land at one end of the mill dam that was Reeves' & appraise the same which land did belong to John Christopher & the price 20 sl. The valuation of 1 a. of land of John Christopher to William Greenstreet was presented 10 Apr 1739 into Northumberland Co Court by ye viewers within named & on ye motion of ye sd Greenstreet ordered to be recorded. Attest: James Fontaine clerk. (Pg 39)

14 May 1739. Deed. Billington McCarty & Ann his wife of North Farnham Parish, Richmond Co for 40 pd sold to George Hunt of Wicocomo Parish, Northumberland Co a 175 a. parcel of land which sd land is pt/o severall trs of land purch by Capt Daniel McCarty of sundry persons, & by the sd Daniel McCarty's will given to his son Billington McCarty bounded by the Main Swamp of Great Wicocomoco, John Pope & John Boyd, William Linkhorn, James Blackerby & Merattico Cr ... . Wit: Dennis Conway, William Thomas, William Linkorn. Ackn 14 May 1739 by Billington McCarty & Ann his wife (Ann McCarty being privately examined by Matthew Quill gent relinquished her right of dower in ye lands) & admitted to record. Attest: James Fontaine clerk. (Pg 39)

14 May 1739. Bond. I Billington McCarty of North Farnham Parish, Richmond Co am firmly bound unto George Hunt of Wicocomoco Parish, Northumberland Co for 200 pd ... the condition of this obligation is such that if the sd Billington McCarty shall well & truly perform, fulfill, accomplish & keep all & singular the articles, clauses & conditions & covenants comprised in one certain indenture [see above] then this obligation to be void ... . Wit: Dennis Conway, William Thomas, William Linkorn. Ackn 14 May 1739 by Billington McCarty & Ann his wife (she being privately examined by Matthew Quill gent relinquished her right of dower in ye lands) & admitted to record. Attest: James Fontaine clerk. (Pg 40)

20 Jan 1737. Bond. I Bennet Boggus (Bogges?) (Boger?) of St. Stephens Parish, Northumberland Co planter am firmly bound unto Lindsey Opie of parish afsd gent for 50 pd ... the condition of this obligation is such that if the sd Bennet Boggus do in all things well & truly stand to observe, perform, fulfill & keep the award, division or final determination of Col William Ball of Lancaster Co in ye sd Col Ball's laying of & surveying of the sd Bennet Boggus' land according to ye courses of the sd Boggus pattent, then this obligation to be void ... . Wit: John Irons, John Boggus. This bond was presented 19 May 1739 & admitted to record. Attest: James Fontaine clerk. (Pg 40)

In obedience to an order of court dated 3 Jan 1738 we John Coppedge, Argail Taylor & John Taylor have met 9 Feb being first sworn by George Ball gent &

appraised the estate of Elizabeth Curtis & delivered by William Barret & has possest Swanson & Charles Prichard with the sd estate: 1 horse, 9 old flag chairs, 1 cow bell, 1 howsin, 1 old wheel & cards, 1 old puter pot, 3 lbs puter, 30 gall cider, 1 old brass kittle, 1 small iron pot, 1 old still, 27 ½ lbs pot iron, 1 old case pistols & sword, 1 old flock bed, bedstead & cord, 1 old table, 1 old fether bed & covering, 1 hide of leather, 1 old chest, 8 new spoons. This appraisement was exhibited 14 May 1739 by Swanson & Charles Prichard & on their motion admitted to record. Attest: James Fontaine clerk. (Pg 40)

11 May 1739. In obedience to an order of court held 10 Apr 1739 we John Rose, John Boyd & Richard Thomas being appointed to value the estate of Dennis Conway decd in the hands of George Conway unto John Dollins the sum of 11 pd 9 sl 1 penny which sd sum wee have possessed the sd John Dollins with all in ye sundry articles hereafter mentioned. 2 cows & calves, 1 feather bed & furniture, 1 oval table, 1 iron pot, 14 ¼ worn puter, 13 lbs old puter, a parcel of earthen ware, 3 old books. 11 pd 10 sl 7 pn. This division & appraisement was exhibited 14 May 1739 by the appraisers & on ye motion of John Dollins admitted to record. Attest: James Fontaine clerk.

11 Jun 1739. Deed of Gift. Phillip Smith of Wiccomoco Parish, Northumberland Co for fatherly love have given unto my dau Mary the following Negro slaves, to wit, my Negro woman Lucy & her two daus Kate & Kertshuch, my Negro girls Phillis & Fanny daus of my Negro man Will & my Negro boy Harry son of my Negro man Piper, & their increase, during her natural life & after her decease to be divided amongst the children of my sd dau Mary if any such & for want of such children to descend & go to the remainder of my daus to be divided amongst them. I do hereby ackn to have put my sd dau Mary into full & immediate possession of the sd six slaves. Wit: T. Edwards. Ackn 11 Jun 1739 & admitted to record. Attest: James Fontaine clerk. (Pg 41)

In obedience to an order of court dated 12 Mar 1739 we Argail Taylor, Joshua James & John Taylor have met & being sworn by George Ball gent have appraised the estate of John Rider decd. Negroes: Man named Jamy, woman named Lucy. Beds & furniture, bedsteads, rugs, cords, 52 ½ lbs of good pewter, 17 lbs of worn pewter, 1 table & cloth, 1 chest, old box, 8 hoes, 3 wedges, 2 narrow axes, 2 hides, 1 cross cut saw, a percell of old iron, 2 old box irons, 2 old chisels & sum trifles, 4 old candlesticks, 2 old wheels, 3 old pr wooliards, 1 gun, 1 small skillet, 1 old spice morter & pestell, 1 pare of old boots, 2 doz glass bottles, some earthen ware, etc. [Not totaled] This inventory was exhibited 11 Jun 1739 by Alice Rider adminr of sd decd with ye will annexed & on her motion admitted to record. Attest: James Fontaine clerk. (Pg 41)

13 Jun 1739. By the directions of an order of Northumberland Co Court dated 9

Apr 1739 we George Ball & Benja Waddy have met & settled the difference between Aaron Taylor adminr of Thos Butcher decd & Michael Tobin & do find that the sd Tobin is indebted to ye sd Taylor 644 lbs of tobacco & we do also find upon a settlement made by Saml Nolan? Between the sd Butcher & sd Tobin that the sd Butcher has made a charge seeking of 2729 per agreement but no sum set & for the allowance thereof we submit to ye court. This report was returned by the auditors & ordered to be recorded. Attest: James Fontaine clerk. (Pg 42)

Thomas Webb's Estate: Sundry debts paid as per order, summons your widow to cash, clerks fees paid by Edward Rogers, commission on ye sales of Webb's estate on 7250 lbs of tobacco. For sundry percells of estate sold to sundry persons. 7215 lbs tobacco.
Thomas Webb's estate in cash: Joshua Nelms, Edwd Rogers on acct of Thos Webb's orphans. Cash recd of Edward Rogers. 15 pd. According to an order of court dated 14 May 1739 we Peter Presley & John Shapleigh did meet & settle ye accounts of Abner Neales agt Thomas Webb's estate & we find the accounts to be as above given. This acct of settlement was returned 11 Jun 1739 by the auditors & ordered to be recorded. Attest: James Fontaine clerk. (Pg 42)

In obedience to an order of court held 14 May 1739 we Aron Taylor, Wm James & John Nutt being first sworn by Thomas Gill gent have appraised the estate of Richd Nelms Junr. 3 pr shoes & stockins, 1 pr britches, some old linen & leather apron, 1 sute of worn cloes, 1 old hat & old acsh, 1 cider casque, 2 heifers, 1 carpenter's adds, 3 flag chairs. This inventory was returned 11 Jun 1739 by Henry Mayes adminr & on his motion admitted to record. Attest: James Fontaine clerk. (Pg 42)

An account of charges on the estate of the decd Benjamin Palmer: Sums paid to Matthew Quill, Capt William Eustace, Thomas Berry, George Mills, Josias Basie, Isaac Palmer, James Blarck, William Harvy, Swanson Pritchard, Charles Coppedge, Richard Hudnall. 27 pd 14 sl 3 pn. Errors excepted per Thos Palmer. This account agt ye estate of Benjamine Palmer decd was exhibited 12 Jun 1739 by Thomas Palmer & on his jmotion ordered to be recorded. Attest: James Fontaine clerk. (Pg 42)

4 Jul 1739. Deed. Farnifold Nutt of St. Stephens Parish, Northumberland Co for 1,000 lbs of tobacco sold to John Doughity (Daughity) of same co a 12 a. parcel of land in the sd parish bounded by the Main Road leading to Parsons Bridge & George Humphry, being pt/o a tr of land which Farnifold Nutt had given to him by his Godfather John Farnifold ... . Wit: James Daughity, John Smith. Ackn 9 Jul 1739 by Farnifold Nutt unto John Daughity (& Sarah his wife being privately examined by Capt Wm Eustace relinquished her right of dower

in ye lands) & admitted to record. Attest: James Fontaine clerk. (Pg 43)

9 Jul 1739. Bond. I Farnifold Nutt of St. Stephens Parish, Northumberland Co am firmly bound to John Daughity of sd parish for 2,000 lbs of good lawfull tobacco ... the condition of this obligation is such that whereas the sd Farnifold Nutt by deed [see above] sold unto John Daughity 12 a. of land, now if the sd Farnifold Nutt shall from time to time & at all times forever hereafter observe, perform, accomplish, fulfill & keep all & every the articles, clauses, provisos & agreements sett down in the sd deed & the sd Farnifold Nutt shall duely ackn the sd deed in form of law in court at ye request of sd John Daughity & that Sarah the now w/o of sd Farnifold Nutt shall relinquish her right in dower to ye sd land at sd court then this obligation to be void ... . Wit: James Daughity, John Smith. This bond was ackn & admitted to record. Attest: James Fontaine clerk. (Pg 43)

9 Jul 1739. Deed. John Harvey of Wicocomoco Parish, Northumberland Co for 35 pd sold to John Ingram of parish afsd a 50 a. parcel of land being pt/o a patten of 350 a. of land dated 3 Apr 1651 & granted to Henry Hurt afterwards by several conveyances pt/o ye sd 350 a. of land became vested in John Bowen decd as per deed 27 Aug 1668 which sd John Bowen was father to Edward Bowen which sd Bowen sold the parcel of land to John Harvey party to these presents, bounded by Hurts Spring Br, corner between Berry & Lattimore & Charles Ingram ... . Wit: Moses Champion, Thos Hurt. Ackn 9 Jul 1739 & admitted to record. Attest: James Fontaine clerk. (Pg 44)

9 Jul 1739. Deed. Thos Hurst of Wicocomoco Parish, Northumberland Co for 50 pd sold to John Harvey of same place a parcel of land being pt/o a patent of 350 a. of land dated 3 Apr 1651 granted to Henry Hurst grandfather of the afsd Thomas Hurst bounded by Cedar Cove, Bowen's line, Lattimore's line, Gaskins line & Champion's line ... . Wit: John Ingram, Moses Champion. Ackn 9 Jul 1739 by Thomas Hurst & Elizabeth his wife being privately examined by Capt William Eustace relinquished her right of dower in ye land & admitted to record. Attest: James Fontaine clerk. (Pg 44)

A true & perfect inventory of all & singular the goods & chattels of Thomas Waddy decd: 14 Negroes young & old, 24 neat cattle, 6 feather beds, 4 boulsters, 4 pillows, 4 bedsteads, 3 hides, 4 blankets, 14 sheets, 2 ruggs, 2 bed quilts, 6 pillow cases, 3 towels, 3 table cloths, curtains, 11 leather chairs, 1 chest of drawers, 2 tables, 1 old safe, 1 pare of small hinges, 1 iron pestle, 2 earthen Chamber pots, 5 earthen pots, 1 pare of money scales & weights, 2 brushes, gallon puter pot, 1 large & 1 small Bible, 3 Common prayer books, 1 duty man, parcel of old books, etc. Outstanding debts & crop growing ye ground at time of the death of Thos Waddy the whole amounts to 6902 ½. Ben Waddy executor.

This inventory was exhibited 9 Jul 1739 & recorded. Attest: James Fontaine clerk. (Pg 45)

Ann Holt's estate. Sums paid to Thomas Webb, John Webb, Will Webb, Winiford Webb, Eliz Webb, Edward Rogers, John Hudnall Junr, 1gallon brandy for ye apraint?, Sarah Berry, Elizabeth Webb. 286 pd 5 sl 4 pn. Tobacco paid to Peter Maron, fee to Wm Hill, Richard Kennedy, Capt Richd Pease, Joseph Hudnall, Corbett Brown, Sam Blackwell, James Daughity, Edward Rogers, Major Jno Waughop, John Corbett, Wm Hobson, Beverley Reeve, Jno Hudnall Junr, Jno Hudnall for sugar for funeral, Saml Helms, John Condra, Jno Williams. 3345 lbs. Received tobacco from Geo Williams. 9 Apr 1739 Errors excepted per Wm Betts & Gervace Ellerton adminrs. This acct was returned 9 Jul 1739 by Wm Betts & Gervace Ellerton adminrs of sd decd by which it appears that the sd adminrs have fully administered which was ordered to be recorded. Attest: James Fontaine clerk. (Pg 46)

9 Jul 1739. Matthew Quill, Travers Colston & Saml Blackwell are firmly bound unto our Sovereign Lord George the Second for 1000 pd ... the condition of this obligation is such that whereas the afsd Matthew Quill is commissioned to be high sheriff of Northumberland Co, if the afsd Matthew Quill do well & truly perform the office of High Sheriff & execute all such writs & precepts as from time to time shall be to him directed & faithfully & truly perform & do all other things pertaining to ye office of High Sheriff then this obligation to be void ... . Sealed & delivered in presence of the Court of Northumberland Co. Attest: James Fontaine clerk. (Pg 46)

4 Jul 1739. By the direction of an order of Northumberland Co Court dated 14 May 1739 I George Ball did meet at George Oldham's & settled the accts of the estate of Thomas Heath decd & do find (after ye deduction of ye legacys & 25 pd it being also a legacy) there is but 21 pd 11 sl 9 pn due to each claimer to ye sd estate & I have allotted Roger Winter his wife's part & Wm Heath's part of ye sd estate accordingly & reported ye same to next court. There being a dispute concerning some cattle supposed to have been sould it was therefore referred for an inquiry & I again met ye sd Winter at sd Oldham's & no proof was made of any cattle being sould. This report & division was returned 9 Jul 1739 by George Ball gent & recorded. Attest: James Fontaine clerk. (Pg 46)

8 7br 1739. Deed of Lease. William Taite & Ann his wife of St. Stephens Parish, Northumberland Co for 40 sl leased to Matthew Quill of same place all their right to 350 a. of land in sd parish on the s side of Chickcone River formerly granted to John Chandler by patent dated 28 Jan 1636 & reserved in his Majestys name 11 Jan 1663 to Daniel Chandler son to the sd John as heir unto his father & sold to Peter Contanuean who by his will dated 20 Apr 1709 gave it

to his son Peter who died without issue intestate & Ann his sister now Ann Taite one of the partys afsd took possession thereof as sister of the whole blood & heir to the sd 350 a. of land adj Bridge Cr ... for the term of 1 year ... . Wit: John Keene, William Taylor, Alexander Anderson. Ackn 10 7br 1739 & admitted to record. Attest: James Fontaine clerk. (Pg 47)

10 7br 1739. Deed of Release. William Taite & Ann his wife of St. Stephens Parish, Northumberland Co for 100 pd released to Matthew Quill of same place a 350 a. tr of land ... [same as above] ... . Wit: John Keene, Wm Taylor, Alexander Anderson. Ackn 10 7br 1739 & admitted to record. Attest: James Fontaine clerk. (Pg 47)

Deed of Gift. Mary Demack of St. Stephens Parish, Northumberland Co for natural love & affection give to my well beloved grandson Leazure Wall of Cople Parish, Westmoreland Co a 50 a. parcel of land now in the tenure of me the sd Mary formerly made over to me by ye name of Mary Leazure by George Eskridge gent decd by deed dated 20 May 1729 & pt/o an escheat deed for 600 a. of land granted to sd Eskridge by the proprietors of Northern Neck 8 Aug 1712 & being pt/o a patent for 1,000 a. first granted John Mucks & William Newman 8 May 1631 which sd 50 a. of land is bounded by land of Leazure & Knoll & Yocomoco River ... . Wit: Danll [?], [?] Harrison, George Harrison. Ackn 10 7br 1739 & admitted to record. Attest: James Fontaine clerk. (Pg 47)

Will. William Hobson of St. Stephens Parish, Northumberland Co. 28 Feb 1737/8. To my son John Hobson & his male heirs all my right of ye land which my brother Thomas Hobson gave me. To my son John Hobson & his male heirs my mill which is now in the hands of my mother during her life. For want of such heirs the sd mill I give unto my two daus Sarah Hobson & Betty Hobson. To my four daus Sarah Hobson, Judith Hobson, Mary Ann Hobson & Betty Hobson 400 a. of land the plantation where I now live where my father lived on to be divided between them & their heirs. If either of my sd daus shall die without lawfull issue the sd land shall revert & come to ye other survivors to be equally divided between them. To my dau Sarah Hobson her first choice of the sd land when it is divided. To my son John Hobson one Negro woman called Peg & her future increase. To my dau Sarah Hobson one Negro boy called Aron. To my dau Judith Hobson one Negro girl called Charrity & her increase. To my dau Mary Ann Hobson one Negro woman called Jane & her increase. To my dau Betty Hobson one Negro boy called Moses. I give the use of one Negro man called Daniel unto my wife Judith Hobson during her widdowhood but in case she marrys I give the sd Negro unto my dau Betty Hobson. I give all ye rest of my whole estate of what nature or quality so ever to be divided amongst my wife, son & daus before mentioned My will is that my son John Hobson receive his part at ye age of 21 & my daus receive their parts at ye age of 18 or at the day of marriage. I appoint my wife Judith Hobson & sister Mrs. Clark (Clarck) Hobson Junr my executors. Wit: Abner Heale, Thomas Frasier. Proved 10 7br 1739 & admitted to record. Attest: James Fontaine clerk. (Pg 48)

Will. Francis Gaskins of St. Stephens Parish, Northumberland Co. 1 Sep 1738. To my son Isaac Gaskin one gun, two iron wedges, all my wearing cloaths & all my tools as coopers, carpenters, shoemakers & all such like & my best feather bed, bedstead & furniture. To my dau Leaseah box iron & heaters, five tongs, & iron [?] & her mothers wearing cloaths & all other things which was known to be her mothers & the next choice feather bed, bedstead & furniture. To my son Jesse Gaskins one feather bed, bedstead & furniture. After my debts pay'd & all quit claims the rest of my estate to be equally divided between my afsd three children. I desire that before the division be made there be an allowance for what is bestowed on my three children's learning & that they may have what can be conveniently purchased of learning for them that is ye garl to read the boys to read write & cipher. I leave my two sons Isaac & Jesse Gaskins for themselves at ye age of 20 years the girl at 18 as ye law directs 7 Sep. I desire my estate to be inventoried & not appraised 8 Oct. I leave Richard Alderson my executor. Wit: Beverley Reeve. Proved 10 7br 1739 & admitted to record. Attest: James Fontaine clerk. (Pg 49)

9 Aug 1739. In obedience to an order of court dated 9 Jul 1739 we Samll Blackwell, John Conway & Richard Smith have allotted Francis Downing a third pt/o reall & ½ of ye personall estate of Edward Downing decd: 1 chest of drawers, 1 feather bed, rug blankets, sheet, boulster, 2 pillows, bedstead, cord, matt, 1 white horse, a new chest, lock & key, a parsell of books, 1 old table, 3 chaffing dishes, 21 ½ lbs good puter, 3 sheep, 5 good cider casks, 3 old leather chairs, 1 wollen wheel, 3 cows & calves, 2 iron pots & some other lumber, choice of Negroes, hoggs, 2 Negroes Bristol & Judy. This report was returned 10 7br 1739 & on the motion of Francis Downing's atty was ordered to be recorded. Attest: James Fontaine clerk. (Pg 49)

9 Oct 1739. Deed. John Evins planter & Jane his wife of St. Stephens Parish, Northumberland Co for 25 pd sold to Rodham Kenner a 25 a. tr of land in the sd parish being pt/o 59 a. of land given by the will of Susanna Lawrence dated 19 Apr 1720 to her son in law John Hartly & Elizabeth his wife & their heirs & then falling to Jane & Elizabeth the daus & coheirs of the afsd John Hartly & Elizabeth his wife, bounded by John Davis & John Lewis … . Wit: Jno Lewis, Edward Mason, Matthew Burel, Lindsay Opie. Ackn 9 8br 1739 by John Evins & Jane his wife she being privately examined by Traves Colston & Robt Jones gent relinquished her right of dower in ye land & admitted to record. Attest: James Fontaine clerk. (Pg 49)

9 8br 1739. Bond. I John Evins of St. Stephens Parish, Northumberland Co
planter am firmly bound unto Rodham Kenner of same place in the penal sum of
60 pd ... the condition of this obligation is such that whereas ye afsd John Evins
& Jane his wife hath by deed [see above] sold unto the afsd Rodham Kenner a tr
of land, therefore if the sd John Evins do well & truly perform, fulfill &
accomplish all & singular the articles, clauses, covenants, grants & agreements
mentioned in the sd deed then this obligation to be void ... . Wit: John Lewis,
Edward Mason, Matthew Burrell, Lindsy Opie. Ackn 9 8br 1739 by John Evins
& Jane his wife & admitted to record. Attest: James Fontaine clerk. (Pg 50)

9 8br 1739. Bond. I Rodham Kenner of St. Stephens Parish, Northumberland
Co gent am firmly bound unto John Evins of same place planter for 100 pd ...
the condition of this obligation is such that whereas the afsd Rodham Kenner
bought a tr of land of Edward Lawrence late of this co & since the afsd purchase
the sd John Evins in right of his wife lays claim to 25 a. of the afsd land which
he the sd John Evins & Jane his wife hath this day ackn in this court to the afsd
Rodham Kenner on condition that he the sd Rodham Kenner allow them the
enjoyment of 12 a. of the afsd land during their natural lives, bounded by John
Davis & Spring Br, if the sd Rodham Kenner doth indemnify & keep harmless
the sd John Evins & Jane his wife afsd during their natural lives & let them have
the liberty for their stock on the other of the afsd Kenner's land nigh adj during
the time afsd then this obligation to be void ... . Wit: Robt Clark Junr, John
Webb, Archibald Johnston. Ackn 9 8br 1739 & admitted to record. Attest:
James Fontaine clerk. (Pg 50)

20 Sep 1739. Deed. John Davis & Elizabeth his wife one of ye daus & coheirs
of John Hartly & Elizabeth his wife late of St. Stephens Parish, Northumberland
Co decd for 800 lbs of tobacco sold to William Hughlet of same place a 25 a. tr
of land in the parish afsd in Cherry Point Neck, adj a br of Coan River, land
which Rodham Kenner bought of Edward Lawrence & land of John Evins,
which land was given by ye will of Susanna Lawrence to her dau Elizabeth
mother of ye above bound Elizabeth Davis ... . Wit: Nath Barret, John Evens,
Richd Tomson, Jane Evens, Eliz Evens. Ackn 8 8br 1739 by John Davis &
Elizabeth Davis she being privately examined by John Shapleigh gent
relinquished her right of dower in the land & admitted to record. Attest: James
Fontaine clerk. (Pg 51)

Will. Isaac Basey (Basye) of Great Wicocomoco Parish, Northumberland Co. 2
Jun 1739. My will is that my land may be divided in manner following, namely
that the division adj James Webb's plantation. To my son William Basey that
pt/o the land on the lower side of ye division with my mannor house. To my son
Jene Basye that pt/o the land being on ye upper side of ye division only the use
of it to my son William Basye during his mother's life. To Edmond Basye &

John Basye a 400 a. tr of land in Prince William Co upon a br of Bull Run to be divided between them & my son Edmond to have his first choice. To my dau Winefort Basye one feather bed & furniture & one cow & calf. To my dau Judith Basye one feather bed & furniture & one cow & calf. My will is & I leave the whole use of all the remainder of my estate, household goods & chattels unto my kind & loving wife Elizabeth Barge during her natural life or day of marriage & after her decease or day of marriage that then my will is that it shall be divided between my four sons & three daus. My will is that my two daus Winefort Basye & Judith Basye shall have what ground they shall have occasion to tend within their inclosure of my two sons William Barye & Gene Barye & lodging home with other conveniences during their single life. My will is that my estate shall not be appraised & that there shall be a just inventory taken of my estate by my executors. I appoint my wife Elizabeth Basye & my two sons William Basye & Edmond Basye executors. Wit: John Hill, William Bend. Proved 8 8br 1739 & admitted to record. Attest: James Fontaine clerk. (Pg 51)

Will. John Wood of Northumberland Co. 21 Aug 1739. To my Godson Saml Porter my great Bible & bed with all its furniture. To my sd Godson one Negro boy named Will, but if he die before he comes of age or without issue then I give the sd Negro to ye use of his two brothers Edward & John Porter. To my Godson John Barret the remainder of my estate. I appoint John Porter & William Barret executors. Wit: Peter Conway, John Porter. Proved 8 8br 1739 & admitted to record. Attest: James Fontaine clerk. (Pg 52)

In obedience to an order of Northumberland Co Court dated 10 7br 1739 we Saml Nelms, Abner Neall & Wm Wildy did meet & being first sworn did appraise the estate of William Hobson decd in money. 14 sheep, 59 lbs puter, some fine earthen ware, some earthen ware, 1 spice morter & pestle paper box, candlestick, skillet, some tin ware, 1 warming pan, 2 fire dogs, 1 cole still, 1 box iron, 2 heaters, 2 pare fire tongs, 1 shovel, 1 flesh fork, 2 botle jugs, 12 leather chairs, 1 chest, 1 table, a small trunk, some books, 1 large looking glass, 1 old cupboard, etc. Servant boy Richd Thomas. Negroes: man Daniel, woman Peg, woman Jane, girl Charity, boy Aron, boy Mous?, girl Winny. This inventory was exhibited 8 8br 1739 by Judith Hobson & Mrs. Clark Hobson Junr executrixes & on their motion admitted to record. (Pg 52)

An inventory of the estate of Francis Gaskins decd made 15 7br 1739: feather beds, rug, 2 blankets, 2 sheets, bolster, bedstead, rawhide, cord, 3 doz puter plates, 1 small puter dish, 8 puter plates, 2 old deep dishes, 1 large old bason, 3 small old basons, 2 good tankards, 2 good porringers, 2 old porringers, 1 brass candlestick, 1 old puter dish & 2 plates, 1 doz spoons, 1 tin funnel, pepper box, 1 large iron pot & hooks, 2 small iron pots, 1 pare of hooks, 2 old frying pans, 1 wooden ladle, flesh fork, 1 large chest, lock & key, 2 wooden boxes, 3 flag chairs, a stoole, etc. Errors excepted per Richard Alderson executor. This inventory was exhibited 8 8br 1739 & admitted to record. Attest: James Fontaine clerk. (Pg 53)

In obedience to an order of court held 11 Jun 1739 we Aron Taylor, Argail Taylor & Charles Coppidge (appointed) to divide the estate of Benjamin Palmer decd & pt/o the estate of Alice Palmer decd have divided & allotted Robert Palmer orphan of Benjamin Palmer his part of the sd estate, viz, 1 feather bed & boulster, 2 blankets, bedstead, cord & hide, 2 sides of [?] leather, 1 old cider cask, tobacco. Robert Palmer's part of ye estate of Alice Palmer decd: 3 lbs of puter, 1 table, 1 pot, 1 sheep, 1 cask, old tub, 1 pare of hors [?], 1 earthen Chamber pot. Have possessed Saml Smith guardian of ye sd Robert Palmer with ye above mentioned goods & tobacco 1 Aug 1739. This report of the division of the estate of Benjamin & Alice Palmer was returned to court 9 8br 1739 & admitted to record. Attest: James Fontaine clerk. (Pg 53)

11 Jul 1739. To Thomas Harrison Junr, John Dickin & Anthony Seale gent of Prince William Co greeting, whereas we trusting to ye provident circumspection & fidelity request you jointly to examine Jane Pursell w/o John Pursell of co afsd whether she voluntarily & of her own free will is willing to sign seal & deliver certain deeds of livery & seizing & bond dated --- 1739 for the conveyance of 155 a. of land in Northumberland Co unto William Fallin of same co & that she is willing that the same shall be recorded ... . James Fontaine clerk. (Pg 53)

27 Jul 1739 In obedience to ye above order we Thos Harrison Junr, John Dickin & Antho Seale have examined Jane Purcell & she freely consents to ye acknowledgment of tha afsd land. This commission & cert was presented 8 8br 1739 & on the motion of William Fallin is admitted to record. Attest: James Fontaine clerk. (Pg 54)

12 9br 1739. Memorandum of the division made between Yarret Hughlet & John Christopher of a parcel of land we bought of [?] Conway adj land formerly Adam Yarret's, Marrow's old field, Conway's old field, Mill Road & Thos Moses? mill, & John Christopher hath taken for his part the place where old [?] Conway lives towards his own land & Yarret Hughlet has got for his part towards Dawkinses & Bice's & the Bridge Swamp & the sd Yarret Hughlet & John Christopher are contented & satisfied with the sd division. Wit: John Richardson, Abner Neale. This division & conveyance from Yarret Hughlet & John Christopher of a parcel of land they bought of [?] Conway to each other was exhibited by Yarret Hughlet & John Christopher & on their motion was admitted to record. Attest: James Font clerk. (Pg 54)

Will. Richard Booth of St. Stephen Parish, Northumberland Co. 26 Sep 1739.
To my wife Martha Booth three Negroes, viz, Dick, Judith & Lucy, five bushels
of wheat & eight barils of Indian corn, four hogs, one large iron pot, one large
chest, a side sadle & three head of cattle, her bed & furniture. To my son
Richard Booth & his heirs my plantation I now live upon & that it be delivered
up next Christmas. But for want of such heirs then in such case it shall revert &
come back to my son John Booth & his heirs & for want of his heirs then it shall
& will come back to my son Adam Booth & his heirs. I give my Negro fellow
Cesar to my son Richard Booth & his heirs. To my son John Booth my sadle,
bridle, coat & chest. To Adam Booth my vest & breeches. To my son James
Booth 200 lbs of tobacco. To my son Wm Booth one pare of shoes, one pare of
Hokins & a gun & hatt. To my dau Elizabeth Short one box iron & heaters.
The rest of my estate to be divided amongst my six children after my debts are
paid. I appoint my son Richard Booth executor. Wit: Thomas Barecroft,
George Duke. Proved 12 9br 1739 & admitted to record. Attest: James
Fontaine clerk. (Pg 54)

An account of what debt is due to the estate of John Rider decd & what crop of
tobacco was made. Wm Garret, Grice? Edwards. 1575 lbs tobacco. Saml
Downing, Wm Hughlet, Francis Taylor. 11 pd 3 sl. Received tobacco from
Hugh Miller, Alexander [?], Isaac Edwards, Wm Eustace, Richd Howson, David
Lattimore, Saml Smith, Aaron Taylor a bushell salt. 891 lbs tobacco. Errors
excepted per Alice Rider executrix. This additional inventory & acct was
presented 18 9br 1739 by Alice Rider extx & on her motion admitted to record.
Attest: James Fontaine clerk. (Pg 54)

A true & just inventory of the estate of Isaac Basey decd. 5 feather beds &
furniture, 2 old beds & furniture, 33 head of hogs, 15 head of cattle, 6 head of
sheep, 2 old horses, 2 chests, 2 old trunks, 4 wooden boxes, 1 spice box, 87 old
books, 6 flag chairs, 2 leather chairs, 3 wooden chairs, 5 wooden stools, 2 oval
tables, 2 small tables, 3 old guns, 1 case of pistols & holsters, 2 old swords, 1
old clock, 1 silver watch, 3 iron pots & hooks, 1 copper pot, 1 iron kittle, 3 brass
kittles, 1 copper kittle, 13 pewter plates, 3 frying pans, etc. This inventory was
exhibited 12 9br 1739 by Elizabeth Basey & William Basey executors & on their
motion admitted to record. Attest: James Fontaine clerk. (Pg 55)

A true & perfect inventory of the estate of John Wood decd taken 2 9br by
David Lattimore, Thos Hurst & Swanson Lunsford appointed by order of court
to be appraised this day sworn by Capt Robt Jones 1739. 1great Bible, 1 feather
bed, furniture, quilt, 1 Negro boy, 2 great coats, 4 suits of cloaths, 2 pare
stockins, 2 pare cotton stockins, 12 pare leather breeches, 2 felt hats, 5 pare of
shoes, 4 knives & forks, 1 chest & some lumber, 2 botles, 1 jug, 3
handkerchiefs, 5 good books, 2 old books, 1 set shoemakers tools, parcel of

thread, 1 old watch, 1 bason, 2 gold rings, etc. [Not totaled] This inventory was exhibited by William Barret executor & admitted to record. Attest: James Fontaine clerk. (Pg 55)

Pursuant to an order of court granted Richd Booth executor of the will of Richard Booth decd we Robt Clark Junr, Edward Barnes & Ormsbee Haynie being first sworn before Major John Waughop have appraised the sd decd's estate in current money. 14 large hogs, 3 hogs, 3 cows, 1 heiffer, 1 bull, 1 stear, 2 yearlings, 1 old black horse, 1 chest, some lumber, 1 cloth jackcoat & breeches, 1 cloth coat, 1 fine hat, spare shoes & Hokins, 1 sadle, bridle & sadle cloth, parcel of nailes, 1 croscut saw, a set of wedges, coopers tools, carpenters tools, 2 narrow axes, 1 whip saw, etc. Servant named Ann King having 5 years to serve. Negroes: woman Lucy, woman Judy, man Cesar, man Dick. [Not totaled] This inventory was exhibited 10 --- 1739 by Richd Booth extr & admitted to record. Attest: James Fontaine clerk. (Pg 55)

8 Dec 1739. Deed. Edward Bowen of Wicocomoco Parish, Northumberland Co for 7,000 lbs of tobacco sold to John Irons of same place a 12 a. parcel of land being pt/o a pattent of 350 a. of land dated 3 Apr 1651 & granted to Henry Hurst afterwards by several conveyances pt/o the sd 350 a. became vested in John Bowen decd as per deed of sale dated 27 Aug 1658 which sd John Bowen was father to the sd Edward Bowen ... . Wit: Moses Champion, John Harvey. Ackn 10 --- 1739 & admitted to record. Attest: James Fontaine clerk. (Pg 56)

8 --- 1739. Bond. I Edward Bowen of Wicocomoco Parish, Northumberland Co am firmly bound unto John Irons of same place for 70 pd ... the condition of this obligation is such that whereas the afsd Edward Bowen by one deed [see above] sold unto the sd John Irons a 12 a. parcel of land, now if the sd Edward Bowen shall well & truly perform, fulfill & keep all & singular the covenants, grants & articles in the sd deed then this obligation to be void ... . Wit: Moses Champion, John Harvey. Ackn 10 --- 1739 & admitted to record. Attest: James Fontaine clerk. (Pg 57)

10 7br ----. To John Waughop, Matthew Kenner & Traves Colston gent of Northumberland Co greeting, whereas we trusting to ye provident circumspection & fidelity request you jointly to examine Ann Taite w/o William Taite of afsd co whether she voluntarily & of her own free will signed, sealed & delivered deeds of lease & release dated 8 & 10 Sep 1739 for the conveyance of 350 a. of land unto Matthew Quill gent of co afsd & that she is willing that the same shall be recorded ... . James Fontaine clerk. 11 7br 1739 In obedience to ye within commission we Matthew Kenner & Tras Colston have privately examined the within mentioned Ann Taite who declared that she did voluntarily sign seale & deliver the deeds mentioned & she is willing & desirous that sd

deeds may be recorded. This commission was returned 8 8br 1739 & recorded. Attest: James Fontaine clerk. (Pg 57)

Will. Saml Lunsford of Wicocomoco Parish, Northumberland Co. 30 8br 1739. To my son William Lunsford my now dwelling plantation with the portion of land belonging. To my dau Betty a feather bed with a new cotton tickin & all the furniture belonging to it. To my dau Sarah the bed wherein I lie with all the furniture belonging to it. To my son Richard Lunsford all that estate that I bought of Bartholomew Richard Dodson which is now on the plantation of the sd Dodson. To my dau Mary one English shilling. It is my will that all the rest of my estate be equally divided between my son John Lunsford & my son Richard Lunsford whom I also appoint executors. Wit: Jesse Robinson, George Mills. Proved 10 --- 1739 & admitted to record. Attest: James Fontaine clerk. (Pg 57)

Will. Thomas Gill of St. Stephens Parish, Northumberland Co. 30 May 1737. To my grandson John Gill 150 a. of land which I purch of John Bales. To my four grandsons Thomas Gill, John Gill, William Gill & Elles Gill nine Negroes & all their increase, viz, Andrew, Ned, Judy, Grace, Jeny, Young Andrew, Sarah, Geney & Young Judy to be divided when the first child shall arrive to age of 21. It is my desire that my extr shall have the care & maintainance of the sd Negroes until the children come to age. To my dau Sarah Hudnal's children nine Negroes, viz, Betty & her three children, Dick, Cesar, Lucey, Caffey & Doll & their three children, viz Lucey, Mark & Lukey & all their increase to be divided among all my dau's children at her death & that my sd dau shall have the whole profits & benefits of the sd Negroes during her natural life. To my son Ellas (Elles) Gill & his heirs the land where I now live on Great Wicocomoco together with all my lands before not given & the mill & for want of such heirs to my grandson William Gill. To my son Elles Gill all the remainder of my Negroes with all their increase & all my personall estate, debts & credits whatsoever & I do appoint him my sole executor. Wit: Wm Hobson, Wm Fallin, Robert Wadinton, Thos Parry. Proved 10 --- 1739 & admitted to record. Attest: James Fonaine clerk. (Pg 58)

In obedience to an order of court dated 10 --- 1739 we Thos Wornom, Wm Wildy & Richard Smith did meet at the house of Thomas Gill gent decd & being first sworn before Capt John Shapleigh gent did appraise the estate of the sd decd for money. 1 large Bible, truckle bedstead, feather bed & furniture, 1 pistol, 1 pare of boots, 2 warming pans, a case of pistols & holsters, 1 pare of bellows, some knives & forks & carrole boxes & trifles, 2 padlocks, 2 pare of sheep shears, 3 pare of Willards & 3 cow bells, 2 spice morters & pestles, 8 old sickles & lumber, 7 candlesticks, 2 mugs, 3 flag chairs, 1 old table, 1 cane, 2 old hors whips, 2 old guns, etc. Negroes: man named Andrew, woman named Judy,

34

man named Ned, woman named Geney, boy named Andrew, girl named Sarah, boy named Jesse, girl named Judy, boy named Abraham, woman named Bess, boy named Dick, boy named Cesar, girl named Lucy, man named Cuffy, woman named Doll, girl named Lucia, boy named Mark, female child named Lukey, boy named Cuffy, child named Billy, man named Tuck?, woman named Jenne, woman named Rose, child named Moses, woman named Mancor?, woman named Hannah, man named Jack, child named Sam, woman named Sue, child named George, child named Dinah, man named Dick, man named Robin, woman named Moll, girl named Sarah, boy named Joseph, man named Davis, woman named Pleasant, man named Billy, child named Ben, man named Jacob, man named Daniel, man named Job. [Not totaled] To cash 76 pd 11 sl 2 pn. This inventory was presented 14 Jan 1739/40 by Elles Gill executor & on his motion was admitted to record. Attest: James Fontaine clerk. (Pg 58)

Pursuant to an order of court dated 10 --- 1739 we John Coppidge, Swanson Prichard & Lar Taylor met being first sworn by Capt Robert Jones & appraised the estate of Samuel Lunsford decd into current money. Cows, heifers, 2 stears, 1 bull, feather beds & furniture, stack of fodder, 1 croscut saw, 1 old plow & harrow, a parsel of corn, 12 sheep, 7 old cask, 5 ducks, 2 sows, 8 pigs, 6 gees, 1 round table, 1 old chest, 2 old guns, 2 old chairs, 1 looking glass, 1 Bible, parsel of old books, 10 glas botles & trifles, 1 iron spit, fire tongs & lumber, 1 set of iron wedges, 1 old horse & harness, 1 old mare 4 pots & hooks, 1 old skillet, etc. [Not totaled] This inventory was exhibited 14 Jan 1739 by John Lunsford & Richard Lunsford executors & on their motion was admitted to record. Attest: James Fontaine clerk. (Pg 61)

3 Jan 1739/40. Deed. John Tully of Christ Church Parish, Lancaster Co sawer for 5,000 lbs of tobacco sold to John Coles of St. Stephens Parish, Northumberland Co a 50 a. parcel of land in St. Stephens Parish on ye side of Great Wicocomoco River adj the land or Richard Hadwell formerly Edward Sanders', John Coles, Howels Cr, land of William Fallin formerly Tobias Pursell's & land of John Coles formerly Nats, together with a grist mill now running & in good order being pt/o a dividend of land which formerly belonging to Tobias Pursell which sd land was sold to Wm Rankins who decd without heirs only a half sister which right of escheat fell to John Tully who intermarried the sd sister who being fully authorized to make sale as by deed will appear dated 27 9br 1739 .... Wit: Clement Lattimer, Jno Conway, Edwd Coles. Memo: Peaceable possession & seizing of the within granted 50 a. of land was this day given & delivered to John Coles by the deliver of turf & twig. Wit: Clement Lattimer, Edward Coles, Wm Edwards Junr. Ackn 14 Jan 1739 by John Tully & Elizabeth his wife she being privately examined by Saml Blackwell gent relinquished her right of dower in the land & admitted to record. Attest: James Fontaine clerk. (Pg 62)

8 Jan 1739/40. Bond. I John Tully of Christ Church Parish, Lancaster Co sawer am firmly bound unto John Coles (Cole) of St. Stephens Parish, Northumberland Co in the penal sum of 10,000 lbs of good & lawful tobacco ... the condition of this obligation is such that whereas the afsd John Tully by one deed [see above] sold a 50 a. tr of land on Great Wicocomoco River unto the afsd John Coles, now if the sd John Tully shall observe, perform, fulfill, accomplish & keep all & every clause, article, conditions, provisoes & agreements mentioned in ye sd deed then this obligation to be void ... . Wit: Clement Lattimer, John Conway, Edward Coles. Ackn 14 Jan 1739/40 & admitted to record. Attest: James Fontaine clerk. (Pg 63)

14 Jan 1739/40. Deed. William Lunsford & Martha his wife of Wicocomoco Parish, Northumberland Co for 4,000 lbs of tobacco sold to Swanson Pritchard of same place a 50 a. parcel of land bounded by the land of sd Swanson Prichard, John Swanson & Grace Edwards ... . Wit: William James, Robt Angell. Ackn 14 Jan 1739/40 & admitted to record. Attest: James Fontaine clerk. (Pg 63)

Pursuant to an order of court dated 14 Jan 1739/40 for settling the acct of the estate of John Lunsford decd in ye hands of George Mills adminr & laying off to Moses Lunsford petitioner his pt/o the sd estate that is moveable we Charles Coppedge, John Coppedge & John Taylor have met & valued to the sd Moses Lunsford his proportional part being 5 pd 10 sl of the sd estate. This report of the division of the estate of John Lunsford decd was exhibited 11 Feb 1739/40 & recorded. Attest: James Fontaine clerk. (Pg 63)

9 Feb 1739. Deed. John Cralle of Northumberland Co gent son & heir of John Cralle late of sd co decd in obedience to a decree & 5 sl doth sell & release unto Willoughby Newton of Westmoreland Co gent a messuage & 280 a. of land ... whereas Richard Flint late of St. Stephens Parish, Northumberland Co decd by deed of feoffment dated 27 May 1698 the sd Flint did sell unto the afsd John Cralle decd a messuage & 280 a. of land then in possession of the sd Richard Flint lying on Mattapony River in Cherry Point & whereas no money or other valuable consideration was really paid by the sd John Cralle to the sd Richard Flint at ye time of executing the deed but the same was made in trust to & for the use, benefit & behoof of the sd Richard Flint & his heirs & the sd Richard Flint accordingly continued in the quiet possession of the sd premises during his life & by his will dated 6 May 1701 devised the same in manner as in the sd will is mentioned & the devisees in the sd will named & those claiming under them from the time of the death of the sd Richard Flint have also continued in quiet possession of the sd premises & whereas the sd Willoughby Newton who is now in possession of the sd premises & claims ye same by purchase from some or one of the devisees in the will of the sd Richard Flint named lately exhibited a

bill in Chancery in the Generall Court of this Colony agt the sd John Cralle party to these presents who lets up a title to these premises under the sd deed of feoffment to deliver the trust afsd to compell the sd John Cralle as son & heir of his sd father John Cralle decd to convey the legal estate in the sd premises to him & the sd cause came on to be heard in the sd Generall Court on 28 Oct last past & upon hearing ye same it was among other things ordered & decreed that the sd John Cralle or his heirs should convey to the sd Willoughby Newton the legal estate in the sd premises ... . Wit: Cavan Dulany, John Lewis, Gress? Fantleroy Junr. Ackn 18 Jan 1739/40 & recorded. Attest: James Fontaine clerk. (Pg 64)

6 Mar 1739/40. In obedience to an order of court dated 11 Feb 1739/40 we Saml Blackwell, Charles Fallin & Argail Taylor having met have allotted John Berry his wife's pt/o her father Geffery Goridge estate: 1 feather bed & furniture, 1 cow, 1 heiffer, 2 small heifers, 2 cows, 1 ram, 1 lamb, 4 young hogs, 1 looking glass, 2 good chairs, 1 frying pan, some earthen ware. 14 pd 16 sl 6 pn. This report of the division of the estate of Geffery Gouge decd was returned 10 Mar 1739/40 & recorded. Attest: James Fontaine clerk. (Pg 65)

17 7br 1739. Power of Attorney. I Hugh Miller merchant have appointed Joseph Hudnall planter of Northumberland Co my atty to ask, demand, sue, recover & receive of every person whatsoever that is indebted to me & to take all lawfull means in my name for the recovery thereof ... . Wit: John Graham, Saml Blackwell gent. Attest: James Fontaine clerk. (Pg 65)

Will. Joseph Millard. 8 Feb 1731/2. To my cousin Elizabeth Millard dau of Christopher Millard one cow & calf & all ye rest of my whole estate to my wife Jane Millard & her heirs forever to whom I appoint executor. Wit: John Flint, George Barret. At a court held 15 Mar 1739/40 John Flint & George Barret evidences to this within will not being found or got to prove the sd will, Thomas Myars came into court & made oath that Joseph Millard decd gave him a paper which he said was his will & desired him to keep it which paper was by him afterward delivered to Jane Millard the executrix within mentioned which he believes to be this very paper. Ann Myars made oath that she saw this will writ & is sure that this will is Joseph Millard's will & that it was writ at his request. This will was presented to ye court by Jane Millard executrix & recorded. Attest: James Fontaine clerk. (Pg 65)

Will. William Eustace of Wicocomoco Parish, Northumberland Co gent. 3 Sep MDCCXXXIX. My will is that my wife Ann Eustace have & enjoy the use of my dwelling plantation & also my plantation at Cabin Neck adj thereto with the use of all my working slaves on the sd two plantations & the use of all my stocks of horses, cattle, sheep & hogs & also the use of all my plate & household furniture during the term of her natural life. My will is that my children remain with my sd wife till they come of age or marry & that she provide them with board out of the stocks hereby given to her & then [?] to my son John. To my son John Eustace my plantation & lands at the Browntown? & my plantation & lands where Richard Lock now lives together with all the stock of horses, cattle, sheep & hogs, & all the remainder of my slaves not before given. To my son John Eustace my plantations & land, slaves, stocks & household goods herein before bequeathed to his mother after her decease. To my son William Eustace my tr of land I purch from George Rust, John Mercer & John Coppedge together with the stocks of horses, cattle & hogs. My will is that my son John by purch or otherwise settle 10 able working slaves on the sd lands sometime within 5 years which sd lands, stocks & slaves I hereby give unto my sd son William at the age of 21 years. It is my desire that the three slaves now on the sd lands (if alive at time when my sd son shall settled the afsd lands) shall be pt/o the afsd slaves. My will is that my sd son John purch for my afsd son William a lot or ½ a. of land in the Town of Falmouth or Fredericksburg & save the same as the law directs in case the same shall not be done at ye time of the purch which sd lot or ½ a. of land I give to my son William when he attains the age of 21. Whereas there is a suit now depending agt me in ye Generall Court for a small pt/o the lands hereby given to my son William in Prince William Co. In case a recovery should be had it is my desire that my son John purch the part so recovered for my sd son William & that my sd son William enjoy the same as it is before to him given. I give to my son Isaac Eustace my lands in Stafford Co on the Pignut Ridge bought of Capt John Lee. It is my will that my son John by purchase or otherwise settle 10 able working slaves on the sd land as also 5 head of cattle & 5 head of hogs some time within 10 years which sd lands, slaves & stocking hereby given to sd son Isaac when he attains the age of 21. I give to each of my daus Elizabeth, Sarah & Anne 400 pd to be paid them ½ thereof when they shall attain the age of 21 or at the day of marriage & the other ½ on the birth of the first child they have. But in case it so happens that either of my sd daus do not arrive to the age of 21 or marry or have a child her part of this bequest shall be divided amongst my surviving children. It is my desire that my son Hancock Eustace as soon as he arrives to the age of 16 years be bound apprentice to some well qualified commander of a London ship to serve till he attains the age of 21 & that care be taken that he be kindly used & sufficiently instructed in the art of navigation & that my executors have power to advance a sum of money with my sd son not exceeding 50 pd & if need be to find him with necessary apparel during his apprenticeship out of my estate. I give unto my son Hancock Eustace when he arrives to the age of 21, 400 pd the sum given with him when he shall be bound apprentice but in case my sd son Hancock shall not arrive to ye age of 21 the afsd 400 pd or what part remains to be divided amongst the rest of my children. In case my wife Ann Eustace shall be unwilling to accept of the legacys herein to her given in lieu of her dower in my estate it is my will that my daus & my son Hancock deduct 50 pd out of their legacys to make good the present disadvantage that may attend my son John in case it should happen as afsd. I give unto my son John Eustace all my store goods & all my book debts & my moneys & tobacco in any land & my goods & all my effects in trade & my will is that my sd son John carry on my trade now begun under the assistance & advice of my friend Matt Quill gent till my sd son John shall arrive to age of 21. I do desire that the tobacco purch in the sd trade be shipt to England & that Thomas Gaskins be retained as an assistant to my sd son John in the store & gathering in the debts after the rate of 5 pd per year during 2 years ... the rest of my estate of what nature I give to my afsd son John Eustace. I appoint my afsd wife & sd son John Eustace executors. Wit: Elizabeth Howson, Thos Edwards, Thos Gaskins. Proved 10 Mar 1739/40 & admitted to record. Attest: James Fontaine clerk. (Pg 65)

In obedience to an order of court held 11 Feb 1739/40 we James Farind?, Ormsby Hayney & Saml Wensted? being first sworn before Capt Matthew Kenner justice to appraise the estate of John Dogget decd in money & have as follows: Negro man called Dick, Negro woman call Sary. 4 young stears, 4 cows, 1 heiffer, 1 yearling, 1 old mare & young horse, 1 ridding horse, saddle & bridle, beds & furniture, 1 cow, 9 young hogs, parcel of sheep, 1 chest, an old trunk, 2 old tables, 1 old chest, old safe, 1 gun, 16 lbs good puter, 14 lbs old puter, 2 axes, 1 old spinning wheel & cards, 1 iron skillet & frying pan, 3 chears, 27 lbs of good feathers, 1 box iron, 1 iron spit, 2 pots & hooks, parcel of leather, some cotton, a parcel of books, etc. [Not totaled] This inventory was exhibited 10 Mar 1739/40 by Mary Dogget adminr & admitted to record. Attest: James Fontaine clerk. (Pg 67)

In obedience to an order of court held 10 Mar 1739/40 granted unto Jane Millard adminr of Joseph Millard decd for appraisement of the sd Millard decd's estate we Richard Claughton, Reinbevton Claughton & Thos Hall being sworn by Traves Colston justice have appraised this 3 Apr year afsd which was brought before us by sd adminr: 9 cows & calves, 3 young stears, 1 heiffer, 6 lambs, 1 ram, beds & furniture, 1 buck skin, a Keny coat & some other waring cloaths, 1 large Bible, 30 lbs of puter, 1 tankard, 18 lbs old puter, 1 spice mortar & pestle, 3 pots & hooks, iron kettle, 2 frying pans, parcel of iron, 3 old chests, etc. [Not totaled] This inventory was exhibited 14 Apr 1740 by Jane Millard adminr & on her motion admitted to record. Attest: James Fontaine clerk. (Pg 67)

In obedience to an order of court dated 10 Mar 1739 we Wm Wildy, Jno Leaband & Thos Womour Junr being met & sworn by Saml Blackwell have valued & appraised the estate of Joseph Wallis decd: 22 lbs good puter, 9 lbs old puter, beds, boulsters, blankets, sheets, bedsteads, parcel of turn'd wooden ware, 1 jacket, breechers, 1 hat, 1 table, old chairs, some other things, parcel of

earthen ware, 1 broad ax, 1 hammer, 2 old hows, box iron & heater, drinking
glasses, 2 old pailes, 1 piggin, 4 good cider cask, 3 old barrils, etc. This
inventory was exhibited 19 Apr 1740 by Ellinor Wallis adminr & admitted to
record. Attest: James Fontaine clerk. (Pg 68)

10 Apr 1740. Power of Attorney. I Margaret Walkden hereby appoint my trusty
friend Richard Thomson my atty to receive & likewise to pay all debts due to &
from me & likewise to prosecute all & every suite belonging to me … . Wit:
Jas Daughity, Wm Hughlet. Proved 14 Apr 1740 & admitted to record. Attest:
James Fontaine clerk. (Pg 68)

14 Mar 1739/40. Award. We John Waughop, John Shapligh & William Taite
elected & indifferently chosen by Lindsey Opie & Parish Garner to settle &
make bounds to ye line of partition & division between their lands as by bonds
given by each party to stand & abide to the award & determination of us, we
accordingly did meet on the lands 14 Mar instant & after having perused the
papers produced & viewed the situation of ye lands we began at a post the
reputed corner for the lands of Wm Keen decd, Thomas Matthews & the land of
Lindsey Opie now in dispute … & posts marked by two of the processioners,
viz, John Lewis & William Taite, we also award & determine that the rayls on
their former reputed lands shall belong to them who before claimed them & it is
likewise our oppinion & award that if at any time hear after the sd Opie is
obstructed or hindered from coming to the first mentioned post by any older
patent or deed then it is our judgment & final award that the above settlement
shall be in no ways binding on the above partys, viz, Linsey Opie & Parish
Garner. The within award was presented in court by Lindsey Opie & Parish
Garner on whose motion the same was admitted to record. Attest: James
Fontaine clerk. (Pg 68)

15 Mar 1739/40. Award. We John Shapleigh & William Taite arbitrators
elected & indifferently chosen by Linsey Opie & Griffin Fauntleroy (Fantleroy)
Junr to settle & make bounds to ye line of partition & division between their
lands as by bonds given by each party to abide & stand to the award &
determination of us, we accordingly did meet on ye land in dispute this 15 Mar
instant & after having perused the papers produced by both & viewed the
situation of the lands & after having run severall lines & reversed others we
agreed & do determine & award the dividing line betwixt the sd Opie &
Fauntleroy … we also award & determine that the rayles of ye land before
claimed by either of ye partys shall remain & belong to the first claimers … .
Wit: John Kennedy, James Straughan, Samuel Bonum. This award was
presented 12 May 1740 by Linsey Opie & Griffin Fauntleroy Junr & on their
motion was recorded. Attest: James Fontaine clerk. (Pg 68)

10 May 1740. Deed. Alexander Rider of St. Stephens Parish, Northumberland Co for 1,550 lbs of tobacco sold to Samll Nelms of same place a 15 ½ a. tr of land on one of the head brs of Great Wicocomoco River bounded by Saml Nelms, Alexander Rider, Isaac Edwards & John Edwards ... . Wit: Wm Nelms, Saml Downing. Ackn 12 May 1740 & admitted to record. Attest: James Fontaine clerk. (Pg 69)

-- May 1740. Bond. I Alexander Rider of St. Stephens Parish, Northumberland Co am indebted to Saml Nelms of same place for 3,100 lbs of tobacco ... the condition of this obligation is such that whereas the afsd Alexander Rider has sold a tr of land [see above] unto the afsd Saml Nelms, if the sd Alexander Rider doth in all things comply with the covenants, agreements &c contained in the sd deed then this obligation to be void... . Wit: Saml Downing, Charles Betts. Ackn 12 May 1740 & admitted to record. Attest: James Fontaine clerk. (Pg 70)

11 Jul 1739. Deed. John Purcell (Parcell) now of Hammilton Parish, Prince William Co for 30 pd sold to William Fallin of St. Stephens Parish, Northumberland Co a 156 a. tr of land in St. Stephens Parish on the n side of Great Wicocomoco River bounded by the lands of John Coles, Mary White, William [?], George Kerterson? & William Rankins decd ... . Wit: Peter Hayes, Wm Harrison, Henry Schofield. Ackn 12 May 1740 & admitted to record. Attest: James Fontaine clerk. (Pg 70)

12 Apr 1740. Deed. William Falling of St. Stephens Parish, Northumberland Co for 50 pd sold to James Philips of same place an 85 a. parcel of land in the sd parish which land was formerly in the possession of William Badger & by the sd William Badger assigned & made over by deed dated 17 May 1727 unto John Mew & by ye sd John Mew assigned & made over unto the afsd William Fallin by deed dated 3 Feb 1735, bounded by Tarpit Cr, land of Col Peter Dresly, Ann Howell decd & Great Wicocomoco River ... . Wit: Richard Smith, Thos Hillman, John Philips. Ackn 12 --- 1740 & admitted to record. Attest: James Fontaine clerk. (Pg 71)

7 May 1740. Deed. John James for a valuable consideration sold to John Hudnall 12 ½ a. of land at & near the n side of the head of Great Wicocomoco River adj Joseph Hudnall & Robert Anderson ... . Wit: Moses Champion, Elizabeth Hudnall. Memo: Quiet & peaceable possession & seizing of the within mentioned 12 ½ a. of land was this day given & delivered to John Hudnall by delivery of turf & twig. Wit: Moses Champion, Elizabeth Hudnall, Winifield Wright. Ackn 12 May 1740 & admitted to record. Attest: James Fontaine clerk. (Pg 72)

19 Dec 1739. Deed. James Ginn (Genn) of St. Stephens Parish, Northumberland Co for 45 pd sold to Robert Alexander of St. Marys Parish,

White Chappel, Lancaster Co, VA a 150 a. tr of land called Denis Eias's old plantation in St. Stephens Parish, now or late in ye tenure & occupation of ye sd James Ginn, bounded by ye Main Swamp of Great Wicocomoco River, Robert Carter esqr decd, Arthur Mash decd, Thomas Smith decd, Richard Walker, Richard Denne & James Sebarees? it being pt/o a patent for 400 a. formerly granted to Denis Conway & Davis Eias in joint tenants by patent dated 11 Mar 1669 & the sd Denis Conway being ye surviving joint tenant to ye same is descended to him & from him to ye sd John Conway as being eldest son & heir of sd Denis Conway ... . Wit: Richard Dinnee (Dennee), John Dinnee (Dennee). Ackn 12 May 1740 & admitted to record. Attest: James Fontaine clerk. (Pg 72)

19 Dec 1739. Bond. I James Genn (Ginn) of St. Stephens Parish, Northumberland Co am firmly bound & obliged to Robert Alexander of St. Marys Parish, White Chappel, Lancaster Co, VA for 90 pd ... the condition of this obligation is such that if the afsd James Genn do well & truly observe, perform, fulfill & keep all & singular the covenants, grants, articles, clauses, conditions & agreements whatsoever mentioned in one indenture of bargain & sale [see above] then this obligation to be void ... . Wit: Richard Dinnee, John Dinnee. Ackn 12 May 1740 & admitted to record. Attest: James Fontaine clerk. (Pg 73)

12 May 1740. Deed. Elizabeth Jones of Wicocomoco Parish, Northumberland Co for 15 pd sold to George Ball of same place ¼ pt/o a water mill upon the s most br of Scotland Mill Cr which sd mill by the will of Bartholomew Schreever late decd is become vested in ye sd Elizabeth Jones & her three sisters as coheirs to their father Saml Heath decd & called Schreevers Mill ... . Wit: John Ball, George Ball Junr, Andrew Chilton. Ackn 12 May 1740 & admitted to record. Attest: James Fontaine clerk. (Pg 74)

12 May 1740. Deed. John Brown of Hammilton Parish, Prince William Co, VA for 3,000 lbs of tobacco sold to Thos Davis of Great Wicocomoco Parish, Northumberland Co a 75 a. tr of land in Wicocomoco Parish bounded by land of John Pope, Benjamin Brown, John Hill & the Coach Road, being pt/o a tr of land devised by ye will of Benjamin Brown to his son John Brown party to these presents ... . Wit: Edwin Fielding, George Dawkins, Elizabeth Hill. Ackn 12 May 1740 & admitted to record. Attest: James Fontaine clerk. (Pg 75)

Will. Francis Vanlandenham Senr of St. Stephens Parish, Northumberland Co planter. 27 Jul 1736. To my son Francis Vanlandenham 1 sl. To my dau Mary Danon? 1 sl. To my son Thomas Vanlandenham 1 sl. All the rest of my personal estate I give unto my wife Elizabeth Vanlandenham during her widdowhood & afterwards to be equally divided between my three daus & two sons, viz, Elizabeth Vanlandenham, Ann Gerited?, Jane Vanlandenham, George Vanlandenham & John Vanlandenham & I do hereby make by wife extx … . Wit: James Oldham, John Backer. Proved 12 May 1740 & admitted to record. Attest: James Fontaine clerk. (Pg 76)

Will. Samuel Mahane. 10 Aug 1737. To my grandson Saml Mahane all my land on the n side of Main Road between the Widdow Watts' line & his own plantation. To my dau Sarah one parcel of land which I bought of Thomas Salberry. To my son Samuel Mahone all my land on ye s side of the road to the Horsehead Swamp & the plantation that Benjamin Chilton lived on with the land, likewise a musket he now has in his possession. To my dau Jane Williams one parcel of land (belonging to ye land where I now live) without the neck fence. To my son Thomas Mahane all my land within the neck fence where now I live. To my grandson Saml Williams one small gun. To my wife Dorothy & all my children my personall estate after my debts be paid but my wife to have the use of my personal estate during her life but not to sell or make waste. I appoint my son Thomas Mahane & my son in law Thomas Williams my executors. Wit: P. Cook, Wm Lattimore, Moses Champion, John Harvey. Proved 12 May 1740 & admitted to record. Attest: James Fontaine clerk. (Pg 76)

Will. Richard Pierce (Pearce) of St. Stephens Parish, Northumberland Co. 30 Mar 1740. To my wife Margit Pearce all & singular & every part & parcel of my estate that I am now possest with & that I have any right, title or reversion thereunto she first paying all my debts. I appoint my wife Margit Pearce my extx. Wit: David Williams, John Hack. Proved 12 May 1740 & admitted to record. Attest: James Fontaine clerk. (Pg 77)

Will. Swanson Prichard of Northumberland Co. 9 Apr 1740. I give all ye land that I now hold to my son Swan Prichard. It is my will that all my Negroes shall be equally divided amongst my wife & all my children at the day of my wifes marriage. It is my will that all the rest of my moveable estate shall be equally divided between my wife & all my children at ye day of my wifes marriage. It is my desire that if any of my daus should die without lawfull issue that their pt/o the Negroes shall go to my son Swan Prichard. It is my will that my wife shall have the use of all my land, Negroes & moveable estate during her widowhood. I appoint my wife Margrit Prichard & my good friend Robert Angell my executors. Wit: Joshua James, Charles Prichard, Elizabeth Curtis. Proved 12 May 1740 & admitted to record. Attest: James Fontaine clerk. (Pg 77)

In obedience to an order of court dated 10 Mar 1739/40 we Saml Blackwell, Saml Nelms, Thos Haynie & John Hudnall having met have allotted Judith Harding her share of her father Thomas Harding decd's estate & likewise her

share of her brother Saml Harding decd's estate.   1 Negro girl Jade, cash, 1 cow
& calf, 1 sow, 6 pigs, 1 iron pot, 1 frying pan, 1 peuter dish, 3 plates, 1 small
chest loc & key, 700 lbs of tobacco, feather bed, 1 spinning wheel, etc.   [Not
totaled] This division was returned 12 May 1740 & recorded. Attest: James
Fontaine clerk. (Pg 77)

An inventory of ye goods & chattels of Capt Wm Eustace decd.   Negroes:
Tony, Will, Emanuel, Arthur, Tom, Judy, Jane, Bess, Bess, Sarah, Moll, Lucy,
Frank, Tom, George, Kent, Henry, Charles, Cain, Tom, Tad, Robin, Benn, Joe,
Dick, Joshua, Nan, Nan, Abigail, Martha, Judy, Bess, Moll.   8 horses, 59 hogs,
18 sheep, 42 cattle, 10 beds, 10 bolsters, 18 pillows, 5 rungs, 5 quilts, 3
counterpains, 8 pare blankets, 17 pr sheets, 19 pr pillow cases, 8 diaper table
cloths, 2 diaper napkins, 12 towels, 5 setts curtains, 8 tables, 2 corner cupboards,
1 chest of drawers, 1 gun, 1 large looking glass, parcel earthen ware, 20 dishes, 5
½ doz plates, 8 basons, 6 potts, 2 kettles, etc. Goods inventoried in 1740
amounting to 417 pd 10 sl 11 pn. Tobacco & money per year 1739 amounting to
225,000 & 230 pd cask goods left in ye store when posted the books 50 pd. Ann
Eustace & John Eustace executors. This inventory was exhibited 12 May 1740
& admitted to record. Attest: James Fontaine clerk. (Pg 78)

12 May 1740. A true inventory of the estate of Robert Gordon decd by Joseph
Nutt. For ready pay: Tobacco paid to Lazarus Sutton, John Ingram, Robt Jones.
For fall pay & bills taken: Tobacco paid to Richard Lunsford, Wm Lunsford,
Charles Prichard, John Richardson, Robert Jones, Wm Barret, Edward Garret,
Christopher Garlington, Saml Snow, Argail Taylor, Thomas Lezenby, George
Mills, Joseph Nutt, Thos Mahane, Wm Wallice. Fall pay in tobacco: John
Webb, John Hurt, Aron Williams, Thomas Gaskins, John Berry, Joshua James,
Randolph Mott, Joseph Hester, Christopher Carpenter, Wm Thomas Wm Barret,
Robert Dridon, Wm Ellet, Joshan Champion, Moses Webb, Thomas Short,
Patrick Fairweather. [Not totaled] Pursuant to an order of court dated 14 Apr
1740 I Joseph Nutt sub sheriff have sold the estate of Robt Gordon decd as
above 12 May 1740. This inventory & sale was exhibited by Joseph Nutt sub
sheriff & was ordered to be recorded. Attest: James Fontaine clerk. (Pg 78)

14 Jan 1739. A true & perfect inventory of ye goods & chattels of Nathaniel
Floyd decd. 1 suit of cloaths, 1 Whitney coat, 3 pare of breeches, 1 pare of
Hokins, 1 fine hat, 1 pare silver clasps, 1 gold ring, 1 pocket botle, 1 stone jug, 1
pen knife, a common prayer book, 1 cane, parcel of lumber, 4 shirts, 1 tailors
goos, 1 chest, 1 side sadle & bridle, 1 pare of sizers, 1 tailors thimble, etc. 10 pd
5 sl 10 pn. In obedience to an order of court 10 Oct 1739 we Benjamin Waddy,
Thomas Winter & Christopher Damiron met at ye house of Madam Mary
Gaskins & being first sworn before Capt George Bell justice did value &
appraise all ye estate of Nathaniel Floyd as above writin. This inventory was

exhibited by Mrs. Mary Gaskins adminr & is admitted to record. Attest: James Fontaine clerk. (Pg 79)

25 Mar 1740. In obedience to an order of court of 10 Mar 1739/40 we Parish Garner, John Reeve & Wm Tayler met at ye house of Wm Taite & being sworn did appraise the goods of Doctor Archibald Johnston. 2 pare of thread stockins, 2 pare of worsted stockins, a parcel of old cloaths, 1 brass skillet, 1 iron morter, 1 brass pestle & mortar, 1 marble morter, 1 pare of bellows, 1 gun in very bad order, 9 books, 2 chests, 20 sheets paper, 1 old trandle bedstead, 1 spatula, 1 probe, 1 forcepes, 1 pare of buckles. This inventory was exhibited 2 May 1740 by William Taite adminr & admitted to record. Attest: James Fontaine clerk. (Pg 79)

7 Jun 1740. Deed. Thomas Davis of Wicocomoco Parish, Northumberland Co & Sarah his wife for 1600 lbs of tobacco sold to William Davis of same place a 40 a. parcel of land in the parish afsd on the s side of the Great Wicocomoco River bounded by Reedy Br, Secretary Carter & Joseph Hail (Haile) ... . Wit: George Mills, Edwin Smith, Ambrose Fielding. Ackn 9 Jun 1740 by William Davis & Sarah his wife she being privately examined by Robert Jones gent relinquished her right of dower in ye land & admitted to record. Attest: James Fontaine clerk. (Pg 79)

In obedience to an order of court dated 12 May 1740 we Richard Clayton, Wm Harding & George Lamkin being appointed to appraise the estate of Francis Vanlandingham being first sworn by ye justices have appraised the sd estate. 9 cows & calves, 1 horse, 15 sheep, 3 sows, 18 pigs, 12 shotes, 3 barrows, beds, bedsteads, pillows & furniture, 2 chests, 1 cupbord, 1 case of bottles, 1 trunk, 1 linnen wheel, 1 wollen wheel, 1 table & form, 7 chairs, 1 looking glass, 1 tea kettle, 2 meale sifters, 1 pitch fork, 6 botles, 2 drinking glasses, 2 books, etc. [Not totaled] This inventory of the estate of Francis Vanlandingham decd was exhibited 9 Jun 1740 by Elizabeth Vanlandingham extrx & on her motion admitted to record. Attest: James Fontaine clerk. (Pg 80)

In obedience to an order of court dated 12 May 1740 we Argail Taylor, John Coppidge & Charles Coppidge have met & being first sworn before Capt Robert Jones have appraised the estate of Swanson Prichard decd in money. Negroes: man named Dick, woman named Jane, child named Solomon, woman named Hannah for 5 years. Feather beds & furniture, curtains, quilt, 1 case pistols, 1 parcel knives & forks, 1 old cupbord, 1 small chest, 1 old table & cloth, looking glass, suit of cloaths, fine hat, parcel of old cloaths, 1 violin, 4 cows, 8 heifers, 1 young stear, 3 sheep, 5 lambs, 3 hogs, 11 small shoats, 2 old guns, 1 horse bridle & sadle, a punch bowl, some earthen ware, 2 spinning wheels, pare of old cards, etc. This inventory was exhibited 9 Jun 1740 by Margaret Prichard & Robt

Angell executors & on their motion admitted to record. Attest: James Fontaine clerk. (Pg 81)

In obedience to an order of court dated 12 May 1740 we Winder Kenner, Richd Kenner & Bertrand Ewell being sworn before Capt John Shapleigh did meet & appraise the estate of Richard Pearce decd in money. A gray mare, beds & furniture, his wearing cloaths, a chest, a table, looking glass, 2 table cloths, 2 towels & trunk, parcel of earthen ware & other lumber, 2 trunks, 2 mens sadles, 2 bridles, 3 old chairs, 1 Bible & other books, a quilting frame, box iron & heaters, a saddle, some sole leather, an old rug, etc. [Not totaled] This inventory was exhibited 9 Jun 1740 by Margit Pearce executrix & on her motion admitted to record. Attest: James Fontaine clerk. (Pg 82

In obedience to an order of court we William Haynie, Saml Nelims, Silvester Welch & Robt Davis having met have allotted Daniel Cotrell his pt/o his brother Thos Entaills decd's estate. 1 cow, 1 cider cask, 13 pd 7 ½ pn. The division of the estate of Thos Cotrell decd was returned 9 Jun 1740 by ye auditors & recorded. Attest: James Fontaine clerk. (Pg 82)

Pursuant to an order of court dated 12 May 1740 we Saml Blackwell, Richard Smith & Joseph Wildy having met have allotted Ransford Flowers his wife's pt/o her decd father John Wom[?] estate. 1 feather bed & furniture, 1 oval table, 1423 lbs of tobacco, horse, 21 lbs pot iron, 1 iron pestle, fish gigg, 1 iron spit, 10 lbs good puter, 4 ½ lbs old puter, 1 cow & yearling, cow & calf, 1 cow big with calf, 1 gun, a saw, 8 shovels, 335 lbs of pork. 24 ½ pd 14 sl 8 ½ pn. This report was returned 9 Jun 1740 by Saml Blackwell gent, Richd Smith & Joseph Wildy & recorded. Attest: James Fontaine clerk. (Pg 82)

In obedience to an order of court dated 13 May 1740 we Wm Taite, Lindsy Opie & John Lewis met at ye house of Jane Miller 4 Jun 1740 & on examining of accts produced to us by ye sd Jane Miller & comparing them with an attested copy of ye inventory of Christopher Miller decd we find a balance due to ye petitioners John Smith & William Gill amounting to 2 pd 3 sl which we have possessed them of. The above report was returned 9 Jun 1740 by ye auditors & recorded. Attest: James Fontaine clerk. (Pg 82)

In obedience to an order of court dated 12 May 1740 we Wm Taite, Lindsy Opie & Jno Lewis accordingly met a ye house of Jane Miller 4 Jun 1740 & on examining of accts produced to us by ye sd Jane Miller & comparing them with an attested copy of ye inventory of Joseph Churchill decd we do find the balance due to Emery Churchill the sd petitioner one of ye orphans to amount to 5 pd 14 sl 3 pn ½ penny which we have possessed her of. This report was returned 9 Jun 1740 & recorded. Attest: James Fontaine clerk. (Pg 82)

6 Jun 1740. Deed of Lease. Daniel Mealy (Mealey) & Ann his wife of Northumberland Co for 5 sl leased to Richard Jackson merchant of Westmoreland Co the old water grist mill called Flints Mill together with ye land belonging on both sides thereof being part in Northumberland Co & part in Westmoreland Co & mill became the right of ye sd Ann as heir to her father Thomas Flint decd ... for the term of 1 year ... . Wit: Willoughby Newton, John Carlyle (Carlile), John Crabb, John Butler. Ackn 14 Jul 1740 by Daniel Mealey & Ann his wife she being privately examined by Robert Jones gent relinquished her right of dower in ye mill & lands & admitted to record. Attest: James Fontaine clerk. (Pg 83)

7 Jun 1740. Deed of Release. Daniel Mealy (Mealey) & Ann his wife of Northumberland Co for 1,000 lbs of tobacco sold & released to Richard Jackson merchant of Westmoreland Co a water grist mill & mill dam called Flints Mill on ye brs of Yeocomico ... [same as above] ... . Wit: Willoughby Newton, John Carlyle (Carlile), John Crabb, John Butler. Ackn 14 Jul 1740 by David Mealey & Ann his wife she being privately examined by Robt Jones gent relinquished her right of dower in ye mill & land & admitted to record. Attest: James Fontaine clerk. (Pg 83)

7 Jul 1740. Deed of Lease. John Reeves & Elizabeth his now wife of St. Stephens Parish, Northumberland Co for consideration hereafter expressed hath farm lett to Ellis Gill of same place a 150 a. tr of land in the parish afsd on ye head of Marriners Cr running into Great Wicocomoco River adj ye Gleeb Line, land formerly Col George Cooper's, Gilberts Cr, Thomas Gill late decd & John Cole, it being pt/o the tr of land whereon Capt Sanders decd lived & left by him to ye sd John Reeves & Elizabeth his now wife ... for the term of the sd John Reeves & Elizabeth his now wife's naturall lives ... the sd Ellis Gill hereby covenants & agrees to & with the sd John Reeves & Elizabeth his wife to satisfy & pay in hand 1,000 lbs of tobacco & pay the quit rents now due & to plant 100 apple trees upon ye sd land & to build a 30' tobacco house & a 20' dwelling house on ye sd land within the term of time & to pay yearly 500 lbs of tobacco to the sd Elizabeth Reeves for rent during the afsd term of her natural life ... . Wit: William Sutton, Wm Wildy, George Berry. Ackn 14 Jul 1740 by John Reeves & Elizabeth his wife & admitted to record. Attest: James Fontaine clerk. (Pg 84)

Will. Robert Hunter of Northumberland County. 22 Jun 1740. To Robert Boyd one cow & calf. To my aunt Joshan Hunter & to my five cousins Sarah Hammonds, Ann Hunter, Robert Hunter, Joshan Hunter & Findly Hunter all the remainder pt/o my whole estate to be equally divided between them. My will is that my aunt Joshan Hunter & John Hornsby be my executors. Wit: Lawrence Parrot, Richard Nash. Proved 14 Jul 1740 & admitted to record. Attest: James

Fontaine clerk. (Pg 85)

In obedience to an order of court dated 9 Jun 1740 we Lindsey Opie, John Lewis, James Straughan & James Farnid met at ye house of George Lamkin & settled & allotted Lewis Lamkin his wife's pt/o her decd father Lewis ab Lewis Lewis' estate: in cash 20 pd 6 sl 3 pn ½ penny. This report was returned 14 Jul 1740 & recorded. Attest: James Fontaine clerk. (Pg 85)

In obedience to an order of court dated 12 May 1740 we Lindsey Opie, James Straughan & John Lewis met at ye house of George Lamkin & settled & allotted Lewis Lamkin his full pt/o his father's estate: 1 cow & yearling, 1 heiffer, 1 old stear, 1 iron pot, 1 pot hook, 12 ½ lbs good puter, 1 bed & furniture, ½ barell of salt, 1 gallon of brandy, 4 barrils of corn, 35 feet of wallnut plank, 1 gun, 1 chest, 1 chair, 4 sheep, 1 oval table, 1 cott, 1 skillet & brass cover, a spoon ladle, 1 mug, 7 lbs of puter, 1 prayer book, 3 bottles. 15 pd 3 sl 1 pn. This report was returned 14 May 1740 & admitted to record. Attest: James Fontaine clerk. (Pg 85)

A true inventory of all & singular ye goods, chattels &c of Saml Garlington decd. No 1: 1 young stear & heiffer, 2 yearlings, 1 cow, 1 ewe, 1 feather bed, bolster rug, pr cotton sheets & stand bedstead, 1 old sow & 3 pigs, 4 unmarked shoats, 1 old trunk, 2 [?] & 1 meale sifter, 1 looking glass, 1 half hower glass, 1 old saddle, 5 forks, 1 knife, 1 candlestick sold Lantham, 1 mug, 1 box iron & heaters, 1 iron pestle, etc. 21 pd 7 sl 9 ½ pn. No 2: 1 heifer, 1 yearling, 1 chest of drawers, 1 bull, 3 bags, 93 lbs of feathers, 1 trundle bedstead, hide & cord, 1 rug, 9 bottles, 1 square table, 4 earthen pots, etc. 21 pd 7 sl ½ pn. No 3: Negro man named Robin. 23 pd. No. 4: Negro woman named Cate, 1 yoke of oxen, 1 large sow & 7 pigs, 1 feather bed, 1 pillow, old rug, 1 blanket, bedstead & cord, 1 old gunn, & old gun baril, 1 old spinning wheel, 1 meale tub, 3 case bottles, 1 old tong, 1 old oval table, etc. 21 pd 8 sl 2 pn. In obedience to an order of court dated 12 May we Benjamin Waddey, Thos Winter & Roger Winter met at ye house of ye decd Saml Garlington & being first sworn before Capt Robt Jones justice have valued & allotted the sd estate of ye sd decd to all & among his children as the severall numbers specify, wit our hands 21 Jun 1740. This division was returned 14 Jul 1740 & recorded. Attest: James Fontaine clerk. (Pg 85)

Pursuant to an order of court dated 12 May 1740 we Jonas Gaskins, Christopher Damiron, & Wm Lattimore did meet & appraise for money the estate of Saml Mahane decd. 1 horse, some old cloaths, linnen shirts & breeches, 2 pare old stockins, 1 pare old shoes, 1 pare garters, beds, bolsters, cord, blanket, rug, 1 table, 3 guns, cupboard, parcel old books, 4 flag chairs, 1 spit, 1 shackle, 9 paper books, 1 tin trunk, 1 desk, 1 pint brandy & botles, old lumber, 2 ½ barils corn, pot rack, 446 gallons cider cask, 2 old tubbs, 4 hogs, 1 pot, kettle, pot rack, etc. [Not totaled] This inventory was exhibited 19 Jul 1740 by Thomas Makague executor & on his motion admitted to record. Attest: James Fontaine clerk. (Pg 87)

An inventory of the estate of Richard Lee decd now in the hands of his late widdow adminr of sd Lee's estate. 2 doz puter dishes, 5 ½ doz puter plates, 1 cullinder, 3 glass salt sellars, 15 drinking glasses, 8 beds &c, 8 bedsteads, 3 pare Holland sheets, 10 pare Lancaster sheets, 4 pare pillow cases, 6 pare fine pillow cases, 2 damask table cloths, 2 diaper table cloths, 8 doz damask napkins 4 linnen table cloths, 1 cart, 19 Negroes, 2 servants til 21 years, 3 trunks, 3 quilts, 3 ruggs, 6 pare blankets, 1 counter paine, 1 chocolat pot, 1 coffey pot, 1 tea kettle, 12 iron pots, 2 pot racks, 6 pare pot hooks, 10 draper towels, 6 butter pots, etc. [Not totaled] This inventory was exhibited 19 Jul 1740 by Judith Lee adminr of sd decd & on her motion admitted to record. Attest: James Fontaine clerk. (Pg 87)

Pursuant to an order of court dated 12 May 1740 we James Fontaine, Abner Neale & Edward Rogers have appraised the estate of John Colton decd in money. 1 feather bed, bedstead, cord, hide, bolster, 1 pillow, five pillow cases, 1 rug, 1 counterpaine, 1 pare of blankets, 2 pare sheets, 9 ¼ lbs old puter, 5 ¼ lbs good puter, 1 warming pan, 1 tin saus pan & a puter tankard, 1 looking glass & towel, 2 maps one of Amsterdam & other of England, a curry comb & brush, 1 pepper box, tobacco box, 2 broken mugs, 1 pare shoe boots, 2 pare shoes, 1 box iron & heaters, 1 hunting sadle & bridle, 1 trooping sadle, sadle cloth & bridle, 1 can, botle glass & ink botle, 1 iron pot, 1 frying pan, 1 pot & pot hooks, 1 iron skillet, 1 sugar box, some spice, etc. [Not totaled] This inventory was exhibited 19 Jul 1740 by Thomas Wornum adminr of sd decd & on his motion admitted to record. Attest: James Fontaine clerk. (Pg 88)

Will. Jarvise Ellistone of Northumberland Co. 10 --- 1740. To my wife Elizabeth Ellistone that pt/o my estate as she has in her possession excepting the Negroes & them? during her widdows life & no longer. To my dau Elizabeth Ellistone my feather bed & all the furniture that belong to it. To my son Cuthbert Ellistone & my dau Elizabeth Ellistone all the rest of my estate. … [blurred] … . Wit: William Betts, Richard Thomas. Proved 12 Aug 1740 & Charles Betts Junr executor made oath to the sd will on whose motion the same is admitted to record. (Pg 89)

In obedience to an order of court dated 14 Jul 1740 we Thos W[?], [?] & Joseph Wildy having mett & being sworn have appraised the estate of Charles Downing decd. 13 hoggs, 9 shoates, 2 piggs, 3 cows & calves, 3 young stears, 1 heifer, 1 young bull, 1 young mare, 1 gun, 1 old desk, 1 old cubbard, 1 chest, lock & key,

1 feather bed, bolster, rugg, blankett, sheet, bedstead, cord & hide, 1 suit of coaths of drugrett new, 1 old great coat, 1 old coat, 1 old jackett, 2 pair of britches, 1 old violin, 1 old saddle, 1 stock lock, 1 pare wosted stockins, 1 fine hatt, 11 ½ lbs good pewter, 2 old iron potts & pot hooks, 1 wash tub, 1 flower tub, etc. [Not totaled] This inventory was exhibited 11 Aug 1740 by John Downing adminr & admitted to record. Attest: James Fontaine clerk. (Pg 89)

Pursuant to an order of court dated 13 Jul 1740 & granted to Edward Mason adminr of the estate of John Penny decd, we John Kennedy, Parish Garner & Bennet Boggess being first sworn before Capt Matthew Kenner have appraised the sd Penny's estate in money. Taylor's [?] & shears, 2 pare sizars, 1 pressing board & yard, 1 horse shoe, wearing apparrill, 2 old wiggs, some thread mohair & other things, 1 fine hat, 1 old hat. 1 pd 10 sl. This inventory was exhibited 12 Aug 1740 by Edward Mason adminr on whose motion the same is admitted to record. Attest: James Fontaine clerk. (Pg 90)

13 Jul 1740. Deed of Lease Alexander Rider of St. Stephens Parish, Northumberland Co for 5 sl leased to William Nelmes of same place an 84 a. parcel of land in the parish afsd bounded by Col Peter Presly, Hannah Edwards, Samuell Nelson & Chichahan Cr ... for the term of 40 years paying the rent of 1 grain of Indian corn upon the feast of St. Michael if demanded ... . Wit: James Daughity, George Humphris, James Genn, Thos Harding. Ackn 11 Aug 1740 & admitted to record. Attest: James Fontaine clerk. (Pg 90)

31 Jul 1740. Deed of Release. Alexander Rider of St. Stephens Parish, Northumberland Co for ... [blurred] ... released to William Nelmes of same place an 84 a. parcel of land ... [same as above] ... . Wit: James Daughity, George Humphris, James Genn, Thos Harding. Ackn 11 Aug 1740 & admitted to record. Attest: James Fontaine clerk. (Pg 90)

31 Jul 1740. Bond. I Alexander Rider of St. Stephens Parish, Northumberland Co am indebted to William Nelms of same place for 14,000 lbs of tobacco ... the condition of this obligation is such that whereas the afsd Alexander Rider has sold an 84 a. tr of land unto the afsd William Nelms [see above], if the sd Alexander Rider shall in all things comply with the covenants & agreements contained in the deed then this obligation to be void ... . James Daughity, George Humphris, James Genn, Thos Harding. (Pg 91)

21 Jun 1740. Deed. Thomas Berry & Patience his wife of Wicocomoco Parish, Northumberland Co for 25 pd sold to Thomas Harvey of same place a 35 a. parcel of land in sd parish bounded by the orphans of Thomas Hardin decd, br issuing out of Edwards Cr & Bowins Cr ... . Wit: George Mills, John Hurst, John Hurst Junr. Ackn by Thomas Berry 11 Aug 1740 & admitted to record.

Attest: James Fontaine clerk. (Pg 92)

14 Jul 1740. Deed of Lease John Reaves of St. Stephens Parish,
Northumberland Co for the consideration hereafter mentioned sold to Elizabeth
Pugh dau of the sd John Reaves of the same parish during the term of her natural
life a 50 a. parcel of land fell to me by Capt Edward Sanders decd's will
bounded by John Coles, Richard [?], land leased to Elles Gill & the e br of
Marriners Cr … in consideration of good & sufficient caution in hand paid but
more in particular for the natural love & affection I bear unto my sd dau … .
Wit: William Sutton, William Wildey, George Berry. Ackn by John Reaves &
Elizabeth his wife 11 Aug 1740 unto their dau Elizabeth Pugh on whose motion
is admitted to record. Attest: James Fontaine clerk. (Pg 92)

11 Aug 1740. Deed of Gift. Robert Robuck of Wicocomoco Parish,
Northumberland Co for natural goodwill & affection have given unto my son
Robert Robuck one Negro woman named Jenny, two Negro boys named Jemmy
& Poll & one Negro girl named Nan … . Wit: Peter Hayes, John Coppedg.
Ackn 11 Aug 1749 & admitted to record. Attest: James Fontaine clerk. (Pg 93)

11 Aug 1740. Deed of Gift. Robert Robuck of Wicocomoco Parish,
Northumberland Co for natural good will & affection have given to my son
William Robuck one Negro man named Tom, two Negro boys named Peter &
Joe & one Negro girl named Frank … . Wit: Peter Hayes, John Coppedg. Ackn
11 Aug 1740 & admitted to record. Attest: James Fontaine clerk. (Pg 93)

28 Aug 1740. In obedience to an order of court dated 12th this instant we
Richard Hull, Thos Wornom & Edward Rogers having met at the plantation of
Jervis Elistone decd & being first sworn by Samuell Blackwell gent have
appraised the sd Elistone's estate in money. 1 mare, 1 box iron, 2 young heifers,
2 young stears, feather beds & furniture, 4 yards flannell, 5 chairs, a parcel of
table lining, 1 water pail, some old hoes, 1 ax, 3 cows & calves, frying pan, etc.
[Not totaled] The above inventory in the possession of the widow according to
the will of the decd. 1 ring, 1 old feather bed, bolster, 2 small pillows, old silk
rug, 2 old sheets, 1 new sheet, old bedstead, old cord, 3 punch bowls, 1 old
basket & old lumber, 2 old chests, 1 old spice morter & pessell, 1 earthen pot &
pitcher, 4 new pewter basons, 16 ½ lbs of pewter, 22 new pewter spoons, etc.
This inventory was exhibited 8 Sep 1740 by Charles Betts Junr executor &
admitted to record. (Pg 93)

In obedience to an order of court held 21 Jan 1735 we Thos Wornom, Jno
Corbell & Daniel Clark being first sworn before Capt John Hack did meet at the
plantation of Samuel Smyth decd's & did appraise ye sold decd's estate in
money. A mair, a small old trunk, a old piggin, 3 Negro children, a Negro

wench, 6 cows, 2 young bulls, 2 heifers, 9 sheep & a lamb, 1 sow, 9 young hoggs, a table & form, 1 old table, 1 old winsuit chest, 1 old cubbord, 1 small box, 3 old flag chairs, 2 leather chairs, 16 buttons, beds, bedsteads, bolsters, rugs, 2 old looking glasses, 13 lbs of good pewter, 18 ½ lbs of old pewter, 1 old whipsaw, 1 old Indian basket, etc. [Not totaled] This inventory was exhibited 9 Sep 1740 by John Shapleigh adminr & admitted to record. Attest: James Fontaine clerk. (Pg 94)

In obedience to an order of court made 11 Aug 1740 wherein it was ordered that we Phillip Smith, Robt Jones & Thos Winter should meet at the house of Mrs. Judith Lee to allot her the third pt/o her decd husband's estate & Peter Conway his wife's filial pt/o her father's estate pursuant to the sd order we have met & proceeded & the amount of the thirds of the decd's estate is 299 pd & allotted as hereunder: Negroes: Man named Tom cooper, man named Solomon, man named Frank, woman named Jane, boy named Moses, boy named Stephen bound till 24 years of age, Negro boy Thomas. 2 draught oxen, 1 stear, 10 cows & calves, 1 bull, 3 young heifers, 4 young stears, 4 ewe lambs, 1 ram, 18 old ewes, 1 sow, 6 barrows, 1 mare, 1 horse, 1 doz plates, 28 lbs pewter, 1 cullender, large spoon, parcell of old tubs, pails, piggins, 1 churn, 1 grid iron, 1 chafing dish, 1 box iron & heaters, etc. (Pg 94)

  To Peter Conway's wife's part which amounts to 85 pd 9 sl 14 ¾ pn: 2 Negroes Will & Anthony. 1000 lbs tobacco, 1 stear, 2 cows & calf, 1 bedsted, bed & furniture, 2 cane chairs, 1 chest of drawers, 4 lbs pewter, 1 doz new plates, 1 bell metle morter & pestle, 1 brass kettle, 1 Lancastier sheets & pr pillow cases, 1 diaper towel, 1 damask table cloath & 2 napkins, 1 croscut saw, 8 sheep, 1 iron pot, etc. This division of the estate of Richard Lee gent decd was returned 8 Sep 1740 & recorded. Attest: James Fontaine clerk. (Pg 95)

In obedience to an order of court directed to us we John Cralle, Wm Taite & Linsey Opie accordingly mett at the house of John Lewis & on perusing the inventory & adding up each page & these sums into one we find Corbin Lewis's pt/o his decd father's estate exclusive of the Negroes to be 89 pd 4 sl 10 pn & consisteth of stock & household goods as per inventory we likewise find there was allotted to the sd Corbin Lewis & Griffin Lewis his brother the following Negroes, Sandle of the price of 20 pd, Jack of the price of 12 pd, Suckie of the price of 15 pd, Congo very old & blind of the price of 1 pd, Tom a boy of the price of 9 pd, Jacob of the price of 9 pd, in all 66 pd but was never divided so could not here certifie his particular Negroes. Likewise perused the book debts & Mr. Hughlet's accounts & tried the sums by adding the articles together & the shares of the crops & found the sums total to be right & find the ballance in Mr. Hughlet's favour to be 1482 5/8 lbs of tobacco & 1 pd 2 pn cash. If Mr. Hughlet's account hereto annexed is allowed of by your worships we likewise find that there is 8 barrells of Indian corn due by the sd Hughlet to sd Corbin

Lewis's estate which we thought we were not empowered to value so left it to your worships. We likewise observed in the bottom of Mr. Hughlet's account a memorandum of several goods & two Negroes which was pt/o the decd's estate & was not allowed to be appraised by John & William Lewis who had them in possession & Mr. Hughlet intermarrying with the adminr to discharge her of her oath as likewise for the interest of the orphan under his care & his own laid it before us but we conceived it to be without the verge of that power given to us in this manner humbly lay it before your worships. This division was returned 8 Sep 1740 & recorded. Attest: James Fontaine clerk. (Pg 96)

The estate of Corben & Griffin Lewis. Sums paid to old Jack a Negro man, old Sucky a wench, Sandy a fellow, Tom a mulatto child, Mrs. Boggess for doctring, Jacob a child, Corbett Griffin, old Jack a Negro man, Cango a blind wench, Elizabeth going to school, to charges of my expence in a suite agt J. Lewis at Williamsburg, buriell of Corbin Lewis. Total 3846. Received 3 hands crops of tobacco 1731. Shares of crop 1044. Memorandum of the estate which John & William Lewis had in their hands of their father's which they would not let come to appraisement, viz, William Lewis's part not appraised to one young Negro wench named Vall about 18 years old which now has a boy 2 years old, 1 white paying horse, 1 bay mare, 1 old feather bed & furniture with suit of VA cloaths, curtains & vallans, 1 spice morter, 1 iron pot, some pewter. John Lewis's part which was not appraised, one Negro wench named Vilat, 2 feather beds with furniture with 3 pillows. Err exd per William Hughlet. This acct allowed by ye Orphans Court & recorded. Attest: James Fontaine clerk. (Pg 96)

In obedience to an order of court dated 14 Jul 1740 we Charles Coppedge, John Coppedge & Laurence PaRutt being first sworn by Capt Robert Jones have appraised the estate of Robert Hunter decd in the hands of Argail Taylor & the orphans of Wm Taylor decd & Aaron Taylor security for the estate of John Hunter decd late father to the sd Robert Hunter decd & posest John Hunter extr with the sd estate: 1 feather bed & furniture, 1 old chest, 1 old table, 3 old chairs, 2 pr mens shoes, 1 pair of womens, 2 barrells of Indian corn, 1 iron pot & hooks, 250 lbs of pork, cows & calves, sheep, 6 glass bottles, 1 old mare, 1 iron pot, 1 old gun, etc. [Not totaled] This inventory was exhibited 13 Oct 1740 by Josken Hunter extr & admitted to record. Attest: James Fontaine clerk. (Pg 97)

Pursuant to an order of court dated 14 Jul 1740 we Richard Hull, Abner Neales & Edward Rogers having mett & being first sworn have appraised the estate of Thomas Frazor decd. 23 ½ lbs good wool, some old wool, 1 new coat, a pattern for vest & britches, a pattern of Whitney for a great coat, 1 kersey coat & other old cloaths, a parcel of old linen cloaths, 1 table & cloath, 1 small looking glass & towel, a parcell of lumber, 1 fine hat, 1 pare new shoes, 1 pare old boots, 3 pare stockins, cask old silver, 1 pare of silver clasps & studs, 1 pr shoe buckles,

1 pare of knee buckles, a box with 3 razors & other trifles, 2 stone juggs, some old wooden & earthen ware, a small brass kittle, ladle & other things, etc. 22 pd 5 sl 6 ½ pn. The within is a true & perfect inventory of all the estate of Thomas Frazer decd that is yet come to my hands. Richard Chickester adminr. This inventory was exhibited 13 Oct 1740 by Richard Chickester adminr & on his motion is admitted to record. Attest: James Fontaine clerk. (Pg 98)

16 Aug 1740. This is to certify all people that I William Teague of Prince William Co carpenter doth a quit & discharge Peter Greenstreet from all service due to me or mine & that I do freely discharge him so that he may be imployed by any person whatsoever. Wit: John Oldham, John Greenstreet. To the worshipfull court of Northumberland Co when seting 26 Sep 1740, then John made oath that the above discharge was truly act of William Teague. John Shapleigh. 18 Oct 1740 this discharge from William Teague to Peter Greenstreet was proved by the oath of John Greenstreet & recorded. Attest: James Fontaine clerk. (Pg 98)

Will. John Keene of St. Stephens Parish, Northumberland Co. 18 Sep 1740. To my wife's dau Sarah Keene Coe & her heirs 1 a. of land out of the tr called Small Hopes & the following Negroes annexed, viz, Sharper, Judy, Ben, Kelter, Moll, Dick, Rachel & Suckils & for default of heirs the land & Negroes to be divided between Elenor Wyat & Eliza Sugget & their heirs. To Sarah Keene Bee the three best beds & furniture & her choice of two chests with three bedsteads & two tables & 150 yards of linnen, ½ oxen brigs?, 38 yards of Dowlass, 37 yards of garlix & 50 weight pewter & three pewter basons each holding three quarts & two doz of plates, 10 gees, two ganders, 12 head of cattle, 12 head of hoggs, 6 sheep, 2 iron pots, 40 pound each, 1 frying pan, 1 iron skillet, all new & 5 60 gallon syder casques, all the above goods to be delivered to her when she comes of age in good order or day of marriage as likewise 30 pd. To my wife Ruth Keene these Negroes, viz Jamy, young Harry, Hannah, Piliana & Doll, these Negroes I only lieve her the use of them for & during her natural life, viz, the afsd Negroes with the plantation I now live on during her widdowhood & if she marrys then I only lieve her ½ of the sd plantation. I likewise give her my sd wife timber for the use of sd plantation from my plantation called Small Hopes & as the still is now fixed it is my will it may stand for the use of my plantation & always goe with the freehold & I likewise leave my sd wife 10 head of cattle, 10 hogs, 10 sheep, 2 iron pots her choice & 50 yards of lining, ½ oznaburgs the other ½ garlic, 2 yokes of oxen, cart & wheels & after my sd wife's decease I leave all the Negroes given her to be divided betwixt my grandchildren, viz, Elizabeth Wyat, John Wyat, Lucy Sugget & John Sugget & their heirs. To my dau Elenor Wyatt her choice of my Negroes not before given, viz, one Negro in lieu of Little Harry which I before had gave her husband Edward Wyatt. I give to her son John Wyatt my tr of land

I now live on after my wife's death & that tr I likewise leave him called Small Hopes as likewise that tr of land called Mother Olivers. To my dau Elizabeth Sugget's son John Sugget my tr of land called Mattapony. To Wineford Rider that Negro called Charity. To my couzin William Lamford all my waring cloaths & 5,000 lbs of tobacco to be paid in 5 years, 1,000 each year. To Rebekah Smith 800 lbs of tobacco. To Elizabeth Allin 500 lbs of tobacco & 500 in goods besides her wages. I lieve Sarah Keene Bee to her mother & my wife Ruth Keene & if she my sd wife should die then I leave the sd Sarah Keane Bee to my surviving executors with her estate. I give each of my daus Elenor Wyat & Elizabeth Sugget 21 sl 6 pn to each of them buy to mourning rings. I give all the rest of my estate to be divided betwixt my grand children, that is, ½ thereof to be divided betwixt Eleanor Wyat's children & the other ½ to be divided betwixt my dau Elizabeth Sugget's children. I appoint my wife Ruth Keene, Edward Wyatt & Edgcome Sugget executors & I desire the favour of Col Peter Presley, Capt Matthew Kenner & Matthew Quill to be my trustees. Wit: Wm Taite, John Lewis, George Conway. Proved 13 Oct 1740 & admitted to record. Attest: James Fontaine clerk. (Pg 99)

13 Oct 1740. To the worshipful court I Ruth Keene do here certify that I am fully satisfied with the legacy left me in the will of John Keene decd my late husband in lieu of my right of dowry & I do hereby renounce all my right of dowry to the sd estate on the payment of the legacy left me in the sd will dated 18 Sep 1740. Wit: Wm Taite, Parish Garner. This relinquishment was proved 13 Oct 1740 & recorded. Attest: James Fontaine clerk. (Pg 99)

19 Apr 1740. Deed. Henry Mayes of Wicocomoco Parish, Northumberland Co for 6,000 lbs of tobacco sold to Moses James of same place a 100 a. parcel of land in the parish afsd on the n side of Scotland Mill Cr bounded by Samuel Ingram, Swanson Lunsford, Church Spring Swamp & William Steptoe ... . Wit: George Mills, Joshua James, Josias Mayes. Memorandum that the within named Henry Mayes hath excepted a ½ a. of ground at the usual burying place to be put to no other use. Ackn 13 Oct 1740 & admitted to record. Attest James Fontaine clerk. (Pg 100)

13 Oct 1740. Be it known that I Elizabeth Mayes of Northumberland Co (the now w/o Henry Mayes of sd co) do appoint my trusty & good friend David Latimore of sd co my atty to appear for me in the sd co court to relinquish my right of dower that I have in a percell of land that my husband Henry Mayes has sold unto Moses James [see above] ... . Wit: Joshua James, Charles Pritchard. This relinquishment of dower was allowed by Northumberland Co Court 13 Oct 1740 & recorded. Attest: James Fontaine clerk. (Pg 100)

Will. Bridgar Haynie of St. Stephens Parish, Northumberland Co. 1 Jun 1739.

To my wife Mary Haynie all my land on the s side of the road forever. To my son Bridgar Haynie all my tr of land on the n side of the road the plantation whereon I now live. To my cousin Wm Haynie adminr of John Haynie decd all my right & title I had in a piece of land in Essex Co on the s side of Rappahannock River which sd land the sd Wm Haynie paid me a reasonable satisfaction for already. My will is that if [?] my son Bridgar nor any of my sons should have any heir at the times of their death the land given to my son Bridgar not disposed of by him nor any other of my sons then I give the sd land to the heir at law which descends either from my brother John of from my brother Maximillion Haynie which shall be called by the name of Bridgar Haynie. I leave the care of my three sons entirely to Capt Daniel McCarty. If my wife should die or marry & I desire that Capt McCarty should sell the land given to my wife Mary Haynie & the land bequeathed to my son Bridgar. I ordain my friend Capt Daniell McCarty executor. Wit: Thomas Machen, Charles Haynie. 2 Sep 1740 Thomas Machen came before me William Hackney & made oath that he saw Bridgar Haynie sign & seal this above will. This will was proved 13 Oct 1740 by Charles Haynie & admitted to record. Attest: James Fontaine clerk. (Pg 101)

10 Sep 1740. Deed. William Moor son & heir of Judith Moor coheir of Thomas Harwood decd & his wife Sarah of Summerset Co, MD for 30 pd sold to Peter Presly gent of St. Stephens Parish, Northumberland Co a 50 a. parcel of land in the parish afsd pt/o a pattent of 384 a. of land granted to Simon Richardson 10 Jul 1661 bounded by Herring Cr & Thomas Webb, which land being ½ pt/o 100 a. formerly belonging to the sd Thomas Harwood decd & descended in right unto Judith & Rose Harwood daus & coheirs of the sd Thomas Harwood .... . Wit: John Shapleigh, Spencer Ball, Thomas Wilkins, Wm James McGoo. Proved 13 Oct 1740 & admitted to record. Attest: James Fontaine clerk. (Pg 101)

In obedience to an order of court dated 11 Aug 1740 we Lazarus Taylor, John Coppedge & Joshua James being first sworn by Capt Robert Jones have valued the estate of Charles Lunsford decd in money. Feather beds & furniture, 3 cows & calf, 2 heifers, 10 hogs, 6 old cattle, 3 old tubs, 1 box iron & heaters, 1 candlestick, 14 lbs good pewter, 1 tin pan & quart pot, 1 small looking glass, 1 spinning wheel & 2 pare of old cards, 1 small trunk, 1 old chest, 1 chest, 1 iron pessell, 77 lbs of pot iron & hooks, 1 water pale & tray, 1 old frying pan, 1 sold iron pot, a percell of hoes & axes, 2 earthen pots, 1 old table & cloath, 4 old chairs, 5 old baskets & lumber, etc. [Not totaled] This inventory was exhibited 13 Oct 1740 by Winefred Lunsford extx on whose motion the same is admitted to record. Attest: James Fontaine clerk. (Pg 102)

In obedience to the above (sic) order we John Cralle, Wm Taite & Parish Garner mett at the house of William Hughlet & there allotted William Lewis his pt/o his brother Corban Lewis decd's estate amounting to 25 pd 19 sl cash this 26 Sep 1740. The within report was returned into court 13 Oct 1740 by the auditors & recorded. Attest: James Fontaine clerk. (Pg 102)

10 Nov 1740. Deed of Lease. Matthew Kenner Junr of St. Stephens Parish, Northumberland Co shipwright for several good causes & considerations but especially for ye improvements that John Hudnall doth covenant & agree to build a substantial framed dwelling house, a shed, with one brick chimney, the two rooms with two fire places, all to be as neatly completed & built as the dwelling house as Richard [?] lived in the year 36 the afsd Hudnall doth agree to & with the afsd Kenner to plant 250 garlentons or bussenten apple trees & to compleat with all the afsd articles of the agreements afsd all to be completely completed in 2 years from the above date to be built & planted on the plantation where the afsd Kenner now lives. Wit that the afsd John Hudnall doth covenant & agree to compleat with all the buildings & improvements & ackn in the lease given by Richard Kenner to Matthew Kenner dated 14 Jul 1736 concluding the afsd buildings & improvements afsd which is in the lease given by Richard Kenner to the afsd Matthew Kenner Junr. Wit the afsd Matthew Kenner shipwright hath farm let by these presents unto the afsd John Hudnall planter a parcel of land excluding the dwelling house & kitchen yard, in St. Stephens Parish containing 69 a. bounded by Absolom Williams, Benjamin Folson & Elias Martin ... for ye full term of 8 years paying 700 lbs of lawfull & merchantable tobacco in cask yearly for 4 years ... . Wit: William Hudnall, John Bransdon. Ackn 10 9br 1740 by Matthew Kenner & John Hudnall to each other & on John Hudnall's motion was admitted to record. Attest: James Fontaine clerk. (Pg 102)

--- 1740. Bond. I John Hudnall of parish afsd Northumberland Co planter am firmly bound unto Matthew Kenner Junr for 100 pd ... the condition of this obligation is such that if the afsd John Hudnall shall & doe for his part in all things well & truly observe, perform, fulfill, accomplish & keep all & singular the covenants, grants, articles, clauses, conditions & agreements mentioned in the [above] lease then this obligation to be void ... . Wit: William Hudnall, John Bransdon. Ackn 10 9br 1740 & recorded. Attest: James Fontaine clerk. (Pg 103)

In obedience to an order of court dated 13 8br 1740 we Thomas Wornum, Winder Kenner & John Corbett did meet at the house of Saml Smith decd & did inspect & settle the accts of the sd estate produced by John Shapleigh adminr & we find that the estate is indebted to ye sd John Shapleigh adminr 1567 lbs of tobacco to be paid amongst the five orphans & we have also allotted to George Barret for his wife's shear of ye Negroes one Negro girl named Rose of 16 pd price provided the sd George Barret pay 24 sl to ye other four children & we also have allotted to be paid to George Barret one young heiffer & one cider cask to be paid by the adminr the cider cask is not to be worth less then 5 sl according to the inventory given under our hands 6 9br 1740. This report was exhibited 10 9br 1740 & recorded. Attest: James Fontaine clerk. (Pg 103)

At the request of Winder Kenner who thinks that when I, John Shapleigh, wrote his grandmother Elizabeth Windser's will that in that pt/o her will which respects the gift of her lands to his brother Richard Kenner that I writ certain words which may be taken in a different meaning to what was intended by the sd Elizabeth Winder, the words are, viz, that I now possess in ye cr called Breartons, set down in that pt/o her will & therefore do of my own knowledge (for I wrote her will) affirm & declare that what construsion may be put on them superfluous words that Elizabeth Winder never meant or intended to invalidate or make voyd her first gift of her land to Winder Kenner. John Shapleigh gent came into court 10 9br 1740 & made oath to ye above deposition & on ye motion of Winder Kenner the same was recorded. Attest: James Fontaine clerk. (Pg 103)

20 Jun 1677. Deed of Gift. I Samuell Smyth of Northumberland Co gent for tender love & affection have given to my son in law Phillip Shapleigh of same co merchant a parcel of land being pt/o the seat of land whereon I now live bound by Hynes Br & Potomack River, including all the land belonging to ye sd Saml Smyth between that & Nulls Thicket Plantation excepting (& always reserving) unto the sd Samll Smyth & his son Saml Smyth Junr all such timber as they or either of them from time to time & at all times hereafter shall use for building during their natural lives ... . Wit: Patr Hamilton, Peter Platt. 13 Jul 1677 recorded. Attest: Thos Holeson. At a court held 9 Mar 174- on the motion of Shapleigh Neale this deed of gift from Samll Smyth certified by Thomas Hobun formerly clerk of this court dated 20 Jun 1677 to Phillip Shapleigh (& not to be found on the records) was by the court allowed & on the motion of sd Shapleigh Neale recorded. Attest: James Fontaine clerk. (Pg 104)

10 May 1739. Bond. I Richard Kenner of St. Stephens Parish, Northumberland Co gent am firmly bound unto Henry Lee of Cople Parish, Westmoreland Co gent for 250 pd ... the condition of this obligation is such that whereas the afsd Richard Kenner on the date above said came to the sd Henry Lee's house & did offer to sell him all his land on the n side of the road that leads to Capt John Footman's which sd land is in Cople Parish, Westmoreland Co adj to that pt/o the land which the sd Kenner hath already leased to Capt John Footman & whereas the quantity of acres of land is unknown to the sd Kenner & Lee the sd Lee did agree with him to give him 2,000 lbs of tobacco & 9 sl 6 pn money for each a. when the sd land shall be surveyed ... if the afsd Richard Kenner shall &

do at any time hereafter when required by the sd Lee deliver & acknowledge for Westmoreland Co Court a lease & release for the effectual conveying the sd land to the sd Lee then this obligation to be void … . Wit: John Wheeler, Dave Currie. At a court held for Northumberland Co 9 Mar 1740 on the motion of Henry Lee gent this bond was recorded. Attest: James Fontaine clerk. (Pg 104)

19 Dec 1740. Deed. Edgcomb Sugget & Elizabeth his wife of Richmond Co for 20 pd sold to Edward Wiat of Glocester Co a 25 a. parcel of land bounded by the land of Capt Matthew Kenner & Lindsey Opie, called Mother Ollivers … . Wit: John Sears, Ed Wiat Junr, Samll Tevisdale. Ackn 9 Mar 1740 by Edgcomb Sugget & Elizabeth his wife she being privately examined by Saml Blackwell gent relinquished her right of dower & admitted to record. Attest: James Fontaine clerk. (Pg 105)

14 --- 1740. Deed. Thomas Hudson of Durum Parish, Charles Co, MD for 5,000 lbs of good tobacco in cask sold to Robert Hudson of St. Stephens Parish, Northumberland Co a tr of land given & bequeathed to him by the will of Henry Hudson decd being pt/o a tr formerly granted to Anthony Linton … . Wit: Richard Claughton, John Claughton, Wm Trunill, Saml Harrison, Rodum Hudson, Fielding Hudson. Proved 9 Mar 1740 & admitted to record. Attest: James Fontaine clerk. (Pg 105)

2 Dec 1740. Bond. I Thomas Hudson of Durum Parish, Charles Co, MD am firmly bound unto Robt Hudson of St. Stephens Parish, Northumberland Co for 10,000 lbs of good tobacco … the condition of this obligation is such that if the afsd Thomas Hudson shall well & truly observe, perform, fulfill, accomplish & keep all & singular the covenants, grants, articles, provisos & agreements mentioned in a deed [see above] then this obligation to be void … . Wit: Richd Claughton, John Claughton, Danl Harrison. Proved 9 Mar 1740 & admitted to record. Attest: James Fontaine clerk. (Pg 106)

11 Feb 1741. Deed of Lease. Shapleigh Neale of St. Stephens Parish, Northumberland Co for 37 pd 10 sl sold to John Graham of same parish a 400 a. tr of land in Wicocomoco Parish on the head brs of Knights Cr adj the lands of Col Carter, Col Peter Presly, Edwin Smith, John Taylor & James Webb … during the term of 10 years & no longer … . Wit: Saml Blackwell, Winder Kenner, William Downing. Ackn 9 Mar 1740 & admitted to record. Attest: James Fontaine clerk. (Pg 107)

11 Feb 1741. Bond. I Shapleigh Neale of St. Stephens Parish, Northumberland Co am firmly bound unto John Graham merchant of same place in the penal sum of 150 pd … the condition of this obligation is such that whereas the afsd Shapleigh Neale by a deed [see above] granted & confirmed unto the sd John

Graham for 10 years & no longer a deed of lease, now if the afsd Shapleigh
Neale shall from time to time & at all times hereafter observe, perform, fulfill,
accomplish & keep all & every article, condition, clause & proviso mentioned in
the sd deed of lease then this obligation to be void ... . Wit: Saml Blackwell,
Winder Kenner, William Downing. Ackn 9 Mar 1740/1 & admitted to record.
Attest: James Fontaine clerk. (Pg 107)

Will. Thomas Burn of Northumberland Co. 12 9br 1740. To my wife Grace
Burn five Negroes, viz, Grace, Frank, Jamy, George, Judy & her child & their
increase. To my son John Burn all my estate of what nature or kind except my
books which I give to my friend Samuell Hamilton. I appoint my wife Grace
Burn & my brother in law George Ball extrs. If it should please God that my
son John die without heirs that then I give to my cousin Saml Garlington all my
land. If my son die as afsd then I give unto my six cousins William, Saml, John
& Morris Garlington & Judith & Elizabeth Bashford all my Negroes & personall
estate. Wit: None. This will was presented in court by George Ball Junr extr
who made oath thereto & being fully proved by George Ball gent, [?] Ball &
Saml Hambleton wits present at the writing the same which wits were severally
examined in open court the sd will is recorded. Attest: James Fontaine clerk.
(Pg 108)

Will. Partin James of Wicocomoco Parish, Northumberland Co. 14 9br 1740 I
give all my whole estate that I die possest with to Sarah Berry. Wit: Thos
Hurst, John Payn (Paine), Aquila Snelling. Proved 9 Mar 1740 & admitted to
record. Attest: James Fontaine clerk. (Pg 108)

Will. Samuell Smith of Wicocomoco Parish, Northumberland Co. 1 Feb
1739/40. I lend the whole use of my whole estate, lands, household goods &
chattels unto my wife Ann Smith during her widdowhood. To my son Samuel
Smith all my land, houses & all the importances thereunto belonging & one
Negro boy named Jeffery. I give all the remainder pt/o my estate unto my five
children Winne Smith, Sarah Smith, Betty Smith, Judy Smith & Samuel Smith
to be equally divided between them. My will is that my wife Ann Smith be my
executor. Wit: Jno Hornsby, Edwin Smith. Proved 9 Mar 1740 & admitted to
record. Attest: James Fontaine clerk. (Pg 108)

Will. Hannah Hill of Wicocomoco Parish, Northumberland Co. 2 Nov 1740.
To my gran sunn Edwin Fielding (Fealding) one cow & calf & three sheep & my
side sadle. To John Fealding son of Edwin one heiffer. To my gran sunn
William Fealding one heiffer. To my gran sunn Ambrose Fealding one mair
coult. I give all the remainder pt/o my moveable estate unto my sunn Ambros
Fealding excepting one small red heiffer which I give unto Absolem Hammond.
My will is that my sunn Ambros Fealding be my executor. Wit: John Hornsby,

Richard Nutt, Britan Hill. Proved 9 Mar 1749 & admitted to record. Attest: James Fontaine clerk. (Pg 109)

In obedience to an order of court dated 13 8br 1740 we Thomas Dameron Junr, John Christopher & Yarnet Hughlet being ordered to appraise the estate of Bridgar Haynie decd accordingly met & were first sworn by Saml Blackwell & appraised as follows: 2 old feather beds & bolsters, 1 quilt, bedsteads, 1 hide, rug, blankets, 28 lbs pot iron, 1 old pare of skillards & pea & frying pan, 7 old chair frames, 7 lbs old puter, 1 old dressing table, 1 old case, 1 old small chest, 2 small boxes, 1 box iron, 1 heater, 1 spice morter, 1 broad ax, 1 candlestick, some old lumber, 1 water pail & surringe, 1 small pare of shears, 1 heiffer, 1 calf, 1 old handsaw. [Not totaled] The inventory was exhibited 9 Mar 1749 by Danl McCarty gent executor & admitted to record. Attest: James Fontaine clerk. (Pg 109)

19 Jul 1740. Deed. William Atkins in North Farnham Parish, Richmond Co planter for 1,100 lbs of tobacco sold to William Hartie painter of parish afsd a 70 a. tr of land on the n side of Great Wicocomoco River as my grandfather John Atkins bought it of Edward Philips bounded by an Indian Field near Henry Bondley's, land that was formerly Bradfort's & land of John Downing ... [blurred] .... Wit: Wm Samford, John Samford, [?] Samford, George Hammond. Quiet & peaceable possession was given to the sd William Hartie by the delivery of turf & twig. Wit: John Downing, Robert Wadington. Ackn 13 Apr 1741 by William Atkins & Elizabeth his wife & proved in court by oaths of Wm Samford, John Samford & George Hammond wits thereto & the afsd Elizabeth came into court & ackn the sd deed she being privately examined by Saml Blackwell gent relinquished her right of dower & admitted to record. (Pg 109)

14 Apr 1741. Deed of Gift. John Cralle of St. Stephens Parish, Northumberland Co for the love that I do bear to my wife Hannah Cralle have given unto her a Negro woman named Rachel & her increase forever. I hereby acknowledge to have delivered up to my sd wife the afsd slave free from al incumbrance whatsoever. Wit: Rodham Kenner, Robt Clarke Junr. Ackn 14 Apr 1741 & admitted to record. Attest: James Fontaine clerk. (Pg 110)

14 Apr 1741. Deed of Gift. I John Cralle of St. Stephens Parish, Northumberland Co gent for the love & natural affection I have & do bear to my only dau Mary Cralle have given unto her two Negro girls namely Jenny & Joane. I acknowledge to have delivered up to my sd dau the afsd slaves free from all incumbrance whatsoever. Wit: Rodham Kenner, Robt Clarke Junr. Ackn 14 Apr 1741 & admitted to record. Attest: James Fontaine clerk. (Pg 110)

19 Feb 1740. Power of Attorney. I William McCall of the City of Glasgow merchant have appointed John Graham of Northumberland Co my atty to ask, demand, sue for, recover & receive of all persons whatsoever indebted to me ... . Wit: Matthew Quill, Adam Crump, Samuel McCall. Proved 13 Apr 1741 & admitted to record. Attest: James Fontaine clerk. (Pg 111)

6 Oct 1740. Power of Attorney. We Edward Tubman & Thos Hartly both of Whitehaven merchants have appointed for ourselves & company James Gordon & Capt Richard Bowman jointly & severally our atty & attys to ask, demand, sue for, recover & receive of & from Joseph Morton of VA merchant or any other person all & any such sums of money, goods, wares & merchandize whatsoever due & payable to us & company ... . Wit: Joseph Casiber, Benjamin Dawson. Proved 3 Apr 1741 & admitted to record. Attest: James Fontaine clerk. (Pg 111)

Settlement. Sums paid to Peter Hayes, Evans & Davis, Mr. Colston, Capt Kenner, Mr. Dulany, Morris Gibbons, Mr. Taite. Sums received by a parcel of land, slaves Jeane, Nan, Joan & Judy. 201 pd 15 sl ½ pn. 14 May 1740 Memorandum: there is a difference in the above acct of the article of 7 pd 11 sl 6 pn which if the sd Lawrence can make to appear to be justly due is punctually to be paid by the sd Richd Kenner for wit whereof we have set our hands & seales, Rodham Kenner & Edward Lawrence. Wit: John Waughop, Matthew Burrell. This acct of settlement between Rodham Kenner & Edward Lawrence was presented into court 14 Apr 1741 by the sd Kenner & on the sd Rodham Kenner's motion was admitted to record. Attest: James Fontaine clerk. (Pg 111)

Deposition. Manly (Mandly) Brown aged 42 years or thereabouts being sworn saith that he went to Economic Church in Apr 1720 & there the sd deponent did in ye open Church before several people see John Miller & Jeane Goodman married together according to law & the sd deponent further saith to the best of his knowledge that the sd John Miller & Jeane Goodman was marryed by Banon? Boickett whom was minister to the parish & the sd deponent farther saith that the sd John Miller & Jeane Goodman was to the best of his knowledge & as fur as he new to be both father & mother to one Rachel Miller now in the care of William Gill. Sworn to 11 Apr 1741 before me Traves Colston. This deposition was presented into court 13 Apr 1741 by Lindsey Opie & on his request was recorded. Attest: James Fontaine clerk. (Pg 111)

11 --- 1741. ... [blurred] ... met on the land with the permission of [?] Mash & did say of ye value 1 a. of land unto Charles Fallin for the building of a water mill according to the tenor of the sd order the value of the land being then paid per the sd Fallin unto the sd Sarah Mash. Yarret Hughlet, Thomas Dameron Junr. This report was returned 13 Apr 1741 & admitted to record. Attest:

James Fontaine clerk. (Pg 112)

Will. John Hartgroves of St. Stephens Parish, Northumberland Co. 7 Mar 1740/41. I do appoint my true & trusty friends Traves Colston & James Furnat my executors. To Sarah Donly all my land in the parish afsd & after her death to be left by her to one of her children & the best bed tick & best feathers for on a bed & furniture also one of the hardest pots to be made choice of by her & the choice of the chests & one small brace kittell & the largest [?]. The rest of my moveables to be set up & sold at publick sale to pay my debts. Wit: Eraphrodelris Sydner, John Hughlett, Wm Stone. Proved 13 Apr 1741 & recorded. Attest: James Fontaine clerk. (Pg 112)

Memo: That on 11 Mar 1740/41 Saml Lucas departed this life but the day before his death he in presence of us John Condre & Thos Watts (said) that it was his earnest desire that his sister Mary Gater should fully posses & enjoy his hole estate after paying lawful & quit debts. This nuncupative will of Saml Lucas decd was presented in court by John Ponder & proved by the oaths of the sd Condre & Thomas Watts wits thereto & the sd wits being severally examined by the court the will was recorded. Attest: James Fontaine clerk. (Pg 112)

Pursuant to an order of court dated 10 Mar 1740 we Richard Smith, Wm Downing & Bertrand Ewell did meet on 23rd of the sd month at the house of Ellenor Gaddes & being first sworn before Capt John Hack did appraise so much of the estate of Adam Armstrong decd as did belong to the orphans of the sd decd & did possess Winder Kenner with the same: Some earthen ware, 2 botles, a small looking glass, beds, bolsters, rugs, blankets, besteads, cord & hide, a bed pillow, 7 sheep, 2 lambs, a mare & young horse, 8 ½ lbs of old peuter, a spit, some hoes, axes, hammers, old fire tongs, a frying pan, a tub, a paile, a pare of small stillards, 2 old pots, a cow & yearling, a sow & barrow. 16 pd 14 sl 5 ¼ pn. This report & appraisement was returned 13 Apr 1741 & recorded. Attest: James Fontaine clerk. (Pg 112)

Pursuant to an order of court dated 9 Mar 1740/1 we John Coles, Richd Smith & Wm Downing did meet on 11 Apr 1741 at the house of James Gaddes decd & being first sworn by the justice did appraise the sd decd's estate in money. 1 horse, 1 old saine, 1 iron pestle, 2 old tubs, 2 old bedsteads, 5 old chair forms, 1 old coat & jacket, 1 old chest & meat sifter, 7 shots & 1 barrow, a plow, 5 jars. 5 pd 19 sl 10 pn. This inventory was exhibited 13 Apr 1741 & admitted to record. Attest: James Fontaine clerk. (Pg 112)

The inventory of James Straughan decd's estate: beds & furniture, 1 large table, 9 leather chears, 8 flagd chears, 2 tables, 3 stools, 1 backgamon table, looking glasses, a pare of money scales, chest lock, pocket knife, 1 pan, spoon molds &

pan pinchers, 1 decanter, parsel of earthen ware, 1 silver spoon, best puter, a large chest, 1 saddle, bridle, 1 case of botles, parsel of books. 1 house bell, 1 gray plow horse, 1 black plow horse, 1 young black horse, 1 old gray horse, 1 gray mare, 1 bay mare, 2 draft oxen, etc. Negroes: woman called Abbe, woman called Nan, man called Darby, boy called Tom, girl called Dinah. 181 pd 2 sl 3 pn. Griffin Fantleroy Junr, Parish Garner, William Taylor. This inventory was exhibited 10 Apr 1741 by Elizabeth Straughan executrix & admitted to record. Attest: James Fontaine clerk. (Pg 113)

The inventory of Thomas Bonum's personal estate taken out of James Straughan decd's estate: 16 old sheep, 2 cows, 2 young stears, 1 large table, 7 young shoats, 2 black horses, 1 bay mare, 1 halbert & 2 chests, 5 leather chairs, 4 flaged chairs, 1 backgammon table, 1 looking glass, 2 punch bowls, candlesticks, 23 lbs pot iron, 1 pare stillards, 17 lbs puter, 1 pot rack, 1 case of botles, parcel of books, 1 cradle, 1 pare andirons, 1 tellescope, 1 saddle, 1 howsin, 1 bridle, etc. 35 pd 7 sl 7 pn. In obedience to an order of court dated 10 Mar last past we Griffin Fantleroy Junr, Parish Garner, William Taylor & John Lewis have set a part & delivered to Lindsey Opie the estate of Thomas Bonum orphan of Saml Bonum decd from the estate of James Straughan decd. This report was exhibited 13 Apr 1741 & recorded. Attest: James Fontaine clerk. (Pg 113)

A true & perfect inventory & appraisement of all & singular the goods & chattels of Thomas Burn decd. Negroes: man named Frank, man named Humphry, man named Charles, Young Humphry, boy named George, boy named James, boy named Frank, boy named Harre, woman named Rose, woman named Jude, girl named Sener, girl named Young Jude, man named Limus, man named Robin. Feather beds, bolsters, pillows & pillow cases, sheets & blankets, 1 rug, suit of curtains & valins, bedsteads, cords & mats, 4 cane chairs, 6 wood chairs, 4 flag chairs, 1 oval table, 2 square tables, 1 old chest, 1 safe, 1 case & 13 botles, 1 sealeskin trunk, old trunk, 3 small boxes, etc. [Not totaled] In obedience to an order of court dated 9 Mar we Benjamin Waddey, Thomas Winter & Roger Winter met at the house of the decd Thomas Burn & being first sworn by Capt George Ball justice have appraised the estate of sd decd that was brought to our view by George Ball Junr 6 Apr 1741. This inventory was exhibited 13 Apr 1741 by George Ball Junr extr & on his motion admitted to record. Attest: James Fontaine clerk. (Pg 114)

9 May 1741. Deed. William Thomas of Great Wicocomoco Parish, Northumberland Co in consideration of 60 a. of land to him sold by George Payne in St. Marys White Chappel Parish, Lancaster Co & 850 lbs of crop tobacco sold to the sd George Payne of St. Marys White Chappel Parish, Lancaster Co a 50 a. parcel of land in Great Wicocomoco Parish which land the

64

sd Thomas bought of Matthew Quill gent ... . Wit: Thos Pitman Senr, John
Mayes, James Balle. Ackn 4 May 1741 by William Thomas & admitted to
record. At a court held 13 7br 1740/1 Darcus Thomas w/o the sd Wm Thomas
came into court & being privately examined by John Foushee gent relinquished
her right of dower in the land unto George Paine on whose motion the same is
admitted to record. Attest: James Fontaine clerk. (Pg 115)

28 Apr 1741. Deed. Edward Fielding of Great Wicocomoco Parish,
Northumberland Co for 30 pd sold to Robt Mitchell of St. Marys White Chappel
Parish, Lancaster Co a 2 a. parcel of land with one water mill built thereon in
Great Wicocomoco Parish bounded by br of Mill Swamp & sd Edward Fielding
... . Wit: William Short, Absalom Hammons, Jeane Tierr. Ackn 11 May 1741
by Edwin Fielding & Judith his wife she being privately examined by John
Foushee gent relinquished her right of dower in the land & mill & admitted to
record. Attest: James Fontaine clerk. (Pg 116)

In obedience to an order of court granted 13 Apr 1741 we Ambrose Fielding,
John Basye & John Hill having met & layd off 1 a. of land for the use of Edwin
Smith's mill & we have valued it to be worth 20 sl. This valuation was returned
11 May 1741 & recorded. Attest: James Fontaine clerk. (Pg 117)

Will. John Shapleigh of Northumberland Co gent. 17 Nov 1740. To my sister
Hannah Shapleigh all & singular my moveable estate not already given, that is to
say, all my Negroes, cattle, hoggs, sheep, horses & mares, household stuffs with
all my cash she paying all my debts out of the same. To my cousin Elizabeth
Alliston one gould ring. To my cousin Shapleigh Neale one gould ring. To my
cousin Prichard Neale one gould ring. To my cousin Lucanna Neale one gould
ring. My will is that my estate be not brought to an appraisement. I appoint my
sister Hannah Shapleigh my executrix. Wit: Clark Hobson, Mary Murphy, John
Hack. Proved 11 May 1741 & admitted to record. Attest: James Fontaine
clerk. (Pg 117)

Will. William Jones of Wicocomoco Parish, Northumberland Co. 25 Nov 1740.
... [blurred] ... Negroes named [?] & Moll ... to my dau Elizabeth Bell my two
Negroes named Dick & Sam ... to my dau Leeanna Jones my Negro man named
Toney & Lucy? Together with a childs pt/o all my household goods & stocks.
To my dau Ann Jones my two Negroes named Peter & Priscilla together with a
childs pt/o all my household goods & stocks. To my son William Jones all my
land being about the falls of Rappahannock part in King George Co & part in
Prince William Co & one Negro man named Harry & a childs pt/o my
household goods & stocks. To my granddau Ann Jones one Negro wench
between the age of 15 & 20 years to be paid to her by my executors at the age of
21 or day of marriage. My will is that all my Negroes except Dick who is to be

delivered to my dau Elizabeth Bell immediately after my death be kept together & all my household goods & stocks for the use of my wife & such of the children as lives with her during her natural life. I appoint my wife, my dau Leeanna Jones, my friend the Rev. Mr. John Bell & his wife Elizabeth Bell, my dau Ann Jones & my son William Jones executors. Wit: Henry Lawson Junr, Charles Lee. Proved 11 May 1741 & admitted to record. Attest: James Fontaine clerk. (Pg 117)

Will. Charles Craven of Wicocomoco Parish, Northumberland Co. 13 Sep 1740. I desire that my wife Rebecka should have the use of all my estate both personal & real while she remains a widdow. To my dau Betty the plantation where on I live with all the land to it & a Negro man called Knail. My desire is that my dau Betty should have the first child that my Negro Rose brings. To my dau Lucy a Negro boy called Simon & a Negro woman named Rose & all her increase (except the child that she is now with which is to be my dau Betty's). To my dau Francine a Negro boy named Sam & a Negro girl named Hagar & all her increase & a feather bed & furniture. To my dau Rhoda my two Negro boys Ned & Harry. To my dau Mary the late w/o William Dasquet 5 sl. My will is that my four daus, viz, Betty, Lucy, Francine & Rhoda should live on my plantation & their estates as long as they remain unmarried. To my cousin Charles Sullivan my gun. To Elizabeth Nickens a heiffer of 3 years old. My will is that the rest of my personal estate (after the death of my wife or at the time of her marriage) be divided between my wife & my four daus, viz, Betty, Lucy, Francine & Rhoda. My desire is that my wife Rebecca & my friend John Coppedge Senr be the executors. I also appoint my friend John Coppedge to act & do in all cases of my estate as he shall see needful or beneficial to my estate & children & to have the same authority as I myself have & to satisfye himself out of my estate for such trouble as he shall see reasonable. Wit: George Mills, John Pursley (Dursley?). Proved 11 May 1741 & admitted to record. Attest: James Fontaine clerk. (Pg 118)

Will. Ann Bogges. 4 Nov 1740. To my mother Mary Bogges all my estate I have of my decd father Hennery Bogges' estate. I appoint my mother the afsd Mary Bogges my executrix. Wit: Richard Thomson, James Fooried?, Francis Brown. Proved 11 May 1741 & admitted to record. Attest: James Fontaine clerk. (Pg 119)

In obedience to an order of court held 9 Mar 1740/1 ordered we the subscribers to meet & settle the acompts of the estate of Benjamin Nutt decd & to possess John Herst? with his pt/o the sd estate have possest the sd Herst as follows: 1 large chest, 1 spice mortar & pestle, 2 old books, 3 old chairs, 3 hogs, 4 sheep, 1 doz spoons, 4 lbs of puter, 2 cows & a heiffer, 2 cider cask, old tubs, 2 quart botles, 1 mare, 1 small feather bed, Indian corn. Charles Coppedge, Josias

66

Basye & Edmond Basye auditors. [Not totaled] This report & division was
exhibited in court by the auditors & recorded. (Pg 119)

In obedience to an order of court dated 13 Apr 1741 we Richd Howson
(Hawson?), John Coppedge & David Lattimore having met & valued as much of
the personall estate of Thomas Taylor decd in the hands of Robert Jones gent as
amounts to 42 pd 8 sl 5 pn & has possest Elles Gill gent with the same & a
Negro woman left in the hands of Robt Jones valued to 25 pd which the sd Robt
Jones & Elles Gill did agree to divide the land at ye fall & the Negro woman
when they were better informed which of them she belond to if wholly to one.
An inventory of the estate as we possest the sd Gill with: 1 Negro man, 1
feather bed & furniture, 4 old chairs, 1 old chest, 1 chest of drawers, 1 cow &
yearling, 1 armed chair, 1 brass sadle & candle snuffers, 1 round table, 3 chairs,
1 hone jug, a parcel of earthen ware, 9 ½ lbs puter, 1 iron pot. This report &
division was exhibited 11 May 1741 & recorded. Attest: James Fontaine clerk.
(Pg 119)

... [blurred] ... 5 May 1741 sworn before ... [blurred] ... & appraise the estate
of John Edwards decd ... [blurred] ... order of court directed to us: 12 hogs, 2
pigs, 1 cow & calf, 1 mare & colt, 1 horse colt, 1 horse, 1 box iron & heaters, 1
broad ax, 1 adz, 1 narrow saw, 1 hand saw, 1 drawing knife, 4 chisels, some
lumber, 6 hows, 1 mans sadle, parcel of old books, a looking glas, 3 ¼ yd linnen,
parcel of botles, parcel of wearing cloaths, parcel of chairs, 3 old chests, 3 jugs,
3 hides, etc. 33 pd 11 sl 6 2/3 pn. The whole estate divided in to three parts 11
pd 3 sl 10 pn a piece. Peter Hayes, Jonathan Betts, Giles Webb. This inventory
was exhibited by Grace Edwards adminr & on her motion is admitted to record.
Attest: James Fontaine clerk. (Pg 120)

In pursuance to an order of court dated 9 Mar 1740 we John Hornsby, Jares?
Basie? & Charles Coppedge having met being first sworn & have appraised the
estate of Saml Smith decd in money. Beds, furniture, covering, 1 Negro boy
named Jeffery, 1 desk, 1 chest, 1 little box, 1 trunk, 3 leather chairs, 7 flag
chairs, 1 broad ax, 1 adds, 2 drawing knives, 2 chisels, 1 auger, 4 compasses, 2
jointer stocks, 2 hand plains, etc. [Not totaled] This inventory was exhibited 11
May 1741 by Ann Smith extra & admitted to record. Attest: James Fontaine
clerk. (Pg 120)

The estate of Robt Sadler decd: Sums paid to Robt Clark Junr, Jno Lewis, Wm
Hughlet, Doctor Robt Eskridge, James Walkden, Jno Keen, Wm Taite, John
Shurly, Thomas Bright. [Not totaled] This acct of the estate of Robt Sadler
decd was exhibited by Peter Bearcroft adminr of the sd decd & approved by the
court & recorded. Attest: James Fontaine clerk. (Pg 121)

A full inventory of Robt Gordon's estate sold by me by order of court returned 11 May 1741. Sold to: Charles Pritchard, Argail Taylor, Saml Snow, Wm Ellet, Wm Thomas Joshua James, Christopher Garlington, John Richardson, Joshan Champion, Thos Gaskins, Edward Garner, Thos Lezenby, Aron Williams, Jno Berry, Randolph Mott, Richd Lunsford, John Webb, Wm Lunsford, Robt Doeden, George Mills, Thomas Short, Moses Webb, Wm Barrett Senr, Jno Hust planter, Joseph Null, Thos Mahan, Joseph Herter, Wm Wallis, Wm Barret Junr, Christopher Carpenter, Capt Robt Jones, Lazarus Sullon, Jno Ingram, Capt Robt Jones, John Ingram. 5806 lbs tobacco. Received of: Patrick Fairweather, Sevenson Lunsford, Joshen Champion, Lazarus Sutton, Swanson Pritchard, Charles Ingram, Jno Hust planter, Elizabeth Swanson, Wm Lunsford, John Ingram, Patrick Fairweather, Hannah Howson, Edmond Conway, Robt Dreddon, Robt Gordon, Joshan James, Benjamin Williams, John Eustace. 2782 ¾ lbs tobacco. This acct of sales & inventory was exhibited by Joseph Nutt sub sheriff & recorded. Attest: James Fontaine clerk. (Pg 121)

8 Jun 1741. Deed. Richard Thomas of Northumberland carpenter for 50 pd sold to James Gordon of Lancaster Co gent a water mill now in the possession of sd Gordon on the head of Great Wicocomoco River on the br that descends to the Great Bridge called Fieldings Bridge the sd mill was conveyed to the sd Richard & his brother Peter Thomas in 1717 & the sd Peter sold his part to the sd Richard Thomas which the sd Peter allows & confirms by his will dated 23 9br 1734 ... . Wit: William Bowen, Bertrand Ewell, H. Tapscott. Ackn 8 Jun 1741 & admitted to record. Attest: James Fontaine clerk. (Pg 122)

8 Jun 1741. Bond. I Richard Thomas of Northumberland Co carpenter do owe & stand bound unto James Gordon of Lancaster Co gent for 100 pd ... the condition of this obligation is such that whereas the afsd Richard Thomas carpenter hath sold a water mill unto the afsd James Gordon gent & past a conveyance of the same [see above], if the sd James Gordon shall have hold, occupy & enjoy the sd mill in the sd conveyance mentioned without any lett trouble or interruption of the sd Richard Thomas or any other person from this time forth forever then this obligation to be voyd ... . Wit: William Bowen, Bertrand Ewell, H. Tapscott. Ackn 8 Jun 1741 & admitted to record. Attest: James Fontaine clerk. (Pg 122)

8 Jun 1741. Deed. William Fallin now of St. Stephens Parish, Northumberland Co for 50 pd sold to Charles Betts of same place a 156 a. tr of land in sd parish on the n side of Great Wicocomoco River bounded by the land of John Coles, Mary White, William Kesterson's orphans, George Kesterson & John Tolly ... . Wit: Richard Smith, John Webb, George Kesterson. Ackn 8 Jun 1741 & admitted to record. Attest: James Fontaine clerk. (Pg 122)

8 Jun 1741. Bond. I William Falling of St. Stephens Parish, Northumberland Co am firmly bound unto Charles Betts of same place for 100 pd ... the condition of this obligation is such that whereas the afsd William Fallin hath by deed [see above] sold unto the afsd Charles Betts a tr of land on the n side of Great Wicocomoco River, now if the afsd William Fallin shall observe, perform & keep all & every the articles, covenants, things & agreements comprised in the sd indenture & ackn the afsd deed in court then this obligation to be void ... . Wit: Richard Smith, John Webb. Ackn 8 Jun 1741 & admitted to record. Attest: James Fontaine clerk. (Pg 123)

--- 1741. Deed. William Linkorn & Jane his wife of Wicocomoco Parish, Northumberland Co for 2,000 lbs of lawfull tobacco sold to George Hunt of same place a 35 a. parcel of land which sd land being pt/o a parcel of land by vertue of a deed of feoffment dated 17 Mar 1735/6 was made & executed by Billington McCarty & Ann his wife unto John Rose & by vertue of a deed of bargain & exchange dated 12 Nov 1737 was made & executed by the afsd John Rose to the afsd Wm Linkorn, bounded by sd Rose & Hunt & the Main Swamp ... . Wit: Richd Doged (Dogged), Billington McCarty, Maryann Tillery. Ackn 8 Jun 1741 by William Linkorn & Jane his wife she being privately examined by John Foushee gent justice relinquished her right of dower & admitted to record. Attest: James Fontaine clerk. (Pg 123)

8 Jun 1741. Bond. I William Linkorn (Linkhorn) of Wicocomoco Parish, Northumberland Co am firmly bound unto George Hunt of same place for 50 pd ... the condition of this obligation is such that if the afsd William Linkorn shall well & truly perform, fulfill, accomplish & keep all & singular the articles, clauses, conditions & covenants comprised in an indenture [see above] & ackn the deed in court then this obligation to be void ... . Wit: Richd Doged, Billington McCarty, Maryann Tillery. Ackn 8 Jun 1741 by William Linkorn & admitted to record. Attest: James Fontaine clerk. (Pg 124)

8 Jun MDCCXDI. Deed of Gift. ... [illegible] ... I have given & made over unto my sd son a parcel of land pt/o my dwelling plantation in sd parish containing 30 a. to be layd off adj to ye lands of Benjamin Waddy & my Negro man Tom & my Negro woman Phillis which sd 30 a. of land & my two sd Negroes do hereby put my sd son into the immediate possession for his present use & do also further agree & conclude that at my decease my sd son Charles shall likewise be intitled to & have hold & enjoy the full ½ of my sd dwelling plantation including my settlement whereon I now live reserving to my wife his mother her widows dower of the same lands in case she happen to survive me to have & to hold the sd 100 a. of land unto my sd son Charles & his heirs & for want of such issue to such of my children as in my will I shall bequeath the same ... . [Signed by] Charles Ingram. Wit: John Coppidg, Joseph Pope, Morley

Mott. Memorandum that this date delivery & seizing of the lands & premises
was given & delivered by the within named Charles Ingram the father to the
within named Charles Ingram the son by delivery of turf & twig .... Wit: John
Tully, William Dameron, John Irons. Ackn 8 Jun 1741 & admitted to record.
Attest: James Fontaine clerk. (Pg 125)

In obedience to an order of court dated 11 May 1741 we Argail Taylor,
Lawrence Parrot & Saml Mahane have met & appraised the estate of Charles
Craven decd in money being first sworn. 1 servant man John Pursley. Negroes:
man named Nail, woman named Rose, boy named Ned, girl named Hagor, boy
named Sam, boy named Harry, boy named Simon, child named James. 15
sheep, feather beds & furniture, 1 horse skin trunk, 2 old trunks, 1 large chest, 1
side sadle & bridle, a parcel of cloaths, 1800 10 lb nailes, 19 ¾ yd cotton, 4 yd
coors linnen, 3 yd linsey woolsey, dear skins, 10 oz thread, 1 razor, 1 funnel,
some pouder & shot, 1 jug & trifles, etc. This inventory was exhibited 8 Jun
1741 by Rebecka Craven & John Coppidge executors & on their motion
admitted to record. Attest: James Fontaine clerk. (Pg 125)

11 May 1741. We John Waughop & John Foushee gent did meet & settle the
accounts due to the estate of Doctor Archibald Johnston which are as follows:
Tobacco & money due from John Cralle, Richard Booth, John Curtis, John
Dogget, Capt Griffin Fantleroy, Griffin Fantleroy Junr, Zachariah Stafford,
Richd Hull, John Kenneday, Edward Lawrence, Morris Gibbons, John Neale,
Lindsey Opie, Michael Ryan, George Turner, Richard Thomson. [Not totaled]
This report & settlement was exhibited 8 Jun 1741 & recorded. Attest: James
Fontaine clerk. (Pg 126)

In obedience to an order of court dated 11 May 1741 we Richard Claughton,
John Claughton & Pemberton Claughton being first sworn before John Foushee
justice did appraise the estate of Jane Miller decd in money & have possest John
Lewis & Lindsey Opie with the same. Beds & furniture, frying pans, 1 large
Bible & other books, parcel of wooden ware, knives & forks, 1 spit, 1 small pot
& hooks, 1 iron skillet, 1 ax, 1 horse, 1 pare of sheep shears, 1 meal sifter, 1
morter & pestle, 28 lbs of puter, a parcel of earthen ware, 1 puter pot, 1 side
sadle & bridle, a parcel of old lumber, 5 baskets, 3 old chests, a box, etc. [Not
totaled] This inventory was exhibited 8 Jun 1741 by John Lewis & Lindsey
Opie who possessed themselves with the same by an order of last court to
indemnify them from being security for the sd Jane Miller in her life time for the
estate of Joseph Miller decd to this court which was ordered to be recorded.
Attest: James Fontaine clerk. (Pg 126)

By vertue of an order of court dated 11 May 1741 we John Stepto, Benjamin
Waddy & Thomas Winter met at the plantation of Major Charles Lee decd &

appraised the sd decd's estate: 9 leather chairs, 1 broken chair, 1 large table, 1 old desk, beds, blankets, bolsters, sheets, pillows, cases, sheets, 2 towels, 1 pare hackles, 1 old table, 1 small wheal, 1 old chest of drawers, 1 old chest, 1 table, 1 cold still, 1 small table, 4 cyder cask, 1 old rum cask, 1 silver seale, 1 pare of oxen, cart wheels, 1 large iron pot, 1 small iron pot, 1 old pot, 17 old hoes, 5 new axes, 1 pare pot hooks, 2 iron pestles, etc. Negroes: Boy Robin, man Sam, man Anthony, man Harry, man Will, woman Nan, Ben, Tony, woman Sarah, woman Judith, woman old Nan, woman Cate, large girl Betty, woman Moll, woman Sarah, woman Martha, girl Sue, girl Lucy, boy Charles, boy Ben, girl Judy, girl Nell, girl Frank, boy Isaac, young child Letty, man Tom, man James. [Not totaled] This inventory was exhibited 8 Jun 1741 by Charles Lee his son one of the decd's executors on whose motion the same is admitted to record. Attest: James Fontaine clerk. (Pg 127)

Mrs. Elizabeth Brent debits to the estate of Charles Lee decd: parcel of old iron, beds, bolsters, pillows, pillow cases, rug, blankets, sheets, 8 leather chairs, 1 table, 9 old chairs, 1 cold still, 2 large bulls, 1 old cider cask, 1 horse Starr, 1 young mare, 2 oxen, cart & wheels, 1 pot, 2 axes, 1 pare of pot hooks, 1 pestle, 1 pot rack, 11 cows & calf, 1 stear, etc. Negroes: Anthony, Harry, Tony, Bob, Kate, old Nan, young Nan, Ben, girl Nel, Lucy, girl Frank, girl Betty. 294 pd 14 sl 4 ½ pn. (Pg 128)

Charles Lee debits to estate of Charles Lee decd: parcel of old iron, beds, bolsters, pillows, pillow cases, rug, blanket, sheets, 1 gun, 3 leather chairs, 2 wheat biddles & 5 old wheels, 1 table & chest, 3 old chairs, 1 chest of drawers, 1 pare of hackles, 4 large bulls, 1 rum cask, 1 horse dragon, 1 copper kettle, 21 lbs old pewter, 1 large pot, 2 new axes, pare of pot hooks, 1 pestle, 1 pot rack, 1 spit, 1 candlestick, 1 frying pan, 12 cows & calves, 2 stears, etc. Negroes: Tom, James, Ben, Will, Judith, Moll, old Sarah, lame woman Martha, girl [?], boy [?], girl Sue. 291 pd 9 sl 1 pn. (Pg 129)

Charles Lee's pt/o his father's estate: Negroes: man Tom, boy Charles, woman Sarah, a child. 2 cows, 1 heifer, 1 yearling, 3 old sheep, 1 lamb, 1 hog, 3 shoats, 1 large table, 200 gallon casks, 1 table, 1 trunk, 1 dictionary, 1 plow, 1 seale, share in silver, 1 large Bible, 1 horse called Pompey. 97 pd 14 sl 7 pn. (Pg 130)

5 Jun 1741. By vertue of an order of court dated 11 May 1741 we John Stepto, Benjamin Waddy & Thomas Winter met & appraised, divided & set apart the estate of Major Charles Lee decd, half to Mrs. Elizabeth Brent guardian to Elizabeth Lee, Margaret Lee & Ann Lee & the other half to Charles Lee executor of the decd Major Charles Lee whereof the inclosed is a just copy. This division was exhibited 3 May 1741 by the auditors & recorded. Attest: James Fontaine clerk. (Pg 130)

13 Jul 1741. Memorandum that it is agreed & concluded by us the subscribers

the buyers & purchasers of the land belonging to the coheirs of Thomas Harwood formerly of this co being 100 a. of land on the Herring Cr (& ye sd land never been parted or divided) the line of division betwixt us does & shall forever hereafter be at the head of the cove on Herring Cr & the line that divides this land from the land of William Webb, & we do mutually agree that this line of partition be & remain the dividing line betwixt us our heirs & assigns forever. Peter Presly & Charles Wilkins. Wit: W. Betts, Richd Seebree. This division & settlement was ackn by both partys & on their motion admitted to record. Attest: James Fontaine clerk. (Pg 130)

Will. James Coppidge of Wicocomoco Parish, Northumberland Co. 23 Apr 1732. I give & bequeath that tr of land whereon I live unto my Godson James Coppidge & his heirs, but if he shall die without such heirs then I give the sd tr of land unto his brother Moses Coppidge & his heirs. To the sd James Coppidge & Moses Coppidge my Negro man Sam & all my moveable & personal estate whatsoever. I appoint my brother Charles Coppidge executor. Wit: Matthew Quill, Elizabeth Quill, David Flicker. Proved 13 Jul 1741 & admitted to record. Attest: James Fontaine clerk. (Pg 130)

28 Jun 1741. We Lindsay Opie, John Lewis & Jno Kennedy met at the house of Jeane Lamkins & by order of court dated 8 Jun 1741 did allot the sd Jeane Lamkins Junr her full pt/o her father's estate: 1 bed & furniture, 1 razer & hone, 1 chest, 1 wheel, 1 mill worm & tubb, 1 cow & calf, 4 lbs of peuter, 1 cask, 1 ½ lbs of wool. 15 pd 2 sl 11 ½ pn. This report & division was exhibited 13 Jul 1741 by the auditors & recorded. Attest: James Fontaine clerk. (Pg 131)

In obedience to an order of court dated 11 May 1741 we William Harding, Geo Lamkin & Francis Vanlandigan met at the decd John Hartgrove's plantation 29 May to appraise the afsd decd's estate. Beds, sheets, pillows, bolsters, besteads, hide, cords, blankets, rug, parcel of [?] ware, 2 table, 1 spinning wheel, 2 pots,. 2 pare of pot hooks, 6 cows, 1 yearling, 2 mares, 2 chests, some lumber, 1 looking glass, pare of fire tongs & shovel, 11 bottles, 1 earthen pot, parsel of earthen ware, 1 Bible, 1 stone jug, etc. [Not totaled] This inventory was exhibited 13 Jul 1741 by Traves Colston gent executor & admitted to record. Attest: James Fontaine clerk. (Pg 131)

18 Jul 1741. Bond. Robert Jones, Cuthbert Spann & John Foushee are firmly bound unto our Sovereign King in the penal sum of ... [blurred] ... the condition of this obligation is such that whereas the afsd bounded Robt Jones if by commission from the Honourable the President of this Colony of VA dated 11 Jun last appointed sheriff of Northumberland Co, if the sd Robert Jones shall well & truly render to the auditor & receiver generall of his Majestys revenues a particular perfect & true acct of all his Majestys rents & dues arising within the

sd co & also due payment make of all other publick dues & fees put into his hands to collect within the sd co unto the severall persons to whom the same shall be due & payable & due performance make of all matters & things relating to the sd office of sheriff during his continuance therein, then this obligation to be void .... Wit: Thos Edwards, James Fontaine clerk. Attest: James Fontaine clerk. (Pg 132)

28 Aug 1740. Pursuant to an order of court dated 13 Jul renewed 12 Aug 1740 I Matthew Quill have perused & examined all the accts in ye books of John Irons late ordinary keeper in this co & find that the persons mentioned in the two following folios are indebted to the sd Irons: Wm Taylor, Jno Kennedy, James Thomson Junr, Linsay Opie, Thomas Manly, Capt Fansbury?, Richd Thomas, Allen Hunter?, John Lewis, David Straughan, John Evans, Archd [?], Joseph B[?], Thos Robinson, Rodham Kenner, Thos Vanlandingham, James Booth, Darly Murphy, Ormsby Haynie, Richd Claughton, Edward B[?], Robt Clark Senr, John Bulgar, John Ducher, Daniel Manly, Richd Broth, Francis Brown, George Brown, Parish Garner, George Turner, John Bogges, Wm B[?], Thos Low, John Hall Junr, Thos Campbell, Wm Fouct?, Spencer Corbell, Andrew Hunt, John Curtis, Farned Burrel, Jonathan Hammontree, Thos Myars, Barrnit Bogges, Richd Couta, John Cralle, Wm Dankins, John Foushee, Thos Taylor, Robt Lindsay, Thos Tubin, George Elmore, Jonas Elinore, Danl Dugins in MD, John Ragley, John Figan, John Donaway, Edward Lawrence, John Wheddon, John France, Robt Rolland, Robt Benatt, Wm Wyatt, John Booth, Owen Williams, James Crow, Peter Lewis, George Clark, Robt Davis, Ben Moor, Thomas Bogges, John Ganur, Vincent Games, John Rout, Thos Webster, Bennet Bogges, Geo Conway, John Hanly, John [?], Thos Hall, George Dawkins, Thos Straughan, David Morgan, John, Burrell, George Riggins, Mitchell Ryan, Benj [?], John Crocket, John Wilson, Matthew Burrell, John Bennet, John Wiggins, Griffin Fantleroy Junr, Alexr Anderson, John Webb, John Connely, Wm Gill, Edmond Cole, Wm Fallin, Richd Partridge, Saml Partridge, John Jones, Wm Harden, James Low, Bradshaw Morris, James Davis, Sarah Wilson, Andrew Bell, Gilbert Harnet, John Dollins, David Morgan. [Not totaled] This report due to ye estate of John Irons late ordinary keeper was returned 11 Aug 1741 & recorded & ordered that the clerk of this court on ye application of Wm F[?] one of ye creditors or pay other creditors from executions agt the sd debtors mentioned in sd report for ye severall sums of money or tobacco to their names annexed not already payd & their proportionable pt/o ye costs. Attest: James Fontaine clerk. (Pg 132)

11 Aug 1741. On the motion of [?] Dulaney atty that Richard Dodson an infant who is heir to lands in this co has been carried away out of this co into Prince William Co by one Thomas Boiert? & that the sd infant not being of age to chuse a guardian it will be necessary to have a guardian appointed him in this

court. It is therefore considered by the court that James B[?] in this co the Godfather & next friend to the sd infant to hereby make his application to the co court of Prince William to obtain an order of the same that the sd infant may be reconvened back to this co & if any guardian should have been appointed to ye sd infant by the sd co court of Prince William that the sd guardianship be set aside for order that a guardian may be appointed to the sd infant in this co according to law which is ordered to be recorded & certified. Attest: James Fontaine clerk. (Pg 133)

In pursuance to an order of court dated 14 Jul 1741 we George Conway, Vincent Garner & James Garner being appointed to value as much out of the estate of John Reeves (mentioned in a certain bill of sale to Leroy Griffin of Richmond Co gent dated 24 Mar 1740) as will amount to the sum of 2,150 lbs of tobacco for the proper use & behoof of Richard & Elizabeth Reeves. We did accordingly meet at the plantation of sd John Reeves & have possessed the sd Elizabeth & Richard Reeves with all the articles hereunder mentioned: 1 cow & yearling, 1 young cow, feather beds, bolsters, rugs, blankets, old iron pot, 1 old white horse, 2 old leather chairs, 1 iron spit & fire tongs, 1 old looking glass, 1 iron skillet, 3 old chests, 2 old dishes, 6 old plates, 2 basons, 2 old tankards, 2 Negro made pans, etc. [Not totaled] This report was returned 11 Aug 1741 by the auditors & recorded. Attest: James Fontaine clerk. (Pg 133)

10 Aug 1741. In pursuance to an order of this court dated 14 Jul last we Saml Blackwell & George Ball Junr have met with Col Wm Ball surveyor of this co & have layd off 1 a. of land belonging to Robt Carter Junr esqr & we doe value the sd acre of land to 15 sl.
    14 Jul 1741. I William Ball have laid off 1 a. of land for Edwin Smith as per the plat [not included here] adj Fieldings Mill Swamp & the Main Swamp ... . The above report & survey were exhibited by Edwin Fielding 11 Aug 1741 on whose motion the same is admitted to record. Attest: James Fontaine clerk. (Pg 133)

By the direction of an order of court dated 13 Jul 1741 have viewed the road through Thomas Mahane's land to an ancient landing now John Harvey's the antient road is [?] & is good except a fence & brush hedge joining to ye sd landing the hedge is of no use but to obstruct the use of sd landing. Given under my hand 7 Aug 1741 George Ball. This report was returned by George Ball gent 11 Aug 1741 & recorded. Attest: James Fontaine clerk. (Pg 133)

29 Jul 1741. Power of Attorney. I Moses Lunsford of Prince William Co appoint William Barret of Northumberland Co my atty to ackn in the court certain deeds of lease & release dated 28 & 29 Jul 1741 from me the sd Moses Lunsford to Thomas Hardin of Northumberland Co & hereby ratifying allowing

& confirming all & whatsoever my sd atty shall do in & about the premises ... .
Wit: Charles Hardin, Joseph Whitehead, Francis Ballinger. Proved 10 Aug
1741 & admitted to record. Attest: James Fontaine clerk. (Pg 134)

28 Jul 1741. Deed of Lease. Moses Lunsford for 5 sl leased to Thomas Harding
of Northumberland Co a 50 a. tr of land in Wicocomoco Parish binding on ye
lands of James Davison & Robert Angel (Angell) ... for the term of 1 year
paying the yearly rent of one pepper corn at the feast of St. Michael ye
Archangel if demanded ... . Wit: Charles Harden, Joseph Whitehead, Francis
Ballenger. Attest: James Fontaine clerk. (Pg 134)

29 Jul 1741. Deed of Release. Moses Lunsford for 3,500 lbs of tobacco
released to Thomas Harden of Northumberland Co a 50 a. tr of land ... [same as
above] ... . Wit: Charles Harden, Joseph Whitehead, Francis Ballenger. By
vertue of a power of atty ackn by William Barret 10 Aug 1741 & on the motion
of Thomas Harding is admitted to record. Attest: James Fontaine clerk. (Pg
134)

7 Aug 1741. Deed. Swanson Lunsford of Wicocomoco Parish, Northumberland
Co for 5,000 lbs of tobacco sold to James Adair of St. Stephens Parish, same co
a parcel of land within Wicocomoco Parish bounded by the land called Scotland,
land of Abraham Ingraham, Richard Swanson, sd Swanson & Richard Hudnall,
formerly in the possession of John Robinson & afterwards in the possession of
Joseph Robinson & granted by the sd Joseph Robinson to John Lunsford by a
deed dated 1717 & afterwards made over by John Lunsford by way of a firm
deed of gift to his son Swanson Lunsford dated 19 7br 1727 & also being pt/o a
pattent of 1,000 a. of land formerly granted to Andrew Boyer dated 2 8br 1662
& by the sd Boyer assigned to Thomas Lane dated 19 Feb 1663 & granted to sd
Thomas Lane by a pattent dated 26 Jul 1665 ... . Wit: Rauleigh Evritt, Moses
Lunsford, George Robuck. Ackn 10 Aug 1741 by Swanson Lunsford &
Elizabeth his wife she being privately examined by John Foushee gent ackn her
right of dower in the lands unto James Adair on whose motion the same is
admitted to record. Attest: James Fontaine clerk. (Pg 135)

-- Sep 1740. Deed of Lease. John Span Webb of Richmond Co for 5 sl leased
to Giles Webb of Northumberland Co all those trs of land near the head of Little
Wicocomoco containing 375 a. being formerly purch by John Span decd of
Charles Wilkins, William Edwards & William McKall & their wives & by the sd
John Span in his will given to his sister Elizabeth mother of the parties after
whose death the same became the property of the sd John Span Webb as her
eldest son & her heir at law ... during the term of 1 year paying the rent of one
pepper corn on the feast of St. Michael the Archangel if demanded ... . Wit:
William Hughlett, Elles Gill, Peter Hayes. Ackn 10 Aug 1741 & admitted to

record. Attest: James Fontaine clerk. (Pg 136)

-- Sep 1741. Deed of Release. John Span Webb of Richmond Co for 50 pd & also in compliance with a decree of the court of Richmond Co obtained by Giles Webb agt the sd John Span Webb released to the sd Giles Webb of Northumberland Co all those trs of land near the head of Little Wicocomoco containing 375 a. … [same as above] … . Wit: William Hughlet, Elles Gill, Peter Hayes. Ackn 10 Aug 1741 & admitted to record. Attest: James Fontaine clerk. (Pg 136)

7 Aug 1741. Deed. James Philips millwright of St. Stephens Parish, Northumberland Co for 45 pd sold to Col Peter Presly of same place an 85 a. tr of land in the parish afsd on the n side of Great Wicocomoco River this land was formerly William Budgar's & by him sold to John Mew & sold from Mew to William Fallin & from Fallin to James Philips, bounded by Tarpit Cr, Col Peter Presley & land formerly Ann Howel's now in the possession of William Edwards Junr … . Wit: James Daughity, George Berry, John Mew. Ackn 10 Aug 1741 by James Philips & admitted to record. 10 --- 1741 Jane Philips w/o the sd James Philips came into court & being first privately examined by John Foushee gent relinquished her right of dower which was recorded. Attest: James Fontaine clerk. (Pg 137)

10 Aug 1741. Bond. I James Philips of St. Stephens Parish, Northumberland Co am firmly bound unto Col Peter Presly of same place for 90 pd … the condition of this obligation is such that if the afsd James Philips shall when required by the sd Peter Presly sign, seale & deliver deeds of conveyance for 85 a. being a tr of land which James Philips bought of William Fallin unto the sd Peter Presley & acknowledge when required in court then this obligation to be void … . Wit: James Daughity, George Berry, John Mew. Ackn 10 Aug 1741 & admitted to record. Attest: James Fontaine clerk. (Pg 138)

At a court held for Northumberland Co on 9 Mar 1740 on ye motion of Ambrose Fielding executor of the will of Hannah Hill decd, Thomas Pitman, Edmond Bane, John Bane & Edwin Smith or any three of them appointed to meet sometime before the next court being first sworn in obedience thereunto we met 31 Mar 1741 & appraised the estate of Hannah Hill decd in money ordered the executor exhibit an inventory thereof upon oath to ye next court appraised & inventoried as follows: Some old waring cloaths, gound, petticoat, old shift, old mantle, old apron, 1 gown & petticoat, old shift & handkerchief & cap. [Not totaled] This inventory was exhibited 10 Aug 1741 by Ambrose Fielding extr on whose motion the same was admitted to record. Attest: James Fontaine clerk. (Pg 138)

Will. Thomas Haynie. 22 Apr 1741. To my wife Martha Haynie the use of all my lands, houses & orchards during her widdowhood & no longer. To my wife Martha Haynie the use of all my moveable estate that I am now possest with all during her widdowhood & no longer. It is my will that if my sd wife do marry that then all my children shall have an equal pt/o all my moveable estate which I lent to my sd wife. I do give to my son Spencer Haynie & his heirs all my land, provided my sd son shall have no right to the sd land till after my wife decease or marriage. It is my will that if my sd son Spencer shall die without having lawful heirs that then I give the sd land to all my daus. I appoint my wife Martha Haynie & Simon Peter Bearcroft my executors. Wit: Thomas Dameson, James Beumer. Proved 10 Aug 1741 & admitted to record. Attest: James Fontaine clerk. (Pg 138)

23 Nov 1740. Deed of Lease. William Hughlet of St. Stephens Parish, Northumberland Co sold & made over to Thomas Tayler & Mary his wife of same place a 100 a. tr of land in the parish afsd on the head of Mattapony Cr bounded by the road that goes from Lewis' Mill along the line of this land & the land of Mr. Straughan, land where Case Moor lived, Long Br & the Main Road in Clapshoo's old field ... during the natural lives of the sd Thos Tayler & Mary his wife & further in consideration for the sd land the afsd Thomas Tayler & Mary his wife do oblige themselves to build what convenient houses they shall want & to plant 100 good apple trees & to keep the same under a good fence from creatures during their lives & after the sd Thomas Tayler & Mary his wife decease then to return to the sd Hughlet & his heirs again ... . Wit: Thos Straughan, Archibald Blaine. Ackn by the parties & admitted to record. Attest: James Fontaine clerk. (Pg 139)

In pursuance to an order of this court dated 10 Aug 1741 we Joshua James, William James & David Flaker having met at the plantation of James Coppedge decd being sworn before Saml Blackwell have appraised all the estate of James Coppedge decd as was brought to our view by Charles Coppedge his executor: Negro man named Sambo. 3 cows & calves, 2 stears, 2 heifers, 2 old feather beds & furniture, a large case of bottles, small case of bottles, a pare of small stillards, some leather, a large chest, 2 small chests, a spinning wheel & old cards, 7 young hogs, 3 sows, 3 pigs, 33 ½ lbs of good puter, 3 candlesticks, pepper box, snuf box, etc. [Not totaled] This inventory was exhibited 14 7br 1741 by Charles Coppedge executor & admitted to record. Attest: James Fontaine clerk. (Pg 139)

In obedience to an order of court dated 10 Aug 1741 we Saml Nelms, Thos Dameron Junr & Thos Harding appointed to appraise the estate of Thomas Haynie decd have met & being first sworn before Saml Blackwell have appraised the sd estate: 11 hogs, 11 sheep, 19 gees, 4 cows & calves, 1 cow bell, 1 gray mare, 1 bay mare, small parsel of tarr, some old tubs, 17 cider cask, 2 washing tubs, 9 old tubs, 3 water pailes, some old wooden ware, 1 gun, 2 stone jugs, 1 earthen pot, 1 sword, cartridge box, 1 belt, 1 baril with some salt in it, 1 old barrill with some feathers in it, 1 old safe, 1 old meale tub, etc. [Not totaled] This inventory was exhibited 14 7br 1741 by Martha Haynie extx & admitted to record. Attest: James Fontaine clerk. (Pg 140)

The estate of Edward Downing decd: … [blurred] … Doctor Coulton, Capt Eustace, John Cole, Wm Hughlet, Elles Gil, Wm Stewart. 8583. Disbursements since the death of Edward Downing: 3 ½ gall brandy at ye childs burial, smith's work to Col Presly, Timo Realy, Jonathan Betts, Moses Williams, Elias Martin, Thos Hightower, Mr. Dulany for attys fee, Hudnall for smith's work, Snow for carpenter's work, Fignor for pork, Daughity for levys & quit rents, Jos Hudnall, Bridman for pork, Foulson for shoes, Foushee for levys, Daughity for levys. 11,673 ½. 8 8br 1741 Saml Blackwell credit's the estate of Edward Downing decd from Jno Downing one of the executors: book debts recd of Saml Downing, recd of Marriner's rent 1736, of Armstrong 1736, Throps rent 1737, Swift's rent 1739, Harrol's rent 1740, Lancaster's rent 1740. Goods sold at outcry: 1 bed & furniture, botles to my self, cow bell, hooks & eyes, pot & hooks, Negro Tom, brandy sold Wildy, brandy sold Plank, hides, tobacco for Hightower. 5802. 8 8br 1741 Saml Blackwell. (Pg 141)

The estate of Edward Downing decd to Wm Fallin one of his executors: tobacco per ye sheriff, Ann Smith, Eliz Harcum, Jno Graham, Wm Steuart, James Philips, Doctor Coulton, Peter Hayes, Jno Throp, Richd Smith, Nathl Floyd, George Berry, Ja McLea, John Harry, Matthew Hopkins, James Daughity, Robt Michell, Ja Patten, Thos Wornum, Bostin? Betts, Jo Lealand, Jo Hudnall, Jo James, Jo Williams, Richard Kenner. 7681. Disbursements since the death of sd Edward: to James Fignor, Geo Kerterson, Jo Fignor, Doctor Adair, Robt Throp, Capt Eustace, Capt Pearce, John Graham, Peter Mason, Capt Spann. 2605 ½. To money when last accounted: James Philips, Thos Morrice, Capt Jones, Thos Hayes, Wm Barret, Matt Welsh, George Curtis. 4 pd 15 sl 10 pn. Book debts received: from Capt Shapleigh, Joseph Williams, John Lancaster. 125 lbs tobacco. Rents received: 1737 & 1739 Lazarus Williams. 614 lbs tobacco. Goods sold at outcry: violin chest young heiffer, servant woman. 1742 lbs of tobacco. 8 8br 1741 Saml Blackwell. In obedience to an order of court dated 10 Aug last in the difference there depending between William Haynie & Frances his wife late widdow of Edward Downing decd & John Downing & William Fallin executors of the will of sd Edward Downing decd I have examined stated & settled the accts of John Downing & William Fallin agt the sd decd Edward Downing's estate & do find due to the sd John Downing & William Fallin from the sd estate the sums of tobacco & money as will appear by their accts hereunto annexed & also what they owe the sd decd's estate …

[blurred] ... . Saml Blackwell. Memorandum: John Downing & William Fallin's disbursements [?] between Mrs. Haynie & her dau of the estate of Edward Downing decd charged in the before accts is 280 lbs of tobacco & 16 sl 5 pn which William Haynie & his wife are not to pay any part. [Not all figures included here] 8 8br 1741 Saml Blackwell. This report & accts were exhibited 10 9br 1741 by Saml Blackwell gent appointed to settle the same & recorded. Attest: James Fontaine clerk. (Pg 141)

The estate of Edward Turner decd: Tobacco paid to Fielding Turner, Elizabeth Thrift, George Lamkin, Richard Claughton, Elizabeth Lewis, Thos Garner, Wm Campbell, Joseph Garner, John Claughton, James Fontaine, Joseph Garner, Fielding Turner, Joseph Garner, Stephen Selfe, John Garner. Cash paid to: Joseph Carr, Jas Thomas, [?] Waswalt?, Christopher Neale. Rent received of Francis Self. Cash received from John Rogers. [Not totaled] This acct of the administration of the estate of Edward Turner decd was exhibited by Fielding Turner extr & approved by the court & recorded. Attest: James Fontaine clerk. (Pg 142)

8 8br 1741 we Lindsey Opie, John Lewis & John Kennedy met at the house of Jane Lamkin & did according to order of court dated 14 7br allot & pay Jane Lamkin guardian to John, Peter & Hannah Lamkin orphans of James Lamkin decd their full pts/o their decd father's estate: 1 weavers loom & gears, 1 pare stillards, 2 linnen wheels, 7 chairs, 1 spit, 1 chest, 25 lbs of peuter, 1 candlestick, 6 shickles, 2 hackles, 1 chest, 1 cradle, 1 croscut saw, file, sheep shears, cutting knife, 1 pare fire tongs, 11 gees, 1 mug, 1 jug, 1 pare snuffers, 1 dock iron & howel ax, 86 lbs of pot iron, 1 tub, 1 paile, 1 sheep bell, 1 grindstone, 1 Bible, etc. Boy named Joseph Stanly. 45 pd 8 sl 10 ½ pn. This report & division was exhibited 10 9br 1741 by the auditors appointed to divide the decd's estate & recorded. Attest: James Fontaine clerk. (Pg 142)

6 Nov 1741. An additional inventory of pt/o the estate of Thomas Burn decd to the crop of tobacco & debts received 6,645 lbs of tobacco to 6 sl cash to 2 cow hides to 358 penny nailes to 1 lb spun cotton to a book called a dictionary to 2 hoggs. This additional inventory was exhibited by George Ball Junr gent extr on whose motion the same is admitted to record. Attest: James Fontaine clerk. (Pg 142)

In pursuant to an order of court dated 14 7br 1741 we Argail Taylor, Charles Coppidge & John Taylor have met & allotted Joan Smith her dower in the lands of David Smith decd. This report & division was exhibited 10 9br 1741 & admitted to record. Attest: James Fontaine clerk. (Pg 143)

In obedience to an order of court dated 7 7br 1741 we Griffin Fantleroy, Traves

Colston & John Foushee did meet at the house of William Taite to allot unto John Graham & Anne his wife her pt/o her decd father William Metcalf's estate & have allotted the following Negroes, viz, Dick, Betty, Nell, Diana, Belinda, London, Adam, Sam & Tony, which amount to 8 pd 13 sl 9 pn more than her third pt/o what slaves was produced to us but Mr. Taite having sold James a slave belonging to the estate of William Metcalf decd it was left to us to settle the matter concerning the sd slave by the consent of both partys & we do agree that Taite pay to Graham 15 pd for his pt/o the sd Negro James. We have likewise possest Mr. Graham household furniture to the value of 26 pd 13 sl & find that there is still due to the sd Graham 48 pd 6 pn & 18 barrils of Indian corn in balance of his pt/o his wife's estate from William Taite. This report & division was exhibited 10 9br 1741 & recorded. Attest: James Fontaine clerk. (Pg 143)

15 7br ----. To John Foushee, Matthew Quill & Matthew Kenner gent greeting, whereas Griffin Fantleroy of St. Stephens Parish, Northumberland Co & Ann his wife by their deed of gift dated 2 7br last past have given unto Griffin Fantleroy Junr two trs of land called Owens Quarter & Allens Quarter each containing 100 a. also 10 Negroes ... [?] ... stocks upon the sd plantation lying in parish afsd & whereas it appears to us that the sd Ann is so sickly that she cannot travel to our co court to make the acknowledgment of the sd gift, therefore having compassion of the [?] of the sd Ann do give unto you power to receive the acknowledgment which the sd Ann shall be willing to make before you, we therefore command you to go to the afsd Ann & receive her acknowledgment ... . James Fontaine clerk. 7 Nov 1741 In obedience to the within precept we Matthew Quill & John Foushee met at the house of Capt Griffin Fauntleroy & received the acknowledgment of Ann his wife ... . This commission was exhibited 10 8br 1741 & admitted to record. Attest: James Fontaine clerk. (Pg 143)

Will. John Boyd of Great Wicocomoco Parish, Northumberland Co. 13 8br 1741. To my son George Boyd & his heirs all my land & plantation I now live upon & in case of his death without heir to my son John Boyd & his heirs. To my son George one Negro named Peter, one feather bed, one cow & calf, my chest, my pistoles & holsters. I give all the rest of my estate both reall & personall to be divided between my son John & the child my wife is now with & in case either of their deaths without heir ... Boyd's will now concluded ... ye remainder of his will is this, his desire is that if either John or the child unborn die without heir that the decd's part should be divided between the other two that is George & John or the child unborn. We the subscribers do swear that the before named John Boyd decd did direct the will before written to be recorded as the same is before written & that the same was finished before he expired & that the above written codicil or addition was written according to his directions after his death within some small time. Henry Tapscott, Robert Boyd. This will was proved 10 9br 1741 by the oaths of Robert Boyd & Henry Tapscott according to their subscription on ye same to be the will of John Boyd decd which was approved & allowed by the court as sufficient proof. Winifrid Boyd widdow of the testator being present & agreeing thereto administration with the will annexed is granted to Joseph Pope & Robert Boyd who made oath thereto on whose motion the will is admitted to record. Attest: James Fontaine clerk. (Pg 143)

Will. John Stepto of Northumberland Co. 12 Sep 1741. My will is that my wife Elizabeth Stepto shall have the use of all my land I now live on during her widdowhood not debarring my son William Hyde of the plantation where he now lives from making ease of the same also the ½ of all my orchards which my desire is that he may have at my decease. My will is that my wife may have the use of all my personall estate during her widdowhood except my store of goods, tobaccos & money which I give ½ to my son William & the other ½ to my son Thomas & their heirs. I give to my son William one Negro man Jack, one Negro woman Bett & one Negro girl Sarah. To my dau Lucy one Negro man Charles, one Negro boy Toby & one Negro girl Silla. I give unto my son Thos one Negro boy Will, one Negro boy Tom, one Negro girl Letty. My will is that whatever estate I have gave to my other children may debar them from any claim from any other pt/o my estate. I appoint my wife Elizabeth, my sons William, John, James & Thomas Stepto my executors. Wit: Thos Pinkard, John Pinkard, Anna Lawson, Edward Robison. Proved 9 9br 1741 & admitted to record. Attest: James Fontaine clerk. (Pg 144)

Will. Richard Thomas of Great Wicocomoco Parish, Northumberland Co. 7 Sep 1741. To my son William Thomas 4 pd. To my dau Ann Sampson 1 sl. To my dau Elizabeth Eldridge 1 sl. To my son Richard Thomas & his heirs my plantation & land that I now live upon in Great Wicocomoco Parish & if he dies without heir to my son Robt Thomas & his heirs. All the rest of my estate to be divided between the last four of my children Richard, Hannah, Robert & Mary. I appoint my brother William Thomas & Henry Tapscott executors. Wit: Dennis Conway, Moses Thomas. Proved 9 9br 1741 & admitted to record. Attest: James Fontaine clerk. (Pg 144)

Will. Daniel Murphy of St. Stephens Parish, Northumberland Co. 1 Sep 1741. I give my whole estate betwixt my four children Mary, Elenor, Merrimon & Benjamin. It is my will that if either of my children die before they come to age or day of marriage ... [blurred] ... . Wit: Wm Betts Junr, Darby Murphy. Proved 9 9br 1741 & Wm Murphy & John Meath executors therein named made oath thereto on whose motion the same was admitted to record. Attest: James Fontaine clerk. (Pg 144)

Will. William Downing of St. Stephens Parish, Northumberland Co. 9 Jun 1741. To my wife Winifrid every slave that came by her during her life but in case of her death to return to my son Samuel & son William Downing but in case of either dying the survivor to heir the whole but in case both my sons dying they are to be at my wife's disposal if she survives them & furthermore if Samuel & William my sons die before my wife (she) shall have her life in the land. To my son Samuel Downing all my land but in case of dying without issue to return to my son William & I give all the rest of my Negroes to be divided between my two sons Samuel & William & in case of either dying without issue to return to the survivor. I give all my stock, household stuff &c to be divided among the three, that is to say my wife & my sons Samuel & William & in case either of them dying to be divided among the other two. I leave my two sons at age when 18 to receive their full parts, I constitute Samuel Nelms my father in law & my wife executors. Wit: John Tolson, Elias Martin, Platt Cook, Thomas Reason. Proved 9 9br 1741 & admitted to record. Attest: James Fontaine clerk. (Pg 145)

Will. James Moon of St. Stephens Parish, Northumberland Co 17 Oct 1741. To my dau in law Winifrid Mason two cows & calves. To John Broady my gun, a coat & two jackcoats, a pair of leather & a pare cloth britches & a hatt. To Spry Broady one years schooling. To my wife Sarah the use of my whole estate both reall & personall during her natural life & after to be divided between my two daus Sarah Anne & Mary & their heirs. For want of such in both my daus then it is my desire that it go to Edward & Winifrid Mason. I appoint my wife Sarah & my friend & son in law Edward Mason executors. Wit: John Lewis, Vincent Garner, Robt Clark Junr. Proved 9 9br 1741 & admitted to record. Attest: James Fontaine clerk. (Pg 145)

In obedience to an order of court dated 9 9br 1741 we Roger Winter, Saml Gaskins & Andrew Chilton have appraised the estate of John Gaines decd & divided the sd estate according to the order of court the orphan's part of the sd estate being 49 pd 4 sl 10 pn. This report was exhibited 19 9br 1741 & admitted to record. Attest: James Fontaine clerk. (Pg 145)

… [blurred] … 1 gun, 1 box iron & heaters, sauspan, some lumber, 2 pots & hooks, 1 frying pan, 1 washing tub, 1 paile, 3 milk pans, 3 old tubs, 28 botles, some wool, 1 hide, 11 gees, 1 chair, 1 great coat, 1 leather britches, 6 yds of callicoa, ½ quier of paper, 3 fouls, 8 chickens, 1 chest of tools, etc. 18 pd 12 sl. William Ball, Wm Murphy, Robt Potts. This inventory of the estate of John Anderson decd was exhibited by Spencer Ball gent adminr of the sd decd & admitted to record. Attest: James Fontaine clerk. (Pg 146)

In obedience to an order of court held 10 9br 1741 we Wm Nelms, Joseph

Lancaster & Shapleigh Neale did meet & did appraise the estate of Thomas Sims decd. 1 set of shoemakers tools, 1 curying knife, 10 sheep, 2 large barrows, 1 sow, 2 pigs, 16 gees, bed & furniture, sheets, rug, blanket, pillow cases, mans new saddle, bridle, womans saddle, 2 bridles, 2 old meal bags, 1 old table, 1 old gun, 3 old flag chairs, 1 curry comb & brush, etc. [Not totaled] This inventory was exhibited 14 xbr 1741 by Sarah Sims adminr & admitted to record. Attest: James Fontaine clerk. (Pg 146)

1 crop of tobacco in 1740. Sums paid by James Adair, Mrs. Hannah Shapleigh, John Foushee, James Daughity, Richd [?], Ann Murphy, Wm B[?] Junr. 1922 lbs tobacco. This additional inventory & acct of the estate of Thomas Sims decd was exhibited 14 xbr by Sarah Sims adminr & admitted to record. Attest: James Fontaine clerk. (Pg 146)

In obedience to an order of court dated 9 --- ---- we appraised the estate of [?] decd in money. Negroes: man named [?], man named Tony, man [?], man named Will, man named Peter, woman named Sue, woman [?], girl named Jude. 2 old whip saws, 1 croscut saw, beds, rug, blankets, bolsters, pillows, sheets, bedstead, cord, 2 oval tables, 1 chest of drawers, 1 desk, 28 lbs pot iron, 1 pare pot hooks, 1 old broad ax, 2 narrow axes, 2 old files, 1 fiddle, 1 large glass, 6 leather chairs, 5 cane chairs, 1 trunk, 1 square table, 1 large chest, 1 old chest, old curtins & vallians, 1 Bible, etc. ... [rest too burred to read] ... . (Pg 147)

In obedience to an order of court dated 9 --- 1741 we Winder Kenner, Richd Kenner, John Coles & Richd Smith did meet at the house of William Downing decd & valued the estate of the decd. Feather beds, bolsters, sheets, blankets, rugs, pillows, bedsteads, cord, hide, 1 large old chest with lock & key, 1 small chest, one old cupboard, 1 old table, 1 gun, 1 sword, 7 flag chairs, 2 old leather chairs, 1 sorrel mare, 1 young gray mare, 1 hipshot mare, 2 raw hides, 12 sheep. 5 hogs, 12 shoats, 3 cider casks, 2 narrow axes, 7 old tubs, 1 pail, 1 old basket, 1 loom & gears, 2 iron wedges, 1 wollen wheel, 2 pare old cards, 32 lbs of pot iron, 1 old frying pan, 1 old iron pot, 1 old handmill, 1 canoe, etc. Negroes: boy [?], boy Garet, boy Peter, man John, woman Moll, woman Bett, girl Rose, child Charles, girl Rachell, girl Judy, girl Lukee, boy Tom, boy James, boy Joe, boy [?], girl Silvia, boy Isaac. [Not totaled] This inventory was exhibited 14 xbr 1741 by Winifrid Downing & Saml Nelms executors & admitted to record. Attest: James Fontaine clerk. (Pg 148)

In pursuance to an order of court dated 10 9br 1741 we George Conway, Wm Thomas & John Rout? being appointed to appraise the estate of John Boyd decd did accordingly meet on the plantation of the sd decd 7 xbr 1741 & have appraised all that sd decd's estate that was presented to our view in money. 2 Negro fellows, young Negro wench. Yoke of oxen, cart & wheels, feather beds

& furniture, bedstead, cord & hide, 4 cows, 4 yearlings, 3 heifers, 2 bulls, 4 hogs, 13 shoats, a mare, 4 old tubs, some tarr, 6 cider casks, 1 stone jug, 1 looking glass, a parcel of books, 1 iron spitt, etc. [Not totaled] This inventory was exhibited 14 xbr 1741 by Joseph Pope & Robt Boyd adminrs & admitted to record. Attest: James Fontaine clerk. (Pg 148)

In obedience to an order of court dated 9 9br 1741 we John Christopher, Garret Haylett? & Thos [?] Junr appointed to appraise the estate of Daniel Murphy decd have met & being first sworn before John Foushee have appraised the estate: 3 stears, 4 heifers, 2 cows, yearlings, 1 young horse, 1 young mare, 1 suit of wearing cloaths, 1 new suit, 1 linnen coat, cotton jacket & breeches, some thread, 1 mans saddle, 2 bridles & cloth, 1 womans saddle & bridle, a bushel of salt, 1 old chest, old barrel, some lumber, some cotton, 23 bottles, 4 stone jugs, 3 stone mugs, earthen ware, 1 large earthen pot, 2 earthen butter pots, some Holland ware, etc. [Not totaled] This inventory was exhibited by Wm Murphy & John Meath executors & admitted to record. Attest: James Fontaine clerk. (Pg 149)

A true inventory of goods & chattels of James Moon's estate decd was appraised by Vincent Garner, James Garner, George Oldham & William Thomas: Beds & furniture, 10 lbs old pewter, 10 chairs, 1 safe, 1 box iron & heaters, 1 looking glass, 1 pare of shoes, 3 pare of stockins, 2 hats, 1 handkerchief, 1 silk handkerchief, 5 shirts, parcel of water ware, a frying pan, 1 spitt, 1 iron ladle, 2 flesh forks, 1 pare fire tongs, 1 razor & hone, 4 drinking glasses, 4 iron pots, 3 pare of hooks, 2 chests, 3 small tables, 1 gun, 1 old spinning wheel, 1 old side saddle, 4 old trays, 3 old bags & ropes, 1 chest, sheep shears, old lumber, 1 hand saw, 1 adz, 2 small casks, 1 great coat, etc. [Not totaled] This inventory was exhibited 14 xbr 1741 by Sarah Moon & Edward Mason executors & admitted to record. Attest: James Fontaine clerk. (Pg 150)

A true & perfect inventory of the estate of Parter (Partin?) James decd taken 31 Mar appointed by an order of court to be appraised by Wm Lattimore, Thos Williams & Edward Boyer sworn by Capt Robt Jones. 4 pare mens worn stockins, 1 carpenters rule, drawing knife, hamer & chisels, 3 ½ yds linnen, 1 pare garters, 2 shirts, 2 mens caps, 1 handkerchief, 1 box & razer, ink horn, pen knife, 1 box 3 ½ doz corks, 1 basket candle snuffers, hinge & staples, 2 pare breeches, 2 shirts, 2 bands, 1 vest, coat, 1 coat vest & breeches, 1 pare shoes, 2 old hats, 1 pare old gloves, 9 buttons, 1 wig, 1 cap, 1 chest, some small lumber, 1 pare of shoe buckles, 1 set of shoemakers tools, 1 volin & saw, 1 pare silver band clasps, 1 pare silver sleeve buttons, ½ quier of paper, parcel of news papers, etc. [Not totaled] This inventory was exhibited 14 --- 1741 by Sarah Berry executrix & admitted to record. Attest: James Fontaine clerk. (Pg 151)

In obedience to an order of court dated 9 9br 1741 we Wm Ball, Wm Murphy & Jno Meath appointed to appraise the estate of James Crupper decd have met & being first sworn before Capt Spencer Ball have appraised the sd estate: parcel of old cloaths 14 sl, pare of shoe buckles 1 pn. This inventory was exhibited 14 xbr 1741 by Saml Walker adminr & admitted to record. Attest: James Fontaine clerk. (Pg 151)

14 Dec 1741. Deed of Mortgage. I Moses Webb of Northumberland Co bargain & agree with my two friends John Porter & John France of Lancaster Co to morgige to ye sd two a parcel of land for ye space of 50 years which land lies in both Northumberland & Lancaster Cos which land the sd Moses Webb now lives on adj land of John Copidge, Charles Copidge, line of Burber's, land formerly called Scrnavers & at head of Scotland Mill Swamp ... . The conditionall agreement is such that the afsd bounded Moses Webb doth mortgage this parsel of land to his two friends afsd to be his security for a sarten sum of money & if the sd Moses Webb pase the sd sum of money that his two friends afsd cums? to no trubell nor cost this mortgage to be voyd .. . Wit: James Saylor, Wm Biven? Ackn 14 xbr 1741 & admitted to record. Attest: James Fontaine clerk. (Pg 151)

8 xbr 1741. In obedience to an order of court ... [blurred] ... which amounted to 285 lbs of tobacco ... . This report & division of the estate of Rance Churchill decd to Willoughby Churchill was exhibited 14 xbr 1741 by Richard Claughton & Pemberton Claughton & recorded. Attest: James Fontaine clerk. (Pg 152)

30 9br 1741. In obedience to an order of court dated 9 --- 1741 we Richard Claughton & Pemberton Claughton have met at the house of Lindsey Opie & have paid Wm Garner his full proportionable pt/o Rance Churchill decd's estate which amounted to 1 pd 8 sl 6 pn paid in tobacco which amounted to 285 lbs of tobacco. From ye estate of Jane Miller decd 1 pd 8 sl 6 pn. This report & division of the estate of Rance Churchill decd to Wm Garner was exhibited 14 xbr 1741 by Richard Claughton & Pemberton Claughton & admitted to record. Attest: James Fontaine clerk. (Pg 152)

30 Nov 1741. In obedience to an order of court dated 9 9br 1741 we Richard Claughton & Pemberton Claughton have met at the house of Lindsey Opie & have paid Daniel Gaines his full proportionable pt/o Rance Churchill decd's estate which amounts to 1 pd 8 sl 6 pn paid in tobacco which amounts to 285 pd of tobacco. This report & division of the estate of Rance Churchill decd to Daniel Gaines was exhibited --- 1741 by Richard Claughton & Pemberton Claughton & admitted to record. Attest: James Fontaine clerk. (Pg 152)

Pursuant to an order of court dated 12 Oct 1741 we John Lewis, John Kennedy

& Lindsey Opie met at the house of Jane Lamkin guardian of Jane Lewis & have allotted & paid the sd Jane Lamkin the sd Jane Lewis' estate which amounted to 5,711 lbs of tobacco payable by bond given on the last of Apr next ensuing. This report & division was exhibited by John Lewis, John Kennedy & Lindsey Opie & recorded. Attest: James Fontaine clerk. (Pg 152)

10 Dec 1741. Pursuant to an order of court dated 9 Nov 1741 we Matthew Quill, Saml Blackwell & Robt Jones met & having first appraised the estate of Thomas Gaskins decd & Elizabeth Schriver decd for money we then divided the same between the orphans of the sd Thomas Gaskins, viz, to Thomas, Edwin, Sarah, Anna, John & Anne Gaskins we allotted 1/5 pt/o the forementioned estates to each 1/5 of the personal estate amounting to 44 pd 4 sl 4 pn & the 1/5 of ye Negroes amounting to 152 pd 19 sl 8 pn besides 63 ½ lbs of tobacco to each of the sd orphans which appears to be due by bills to the forementioned estates. We also divided the corn & adjudged Richard Hull & Thomas Gaskins to pay to Collin Campbell & Mary his wife 7 barrils besides what they had already in possession at home being what falls short of their & the two orphans share of the corn, John & Anna Gaskins, all which may more fully appear by the respective inventorys of goods & Negroes delivered to them & signed by us & as the present crop of tobacco is not ye inspected we could make no division of the same. This report & division was exhibited 14 xbr 1741 by the auditors & admitted to record. Attest: James Fontaine clerk. (Pg 152)

In obedience to an order of court made 14 7br 1741 wherein it was ordered that we George Ball, Robt Jones & Thos Winter should meet & allot Charles Lee his wife's filial pt/o her father's estate accordingly we mett at the house of Mrs. Judith Lee the 4th this instant & allotted him 85 pd 5 sl 4 pn 3 farthings it being his just part paid in manner following: Negro woman named Judy, Negro boy named Ax?. 2 cows & calves, 2 yearling heifers, 1 broken bell mettle skillet, 1 chest, 1 iron pot, 1 linnen wheel, 1 pare of blankets, 3 Holland sheets, 1 round folding table, 1 copper coffee pot, 1 pare money scales & weights, 1 pare brass fire tongs, 1 brass candlestick, 1 pare pot hooks, etc. Note: Charles Lee owes the estate 3 pn. This report & division was exhibited 19 --- 1741 by the appraisers & admitted to record. Attest: James Fontaine clerk. (Pg 152)

By vertue of an order of court dated 9 9br 1741 we being first sworn before a justice of the peace appraised the estate of John Stepto decd: beds & furniture, 1 standing looking glass, leather seat chairs, 1 stool, 1 pare blankets, 1 new quilt, 2 counterpaines, sheets, 1 old box no lock nor key, 1 table, 2 oval tables, 1 old armd chair, 2 old gunns, 1 square table, 1 small looking glass, 1 sett of china, 4 little silver spoons & tongs, 4 punch bouls, 11 tea cups, etc. Negroes: man Jack, man Jacob, man Charles, boy Toby, boy Will, woman Liddy, woman Dinah, boy Tom, woman Betty, girl Silla, girl Letty, boy Moses. [Not totaled] This inventory was exhibited 11 Jan 1741/2 by William Stepto extr & admitted to record. Attest: James Fontaine clerk. (Pg 153)

In pursuance to an order of court dated 9 9br 1741 we George Conway, John Rout & George Dawkins appointed to appraise the estate of Richard Thomas decd did accordingly meet & have appraised all the sd estate of the decd that was presented to our view in money: 1 large barrow, 2 other hogs, cows, yearlings, heifers, pare of old cart wheels, a small grindstone, old saddle & bridle, 1 iron wedge, 1 old hone, 1 young stone colt, 4 sheep, feather beds & furniture, bedstead, cord, hide, 4 old flag chairs, some earthen ware, some wooden ware, 1 old meale sifter, 74 lbs of pot iron, 3 pare of old pothooks, a parcel of carpenters & joiners tools, 2 tennant saws, etc. [Not totaled] This inventory was exhibited 11 Jan 1741/2 by William Thomas & Henry Tapscott executors & admitted to record. Attest: James Fontaine clerk. (Pg 155)

Will. John Hill of Great Wicocomoco Parish, Northumberland Co. 15 Jul 1737. To my wife Mary the use of all my estate until William & Charles Costans sons of my sd wife Mary attain to the age of 18 years then to be divided between them. My will is also that if my wife Mary should marry or waste my sd estate my desire is that my friend George Mills should take the sd estate until the sd William & Charles Costans arrive at the age of 18. I appoint my wife Mary executrix. Wit: Henry Mayes, John Swanson. Proved 11 Jan 1741/2 & admitted to record. Attest: James Fontaine clerk. (Pg 156)

Will. Winifrid Rider in Cherry Point, Northumberland Co. 5 Oct 1741. To my sister Hannah Rider one Negro woman named Charity & her increase, also all my pt/o my father's estate which is 16 pd due to me or Denland in Elec? Moorhead's hands & also all other debts that can be found due to me. I leave my sister Hannah Rider executrix paying all my debts & funerall charges. Wit: Thos Anderson, Ruth Keen, Hannah Lewis. Proved 11 Jan 1741/2 & admitted to record. Attest: James Fontaine clerk. (Pg 156)

9 Jan 1741/2. Deed of Gift. Henry Dawson of St. Stephens Parish, Northumberland Co planter & Anne my wife for natural love & affection have given unto our son John Dawson a 60 a. tr of land in the afsd parish whereon we now live binding on the lines of John Claughton & William Harding ... . Wit: Matthew Quill, Richd Claughton, Thomas Tayler. Ackn 11 Jan 1741/2 ... [blurred] ... . (Pg 156)

--- 1741. Deed. John Foulson of St. Stephens Parish, Northumberland Co in consideration that Mary Foulson should deliver ½ of the estate that belonged to William Foulson decd or otherwise the ½ of what is now in her possession sold to the sd Mary Foulson mother of the sd John Foulson one messuage of land that the sd John Foulson now lives on with free priviledge to plant, tend & manure or occupie & to possess & enjoy all benefits as is necessary upon the sd land during my mother Mary Foulson's life & for the true performance of the same I have hereunto set my hand & fixed my seale. Wit: Richd Smith, Wm Betts, Edward Coles. Ackn 11 Jan 1741/2 by John Toulson & Hannah Toulson his wife being privately examined by John Foushee gent relinquished her right of dower in the land conveyed unto the afsd Mary Foulson on whose motion the same is admitted to record. Attest: James Fontaine clerk. (Pg 157)

20 Dec 1741. In obedience to an order of court dated 14 xbr 1741 we Griffin Fantleroy, Matthew Kenner & John Foushee did meet at the house of Wm Taite guardian of Betty Metcalf one of the daus & coheirs of William Metcalf decd & hath allotted Betty Metcalf's pt/o her decd father's estate. The names of the Negroes allotted for her use are: Beale, Judy, Jenny, Wenny, Jacob, Dick, Lucy, Sam, Judie, Letty, we having therein allowed her pt/o a Negro sold by the sd Taite named Jamie & we find due to her in personal estate 63 pd 6 sl. This report & division was returned 11 Jan 1741/2 & recorded. Attest: James Fontaine clerk. (Pg 157)

In obedience to an order of court dated 14 xbr 1741 requiring us on the prayer of Spencer Ball gent adminr of the estate of John Anderson decd with whom the sd adminr had made agreement for the life of the sd Anderson to finish the carpenters & jointers work of his dwelling house & the sd Anderson dying before the same was finished to view the work of the sd house that was left unfinished at his death which we have accordingly done & are of opinion that what work was left unfinished of the sd house by the sd Anderson according to his covenant or agreement with the sd Spencer Ball is worth 25 pd which is certified under our hands this 11 Jan 1741. George Hunt, Thos Hunt, James Davison. This report was returned 11 Jan 1741/2 & recorded. Attest: James Fontaine clerk. (Pg 157)

In obedience to an order of court dated 14 xbr 1741 we Abner Neal, Motly Wildy & Rich Hull who were appointed did meet at the house of John Downing this 6 Jan 1741/2 & have audited & settled the accts agt the personal estate of Charles Downing decd & have allotted to Hannah Downing her part thereof: 1 suit of Douget cloaths, 1 feather bed & furniture, 2 young stears, 1 young cow & calf, 2 ½ lbs new peuter, 4 ¼ lbs old peuter, 1 young stear, 36 lbs pot iron, 1 Negro man Cesar. We do find in the settlement of the accts as appears due to the adminr from the estate of Charles Downing decd 916 ½ lbs tobacco & 1 pd 11 sl 2 pn, the ½ of which the sd tobacco & money is to be paid to the sd adminr from ye sd William Haynie guardian to the sd Hannah Downing. As to the acct of the crops it does not appear to us the quantity (of) tobacco not being striped & inspected we leave it unsettled. This settlement, report & division was returned

11 Jan 1741/2 & recorded. Attest: James Fontaine clerk. (Pg 157)

List of Col Peter [?] taken by George Conway: ... [names illegible] ... Wm
Barret, Wm Mack, Moody Mott, John [?], Christopher Dameron, Wm Hughlet,
Abner Neal, Aron Williams, Motly Wildy, Jonathan Betts, Owen Jones, James
Fignor, Silvester Welsh, Ellis Gill, Saml Downing, Thos Manes, John Hurt, Wm
Wildy, Robt Alexander, John Bransdell, John Humphris, George Dawkins,
Joseph Pope, Thos Dameron, Joseph Wildy, Andrew Chilton, Wm Dameron,
Saml Jackson, Abraham Shears, Joseph Gaskins, Charles Dameron, Edward
B[?], John M[?], James Daughity, Yarret Hughlet, John [?], Wm Nelms, Thomas
[?]burn, Alexander Moorhead, Richd Price, Thos Hayes, Moses Williams, John
Conway, Fignor Fallin, Edward Coles, Richd Waller, Wm Webb, J[?] Nelms,
Richd Hadwell, Peter Bearcroft, Robt Short, Francis Beatly, John Bearcroft,
John James, John Corbell, Stephen Haynie, Henry Haynie, Saml Wisestead,
Vincent Garner, John Rice, Robt Boiant, Richd Claughton, Danl Gaines, Penly
Dawkins, Pemberton Claughton, Thos Bridgman, John Jones, Thomas Hall,
Isaac Edwards, James Lewis, James Thompson, James Mash, John Allgood,
Parish Garner, John Daughity, Saml Manes, George Berry, George Pickerin,
John Thomas, Tarkle Tarkleson, Richd Rowt, Thos Rowt, Richd Seabre, Wm
Greenstreet, George Oldham, Griffin Fauntleroy Junr, John Christopher, John
[?], George Humphrys, John [?], George Conway Junr, John Harvey, Thomas
Hughlet, Wm Knot, Wm Dowly, John Ingram, Daniel Clark, John Hill, John
Richardson, Benjamin Swanson, John Rea, David Lattimore, Wm Betts, John
Gaskins, George Kutzman, Edmond Basey, Dennis Conway, Wm Kelly, John
Basey, John Stot, Edward Rogers, Richd Whey, John Smith, Richd Cruit, Wm
Garner, Francis Vanlandigan, Thos Ginn, John Claughton, Peter Hayes, Wm [?],
Edward Ryon, Wm Dawkins, Richd Howson, Wm Thomas, Wm Thomas, Wm
Linkhorn, Thos Wornum Junr, Joseph Lunsford, Willoughby Newton, Richd
Cornish, Philip Smith, Matthew Kenner, John Cralle, Edward [?], Wm Fignor,
Wm [?], James Smith, Bennet Bogges, [?] Ball, Collin Campbell, Henry Keller?,
John West, John Oldham, Moses Oldham, John Edwards, Ormsbea Haynie,
Tarply Oldham, Thomas Davis, Wm Lattimore, Wm Harding, Geo Conway,
Wm Nelms, George Lamkin, Thos Dameron, Argail Taylor, Jesse Basie, Wm
Taite, Saml Blackwell, John Hack. 17 Nov 1741 George Conway. Copy attest:
Robt Jones sheriff. Attest: James Fontaine clerk. (Pg 158)

A list of Saml Blackwell's votes taken by Saml Nelms: Richd Hudnall, John
Nutt, Richd Nutt, George Mills, John Downing, John Maise, Wm Mash, Joseph
Lancaster, Charles Coppidge, Mosely Mott, Shapleigh Neale, Lawrence Parrot,
John Coppidge, Abner Neale, Motly Wildy, Owen Jones, James Fignor, Saml
Downing, Willoughby Churchill, Charles Pritchard, Wm Webb, Wm Lunsford,
Edward Rion, Abraham Low, John Sutton, Wm Wildy, Robt Alexander, George
Paine, John Lealand, Joseph Pope, Joseph Wildy, John Webb, Griffin White,

Lazarus Sutton, Edward Bowen, Argail Palmer, Isaac Palmer, Yarret Hughlet, Uriah Angel, John Smith, Wm Short, John Webb, John Conway, Fignor Fallin, Elizamond Basie, Thos Evritt, Richd Lansdell, Richd Walker, James Seebre, Wm Webb, Ben Lansdell, Aron Nelms, Josia Basie, James Webb, Robt Short, John Hurst, Mallachy Burbury, Joseph Nutt, Britain Hill, Saml Nelms Junr, Edward Garner, John Bearcroft, Moses Champion, John James, Saml Mahane, Saml Snow, Saml Temple, Wm Barret, Char Wilkins, Richd Pope, Rawleigh Evritt, Wm James, Wooldridge Smith, John Alexander, John Pope, Isaac Edwards, James Mack, Wm Fletcher, Robt Angell, John Daughity, Joseph Reiter?, John Taylor, Thos Hurt, Edwin Smith, Joshua James, Pitts Curtis, Moses James, John Hudnall, Aron Taylor, Richd Denny, Joseph Knight, Saml Ingram, David Flicker, Thos Hughlet, Wm Bowly, James Davis, John Hill, Geo Kesterson, John Gaskins, Edmond Basey, Denis Conway, John Basie, Farnifold Nutt, Edwin Fielding, Thos Jones, Thos Palmer, Swanson Lunsford, Roger Winter, Wm Basie, Benjamin Curtis, Abraham Fielding, Wm Linkhorn, John Hornsby, Joseph Lunsford, Richard Cornish?, Matthew Kenner, [?] Fignor, John Edwards, Thos Davis, Wm Lattimore, Winder Kenner, Will Hardin, Wm Nelms … [rest of the names illegible] … 17 Nov 1741 Saml Nelms. Copy attest Robt Jones sheriff. Attest: James Fontaine clerk. (Pg 158)

Major John Waughop's list of votes taken by James Stepto: Rodham Kenner, Griffin Fauntleroy, Lindsey Opie, Thomas Toby, James Booth, Richd [?]uky, Daniel Shurly, James Grigs, George Harrison, Landon Carter, Richd Warrick, John Lewis, Thomas Bearcroft, Thos Pew, John Shurly, Spencer Corbin, Wm Hughlet, John Reeves, John Evins, Patrick Mealy, John Rogers, George Dawkins, John Butler, John Beachum, John Baker, Richd Thompson, James Daughity, Gilbert Harrell, Geo Brown, John Oldham, John Shadock, Richd Rice, John Tullos, Thomas Bayley, Peter Bearcroft, James Crane, John Rice, Robt Bryan, Benly Dawkins, Thos Wraughan, Robt Mitchell, Daniel Beachum, Parich Garner, John Kennaday, Winder Kenner, Thomas Wrout, Richd Wrout, Wm Grisestead, Geo Oldham, John Christopher, Henry Dawson, Thos Miflandigen, Wm Kelly, Edward Rogers, Richd Whay, Matthew Quill, Charles Fallin, Robt Middleton, Richd Cruit, Thomas Ginn, Lewis Lamkin, James Blinker, Robt Hutson, Richd Kenner, Wm Dawkins, Richd Booth, James Garner, Wm Thomas, George Riggins, Willoughby Newton, Philip Smith, Bennet Bogges, Moses Webb, Geo Conway, William Fallin, Traves Colston. 17 Nov 1741 James Stepto. Copy attest Robt Jones sheriff. Attest: James Fontaine clerk. (Pg 159)

[?] Colston? list of votes taken by Wm Fallin: … [some names illegible] … George Harrison, Wm Jones, Landon Carter, Richd Warrick, John Lewis, Thos Bearcroft, Thos Pew, John Shurley, Spencer Corbell, Thomas Hickman, John Greenstreet, Shapleigh Neale, John Coppidge, John Reeves, John Evans,

Willoughby Churchill, Patrick Mealy, John Rogers, George Bair, John Lealand,
John Butler, John Beachum, John Baker, Wm Haydon, Richd Thompson,
Gilbert Harrel, Geo Brown, Geo Lamkin, John Oldham, John Shadock, John
Tullos, Wm Vanlandenham, Wm Lewis, John Hurst, Jos Nutt, Saml Nelms Junr,
Moses Champion, Saml Mahane, James Coane, [?] Garner, Rawligh Evritt,
Richd Claughton, Daniel Gaines, Pemberton Claughton, Thomas Straughan,
John Jones, Thos Hall, James Lewis, James Thompson, Daniel Beachum, John
Allgood, John Kennedy, Tarkle Tarkelson, Thos Hurst, Francis Timberlake,
Joshua James, Elias Edmonds, Richd Seebre, Moses James, John Hudnall, John
Gouge, Wm Nott, David Flicker, Henry Dawson, Thos Vanlandenham, Thos
James, Thos Palmer, Matthew Quill, Charles Fallin, Robt Middleton, John
Smith, Wm Garner, Francis Vanlandenham, John Claughton, Lewis Lamkin,
Thomas Berry, John Berry, Robt Hudson, Richd Kenner, Wm Trusel?, Thos
Pitman, Richd Henson, Richd Booth, James Garner, Geo Riggins, Geo Hunt,
Richd Yates, Robt Clark, John Cralle, Wm Gill, Edward Barnes, Wm Taylor,
Griffin Fantleroy, Richd Hull, James Smith, Wm [?], Collin Campbell, Henry
Miller, John West, John Oldham, Moses Oldham, Ormsbee Haynie, Tarply
Oldham, John Downing, Wm Fallin. 17 Nov 1741 Wm Fallin. Copy attest Robt
Jones sheriff. Attest: James Fontaine clerk. (Pg 159)

[?] list of votes taken by John Alexander: … [some names illegible] … Aron
Williams, Jonathan Betts, Wm Webb, Griffin White, John Harrison, Wm Nelms,
James Sims, John Smith, Thomas Hayes, John Tully, Richd Cockril, Moses
Williams, Richd Lansdell, John Cole, Henry Haynie, Charles Wilkins,
Woldridge Smith, Thos Bridgman, Alexr Moorhead, George Berry, George
Pickrell, John Thomas, Pitts Curtis, Elias Edmonds, Richd Denery, George
Humphris, John Denny, George Conway, John Humphris, Silvester Welsh, Robt
Davis, Joseph Humphris, Saml Nelms, Moses Webb, Thomas Hardin. Attest:
John Alexander. Copy attest: Robt Jones sheriff. Attest: James Fontaine clerk.
(Pg 160)

George Ball's list of votes taken by Saml Hamilton: Wm Ball, Jacob Haynie,
John M[?], Ben Haynie, Christopher Dameron, Charles Pritchard, Thos Mahane,
Amos Love, Wm Lunsford, John Hurst, John Sutton, Abraham Love, Thomas
Dameron, Andrew Chilton, Wm Dameron, Saml Gaskins, Abraham Shears, Wm
Hayden, Josia Gaskins, Charles Dameron, Lazarus Sutton, Edward Bowen, Isaac
Palmer, Wm Gardner, Thos Hurst, John Waddy, Richd Pope, Wm James, Robt
Angell, Saml Mahane Junr, Joseph Hester, Wm Garlington, Joseph Robinson,
John Gruga, Thos Harvey, John Harvey, Saml Ingram, Wm Ellis, James Davis,
John Ingram, John Richardson, Benjamin Swanson, Swanson Lunsford, Roger
Winter, Wm Basie, Randolph Mott, Wm Smith, John Hornsby, Wm Hardin. 17
Nov 1741 Saml Hamilton. Copy attest: Robt Jones sheriff. Attest: James
Fontaine clerk. (Pg 160)

[?] list of votes taken by George Mills: ... [some names illegible] ... [?] Parrot,
[?] Wright, [?] Palmer, Uriah Angel, Elizamond Basey, Josias Basie, James
Webb, [?] Burbro, Edwd Gardner, John Waddy, Saml Temple, Robt Mitchell,
Wm Fletcher, John Taylor, Francis Timberlake, Edwin Smith, Wm Garlington,
Aron Taylor, Joseph Knight, Thomas Harvey, Randolph Mott, Thos Winter,
George Mills. 17 Nov 1741 George Mills. Copy attest: Robert Jones sheriff.
Attest: James Fontaine clerk. (Pg 160)

9 Mar 1742. Deed. John Robison, Gilbert Thomas, Gilbert & John Burton
(Burtan) & Sarah his wife formerly Sarah Gilbert dau of Mary Gilbert all of NC
for 30 pd sold to Peter Presly of St. Stephens Parish, Northumberland Co all
their right & title to a tr of land in St. Stephens Parish bounded by the Main Br
of Herring Cr, Beaver ... [illegible] ... the same being parcel of James Ashton's
patent formerly of this co being 340 a. & devised to sd John Robinson, Gilbert
Thomas, Gilbert & Sarah w/o John Burton by the will of Nicholas Robison decd
... . Wit: Robert Jones, James Daughity, John Corbell, Edward Rogers, Daniel
Cottrell. Proved 13 Apr 1742 & admitted to record. Attest: James Fontaine
clerk. (Pg 160)

5 Mar 1741. Deed. Richard Cornish of St. Stephens Parish, Northumberland Co
for 1,000 lbs of tobacco sold to Charles Betts Junr of same place a 25 a. parcel
of land binding on land of William Haynie formerly Daniel Holland's, land of
Col Presly formerly Corbill's, land of Col Presly formerly Joseph White's &
land of William Betts formerly Jonathan Royston's, it being pt/o a tr of land
taken up by my grandfather William Cornish dated 9 Dec 1662 ... . Wit: Wm
Betts, Wm Betts Junr, John Leach. Ackn 15 Apr 1742 & admitted to record.
Attest: James Fontaine clerk. (Pg 161)

5 Mar 1741/2. Bond. I Richard Cornish am firmly bound unto Charles Betts
Junr in the penal sum of 2,000 lbs of tobacco ... the condition of this obligation
is such that if the afsd Charles Betts shall have, hold, occupy, possess & injoy
the 25 a. of land & premises which by the sd Richard Cornish is sold by deed
[see above] according to the true intent & meaning of the sd deed expressed then
this obligation to be void ... . Wit: Wm Betts, Wm Betts Junr, John Leach.
Ackn 13 Apr 1742 & admitted to record. Attest: James Fontaine clerk. (Pg 162)

25 Feb 1741/2. Deed. John Thomas of St. Stephens Parish, Northumberland Co
for 2500 lbs of tobacco sold to Joseph Robinson son of Joseph Robinson of same
parish a 65 a. tr of land in St. Stephens Parish binding on the land of Thomas
Hobson late decd, John Bearmonale Holt, Waddington decd's line & a br of
Herring Pond ... . Wit: Abner Neale, John Lancaster, David Price. Ackn 12
Apr 1742 by John Thomas & Ann Thomas his wife she being privately
examined by John Foushee gent relinquished her right of dower & admitted to

record. Attest: James Fontaine clerk. (Pg 162)

2 Feb 1741/2. Bond. I John Thomas of St. Stephens Parish, Northumberland Co am firmly bound unto Joseph Robinson Junr son of Joseph Robinson of same parish for 5,000 lbs of lawfull tobacco ... the condition of this obligation is such that if the afsd John Thomas shall any time hereafter at the request & charge of the sd Joseph Robinson Junr make seale & deliver unto him such conveyances as to him the sd Joseph Robinson Junr shall reasonably devise for the sure making & confirming a tr of land unto the sd Joseph Robinson Junr called Thomases Island [see above], in consideration thereof hath ingaged to pay the sum of 2500 lbs of tobacco & the sd John Thomas with his now wife at the next court shall ackn the deed on demand in court then this obligation to be void ... . Wit: Elles Gill, David Price, John Swords Ackn 12 Apr 1742 & admitted to record. Attest: James Fontaine clerk. (Pg 164)

XXII Mar MDCCXLI. Deed of Mortgage. Richard Kenner of St. Stephens Parish, Northumberland Co gent for 2,709 lbs of tobacco & 23 pd 17 sl 3 pn sold to Thomas Edwards of Lancaster Co gent my Negro woman Nell & her son Bristow ... provided that if the sd Richard Kenner shall on or before XII Dec next well & truly pay unto the sd Thomas Edwards 2,709 lbs of tobacco & 23 pd 17 sl 3 pn with interest then this present deed of sale shall cease & be utterly voyd ... . Wit: J. Eustace, Richd Dudly, Wm Lavender. Proved 13 Apr 1742 & admitted to record. Farther proved 10 May 1742 & admitted to record. Attest: James Fontaine clerk. (Pg 164)

10 Apr 1742. Deed. Thomas Berry Senr of Wicocomoco Parish, Northumberland Co for 20 pd sold to John Hart of same place a 50 a. tr of land (except 1 a. binding on the Main Swamp) in the sd parish being pt/o 100 a. of land formerly holden of David Orland a Dutchman who died [?] of the same he the sd Thomas Berry escheated the same by deed from the Proprietors Office dated 1 Dec 1730 bounded by Flax Pond Cove, Vulcans Cr & John Holt ... . Wit: David Lattimore, Saml Gaskins. Ackn 12 Apr 1742 & admitted to record. Attest: James Fontaine clerk. (Pg 164)

3 Aug 1741. I Thomas Berry of Wicocomoco Parish, Northumberland Co am firmly bound unto John Hart of same parish for 40 pd ... the condition of this obligation is such that if the afsd Thomas Berry do ackn unto the sd John Hart a 50 a. tr of land less 1 a. excepted for building a mill [see above] then this obligation to be void ... . Wit: John Edwards, Wm Berry. Ackn 12 Apr 1742 & admitted to record. Attest: James Fontaine clerk. (Pg 165)

In pursuant to the within order I have heard the partys within named & their evidences & do award that the sd John Hill pay unto the sd Ambrose Fielding 13 pd 14 sl 7 pn of the estate of the within named Hannah Hill decd in his hands together with the costs by him the sd Ambrose in this behalf expended the lawyers fee excepted & of this I do make my report given under my hand this 11 Jan 1741. Saml Blackwell gent. This report was exhibited 13 Apr 1742 & admitted to record. Attest: James Fontaine clerk. (Pg 165)

We Joshua James, David Flicker & Robt Angell in obedience to an order of court held 11 --- 1741/2 being first sworn before Saml Blackwell have appraised all the estate of John Hill decd that was brought to our view in money. Feather beds, rugs, blankets, bedsteads, cords, hides, a mare & colt, saddle & bridle, 4 small hogs, 9 sides of leather, 2 ¼ yds coons linnen, 1 ½ yds breadcloth, a parcel of old cloaths, 36 ½ lbs good peuter, mustard pot, spice morter & pestle, bell metle skillet, a cowbell, box iron, 2 chests, 2 candlesticks, copper pot, grater, parcel of earthen ware, 1 stone jugg, an old Bible, a broad ax, some hows, hand saw, parcel of lumber, etc. [Not totaled] This inventory was exhibited 12 Apr 1742 by Mary Hill extx & on her motion the same is admitted to record. Attest: James Fontaine clerk. (Pg 166)

Pursuant to an order of court dated 11 Jan 1741 we Jonathan Betts, George Basy & George Kesterson being first sworn by a justice of peace have appraised the estate of John Philips decd. 1 chest, bed, blankets, rug, bedstead, cord, 8 lbs of old pewter, 1 table, 1 paile, 1 can, 1 iron pot & hooks, 3 flag chairs, a parcell of dry beef, 1 stear hide, 3 pecks of salt, 1 hand saw, 1 spinning wheel, old bolster & some feathers, 2 knives & forks, 1 candlestick, 1 frying pan, 1 white mare, 2 old baskets, 1 old box, 1 large earthen pot, 1 meale bag, 4 qt bottles, jug, 1 drinking glass, 1 small butter pot, etc. [Not totaled] This inventory was exhibited 12 Apr 1742 by Peter Presly gent adminr & on his motion admitted to record. Attest: James Fontaine clerk. (Pg 166)

In obedience to an order of court dated 11 Jan 1741/2 we John Lewis, John Kennedy & Rodham Kenner being first sworn before Matthew Quill justice of peace did accordingly appraise & value the estate of James Straughan decd in the hands of Thos Tobin in money. Beds & furniture, cord, bedstead, 1 trunk, 2 baskets, 3 pare lards & some woll, 2 stone jugs, 1 bag with feathers, a parcel of old curtins, 1 chest, a parcel of books, 1 pare of dove tails, 1 trunk, 1 chest, a parcel of chairs, 1 table, 1 pare scales & weights, lock, 1 pare willards, 1 table, knife & fork, 1 looking glass, 1 spinning wheel, 1 spit, a skimmer, flesh fork & ladle, 15 ½ lbs old puter, etc. Negroes: Darby a man, Dinah a girl, old Abby a girl, old Nan a girl, Tom a boy. [Not totaled] This inventory was exhibited 12 Apr 1742 by Winiford Straughan adminr & admitted to record. Attest: James Fontaine clerk. (Pg 166)

An inventory & appraisement of that pt/o the estate of Benjamin Waddy decd in

Westmoreland Co that was shewed us by Mrs. Jane Waddy the adminr: Negroes: man called Jack, woman called Nan, woman called young Nan, woman called Nell, child called Frank, girl called Nan Goard. 1 old cupboard, 3 cow hides, 7 lbs old peuter, 2 old narrow axes, 8 lbs old iron, 1 old cracht iron pot, 4 butchers knives, 4 old broad hows, 1 old homony pestle, 1 old hand saw, 5 young stears, 12 bull calves, 4 young heifers, 4 cows, 2 small heifers. 151 pd 17 sl. In obedience to an order of this court Nicholas Minor Junr, Edward Ransdell & John Barnett to value & appraise what of the estate of Benjamin Waddy decd as should be shewed us by Mrs. Jane Waddy the adminr have done the same accordingly. (Pg 167)

27 Jan 1741 Mrs. Jane Waddy, James Waddy & Charles Ingram his wife's pt/o Benjamin Waddy decd's estate paid them. 1st lott: 1 Negro man called Jack, at Mrs. Waddy's, due to estate by Mrs. Waddy: 8 pd 12 sl 10 ½ pn. 2nd lott: 1 Negro old Nann, due to the estate 12 pd 10 ½ sl. 3rd lott: 8 small heifers, 1 large heiffer, Ingram's part, due to the estate 10 ½ sl. ... [illegible] ... Jane Waddy adminr. Nicholas Minor Junr, Edward Ransdell, John Barnett. This inventory & division was exhibited 12 Apr 1742 by Mrs. Jane Waddy adminr & on her motion admitted to record. (Pg 166)

Will. Mary Tolson of Northumberland Co. 24 Jan 1741/2. To my dau Mary Parker the use of my Negro fellow named Tom during her natural live & after her death I give the sd Negro to my grandson Tolson Parker. To my dau Mary Parker my riding horse, saddle & bridle. To my granddau Elizabeth Tolson a feather bed & furniture as I gave her some time ago, two dishes, six plates, two basons, a great eyard? pot, a candlestick, a salt seller, her riding mare, saddle & bridle, a cow & yearling that is commonly called hers, her chest, a box & a trunk. My will is that all the rest of my estate be divided amongst my children. I appoint my good friends Winder Kenner & John Tolson executors. Wit: Winder Kenner, John Tolson. Proved 12 Apr 1742 & admitted to record. Attest: James Fontaine clerk. (Pg 167)

Will. Daniel Beachum of St. Stephens Parish, Northumberland Co. 7 Jul 1736. To my two eldest sons John Beachum & Daniel Beachum all the land on the e side of a right line adj land sold to Hughlet & the road which leads to Mrs. Belfield's Quarter. If either of them dies without heirs my desire is that my son William Beachum may have their part. To my son Isaac Beachum all the land I bought of John Litreil together with all my land lying on the n side of the afsd road which leads to Belfield's Quarter. If he dies without heirs my will is that my son William may have except if either of the afsd parts should fall to him then my will is that the child my wife is now with may have it if it be a boy & if not to be divided amongst all my sons. To my son Abraham Beachum my dwelling plantation together with all my lands except as before bequeathed. If he dies without heirs to belong to my son William except as afsd. To my son

William Beachum my sorrel mare & colt with all her increase. To my dau Mary
Beachum the sorrel mare colt I had of John Watts. To my dau Ann Beachum the
coult which my old gray mare brought this year. All the rest of my estate
together with my household goods & moveables to be divided between my wife
Rebecca & my son William & my four daus Mary Magdaline, Ann, Rebecca &
Winifred & the child by wife is now with. I constitute my wife Rebecca & my
trusty friend William Westly my executors. Codicil: 9 Jan 1741 being it hath
pleased God to spare me till this day & that my sons Daniel & William have
departed this life my desire & will is that my son Isaac may have the land above
bequeathed to my son Daniel decd & for want of heirs to be divided amongst my
surviving sons & the land above given to my son Isaac I give to my son
Abraham & for want of heirs to be divided amongst my surviving sons. The
land above given to my son Abraham I give to my son Joab & for want of heirs
to be divided amongst my sons as afsd. I give my Negro woman called Jug to
my wife Rebecka. Wit: James Self, Benedict Short, David Williams. Proved
12 Apr 1742 & admitted to record. Attest: James Fontaine clerk. (Pg 167)

Will. John Shirly of St. Stephens Parish, Northumberland Co. 30 Mar 1742. To
my wife Betty Shirly & the child wherewith she now goes with my moveable
estate of any kind whatsoever. ... [illegible] ... I appoint my wife Betty Shirly
my executrix ... [illegible] ... . Wit: Peter Bearcraft, Susan Gounsteed, Robt
Clark Junr. Proved 12 Apr 1742 by the oaths of Peter Bearcraft, Susanna Shirly
& Robt Clark Junr wits thereto & Betty Shirly & Archland Shirly executors
made oath to the sd will on whose motion the same is admitted to record.
Attest: James Fontaine clerk. (Pg 169)

Will. Thomas Hall of Northumberland Co. 28 Feb 1738/9. To my son John
Hall all my land & plantation but if he dies without heir to go to my dau Betty.
To my son John Hall at the time of my death all my wearing cloaths. To my
wife Hannah Hall one servant wench named Ann Jones during life. To my wife
Hannah one new feather bed & furniture that now belongs to it during her life &
then to my son John. To my dau Betty one feather bed & furniture that she has
now in possession. To my dau Betty one cow & calf. All the rest of my estate
to be divided betwixt them & my son John Hall sole executor. Wit: Gibbord
(Gilbert) Harril, Richard Booth Junr. Proved 12 Apr 1742 & admitted to record.
Attest: James Fontaine clerk. (Pg 169)

Will. Mary Palfry. 13 Jan 1741. ... [illegible] ... . (Pg 169)

Will. Joseph Hudnall of Northumberland Co. 11 Aug 1736. To my wife Sarah
Hudnall that parcel of land that fell to me by my mother's death during her
natural life. I give my sd wife all that land I bought of John James on the head
of Great Wicocomoco River during her natural life. To my wife all that land

bought of Timothy Baley on Fielding Swamp next Thomas Mill during her
natural life. My will is that if my sd wife shall hereafter have a child by me then
my desire is that he or she as they may have all the afsd lands when they come to
age & in case my wife shall have no living child as afsd then my desire is that
my dau in law [?] Cottrell shall have that land bought of John James after my
wifes death. My will is that Lucretia Cottrell shall have that land bought of
Timothy Baley after my wifes decease. I give unto my brother's son John
Hudnall that land that fell to me by my mother's death after my wife's death &
in case she has no child. But if the sd John Hudnall ... [illegible] ... if no child
to be divided between Thomas Cottrell & Lucretia Cotrell. My will is that my
estate be not appraised. My will is that my wife be my executrix. Wit:
William James McGee, Elles Gill. Proved 12 Apr 1742 & admitted to record.
Attest: James Fontaine clerk. (Pg 170)

Will. Robert Anderson of St. Stephens Parish, Northumberland Co. 10 Jul
1740. To my son William Anderson all my lands that I am now possest with. If
the sd William dies without issue then my will is that my land shall fall unto my
son John Anderson. If my son John Anderson should die without issue then my
land shall fall unto my dau Elizabeth Anderson. All my personall estate shall be
divided between my wife Elizabeth Anderson & my three children William,
John & Elizabeth Anderson. I appoint Abner Neale & Motly Wildy executors.
Wit: Wm Fallin, John Edwards. Proved 12 Apr 1742 & admitted to record.
Attest: James Fontaine clerk. (Pg 170)

... [illegible] ... I give to my son Henry Turner my tr of land called Opies
Quarter which I bought from Rodham Kenner being 124 a. & for default of heirs
I give the tr to my son George Turner & for default of heirs to my son Edward
Turner. My Negro lad called Sain to my son Harry. The above land to be
delivered to my son Henry when he comes of age or marries. I give my Negro
girl called Kate to my son George Turner to be delivered to him at the day of
marriage or at the age of 21. I likewise give my Negro girl called Lucy to my
son Edward Turner to be delivered at the age of 21 or day of marriage. I give to
my dau Elizabeth Hayden my Negro boy Adam which her husband hath in
possession for full of her part. I give to my dau Monaca Turner my Negro boy
called Davie to be delivered when she comes of age or day of marriage. I give
to my dau Prisilla Turner my Negro boy called Jacob to be delivered when she
comes of age or day of marriage. I give my dau Ann Turner my Negro boy
called Will to be delivered to her when she comes of age or day of marriage.
My will is that my crop of corn & tobacco shall not be appraised or my estate for
I leave it to pay my debts & defray my funeral expences & the rest to maintain
my children & my will is that my children should live together & be maintained
out of the crops at the direction of my executors. ... [illegible] ... [Signed] John
Turner. Proved 14 Apr 1742 by the oaths of William Taite, James Lewis &

[illegible] wits & Febbe Turner & John Turner executors therein named made oath to the sd will on whose motion the same is admitted to record. Attest: James Fontaine clerk. (Pg 171)

Will. Charles Wilkins of St. Stephens Parish, Northumberland Co. 24 Dec 1731. To my wife Catherine Wilkins & my dau Jane Wilkins all my land to be divided between them during my wife's widdowhood & after her widdowhood it is my will that my dau Jane Wilkins should have all my sd land. But in case she should die without heir then it is my will that my youngest child should have the land & the heirs of his body. I give unto my dau Jane Wilkins one young heiffer of 2 years old & her increase. I give all the rest of my estate to be divided between my wife Catherine Wilkins & my dau Jane Wilkins & my son Charles Wilkins & my youngest son. I appoint my dau Jane Wilkins my executrix. Wit: John Ashburn, William Hobson. Codicil: 20 Feb 1741/2. I give unto my son John Wilkins two young heifers with their increase. I give to my son Charles Wilkins one book called the Whole Duty of Man & one singing book. Wit: James Daughty. ... [rest illegible] ... . (Pg 171)

Will. Tarkle Tarkleson. ... [illegible] ... to my dau Mary plantation where I now live. To my dau Elizabeth Tarkleson the plantation whereon my father now lies. My will is that my dau Sarah Tarkleson shall have all my personal estate of what kind. In case my dau Elizabeth Tarkleson should have no right to that plantation whereon my father now lives then my will is that my personal estate should be divided between my daus Eliz & Sarah Tarkleson. My will is that the profits of my estate should be for the maintenance of my children till they come of age or marry. I appoint my brother John Cox & my friend William Hammond my executors. Wit: Thos Dinkard, John Dinkard. Proved 12 Apr 1742 & admitted to record. Attest: James Fontaine clerk. (Pg 172)

Will. John Power. 4 May 1742. To my son Peter Power two of my best feather beds & four sheets, [?], two bolsters, one pillow & one standing bedstead. To my sd son Peter Power 15 new pewter plates, four new puter basons, two new pewter dishes, one big & the other small, two new pewter ten hards?, three new pewter porringers & one bett of iron wedges ... [illegible] ... . To my son Joseph Power one large feather bed & the furniture. To Mary Watts one cow. To my dau Catherine Donaway one young cow which is at Richard Partridge's & one red pied steer, four sheep, three hogs & one broad bason. To my son Joseph Power my mare & two cows . It is my desire that after my decease the remainder of my estate shall be divided amongst my three children Joseph, Catherine & Peter. I appoint my son Joseph Power & Ezekiel Hill executors. Wit: Thos Dameron, John Webb, Samson Finch. Proved 10 May 1742 & admitted to record. Attest: James Fontaine clerk. (Pg 172)

Will. John Sutton of Wicocomoco Parish, Northumberland Co. I leave my land
to my wife Mary during her naturall life & after her decease to my son William.
To my son William a pare of pistols & holsters & sword & chest. To my son
Wm that feather bed & furniture that he hath now in his possession. To my dau
Ann a bed & furniture which she hath now in possession. To my dau Elizabeth
a feather bed & furniture which she has in possession. To my son John ...
[illegible] ... . The rest of my estate to be divided between my wife & five
children, viz, John, Mary, Dorothy, Richard & Sarah Ann. ... [rest illegible] ...
. Proved 10 May 1742 by the oaths of George Mills & Thomas [?] & admitted
to record. Attest: James Fontaine clerk. (Pg 172)

29 Jul 1741. Bond. Moses Lunsford & Charles Harding of Overwharton
Parish, Stafford Co are firmly bound to Thomas Harding of Wicocomoco Parish,
Northumberland Co for 8,000 lbs of tobacco ... the condition of this obligation
is such that if the afsd Moses Lunsford & Charles Harding do upon the
reasonable request of the sd Thomas Harding after 10 7br 1741 make a deed &
ackn the same to the sd Thomas Harding for a 50 a. parcel of land bounded by
James Davison & Robt Angell then this obligation to be voyd ... . Wit: Nath
Sharman, Wm Smith. Ackn 10 May 1742 & admitted to record. Attest: James
Fontaine clerk. (Pg 173)

10 May 1742. George Conway & Ann his wife dau of Saml Heath gent decd of
Wicocomoco Parish, Northumberland Co ... [illegible] ... George Ball ... by the
will of Bartholomew Schreever lately decd became vested in the sd Ann
Conway & her [?] as coheirs to their father Saml Heath decd & called
Schreevers Mill ... the sd George & Ann Conway doth covenant & grant to &
with the sd George Ball the sd water mill ... . Wit: Henry Miller, James Webb,
John Ball. Ackn 10 May 1742 by George & Ann Conway unto George Ball gent
& the sd Ann Conway being privately examined by Traves Colston gent in court
relinquished her right of dower in the lands & mill conveyed by the sd deed unto
the sd Ball on whose motion the same is admitted to record. Attest: James
Fontaine clerk. (Pg 173)

10 May 1742. Bond. George Conway & Ann Conway his wife of Wicocomoco
Parish, Northumberland Co are firmly bound unto George Ball of parish afsd for
[?] thousand fifty lbs of tobacco ... the condition of this obligation is such that
whereas the afsd George Conway & Ann his wife by one deed [see above] hath
sold unto the sd George Ball ¼ pt/o a water mill, now if the afsd George
Conway & Ann his wife shall well & truly perform, fulfill & keep all & singular
the covenants, grants & articles mentioned in the afsd deed then this obligation
to be void ... . Wit: Henry Miller, James Webb, John Ball. Ackn 10 May 1742
by George Conway & Ann Conway unto George Ball gent on whose motion the
same is admitted to record. Attest: James Fontaine clerk. (Pg 174)

10 May 1742. Deed. Between John Litreel of St. Stephens Parish,
Northumberland Co planter of the first part & Abraham Beachum son of Daniel
Beachum decd late of St. Stephens Parish, Northumberland Co of the second
part ... whereas James Litreel father to the afsd John Litreel bought a 100 a. tr of
land of Dennis Cornwell in St. Stephens Parish & did bequeath the same to the
afsd John Litreel ... now this indenture wit further that the sd John Litrell having
contracted a bargain & sale of the sd 100 a. of land except 15 a. which the sd
John had sold to John Turner before with the afsd Daniel Beachum who died
before the ensealing of the deed whereby the inheritance of the land is still
remaining in the sd John Litreel & whereas the sd Daniel Beachum by his will
dated 9 Jan 1741 did bequeath the sd land to his son Abraham Beachum party to
these presents & the sd John Litwell being justly & truly paid for the same &
willing to satisfy & perform the will of the dead & for 5 sl do hereby sell &
confirm unto the sd Abraham Beachum the afsd 100 a. of land except the 15 a.
afsd in St. Stephens Parish bounded by George Knot & Marshy Swam belonging
to Edward Lewis decd ... [rest illegible] ... . Wit: Geo Clark, William Dogget,
Adcock Hobson. Ackn 10 May 1742 & admitted to record. Attest: James
Fontaine clerk. (Pg 174)

11 Apr 1738. Memorandum. It is agreed by & between Peter Bearcroft of the
one part & Rodham Kenner of the other part that for the ending & determination
of all disputes & suits & controversys had depending between them for &
concerning any lands in their or either of their possession it is mutually agreed
between us that a dividing line to conclude us & our heirs forever hereafter, that
runs from the cedar now markt to King Cr & the corner of the sd Bear croft's ...
[illegible] ... we shall enter into & pass to each other a deed to confirm the sd
bounds or division between us & our heirs forever hereafter. Wit: Thos
Edwards, James Stepto. Ackn 10 May 1742 to each other in court & admitted to
record. Attest: James Fontaine clerk. (Pg 175)

15 8br 1741. In obedience to an order of court dated 14 Sep 1741 we Thomas
Pitman, Argail Taylor & James Genn have met & layd off Capt Jones' wife's
dower of the land of her husband Thomas Taylor decd. This report of the
division of Thomas Taylor's land to Robt Jones gent was exhibited 10 May 1742
by the auditors & recorded. Attest: James Fontaine clerk. (Pg 175)

In obedience to an order of court dated 11 Jan 1741/2 we George Conway, John
Rout & William Thomas being appointed to allott Winifrid Boyd 1/3 of her decd
husband John Boyd's estate we did accordingly meet & have possessed her with
the same in the articles hereunder mentioned. A Negro fellow named Daniel. 2
looking glasses, a silver dram cup, 2 old trunks, pare arm chairs, a box iron &
heaters, a mare, 1 white faced cow & yearling, a black heifer & yearling ...
[illegible] ... a warming pan, pare fire tongs, 1 iron pestle, 1 old oval table, 1

square framed table, flag chairs, iron spit, earthen ware, 1 old tub, 1 frying pan, flesh fork, brass skimer, some wooden ware, spinning wheel, etc. 51 pd 8 sl 6 ¼ pn. This report & division was returned 10 May 1742 & recorded. Attest: James Fontaine clerk. (Pg 175)

In obedience to an order of court dated 12 Apr 1742 we John Claughton, Richd Claughton & Wm Garner being first sworn before Traves Colston met at the plantation of John Hall & valued in money the estate of Thos Hall Junr decd in ye house of John Hall & possessed the guardian of Rodham Hall appointed by the court Ormsbe Haynie with the sd estate: 1 bed & furniture, 1 chest of drawers, 1 chest, 7 chairs, 2 old potts & pothooks, pott rack ... [illegible] ... quilting frame, 1 sifter & salt box, parcel of wooden ware, brass candlestick, ladle, 1 cannister, 1 Negro woman, 1 Negro boy. 69 pd 5 sl 9 ½ pn. This report & division of the estate of Thomas Hall to Rodham Hall an infant delivered to Ormsbe Haynie his guardian was exhibited by the auditors & recorded. Attest: James Fontaine clerk. (Pg 176)

1 May 1742. In pursuant to an order of court granted to Peter Bearcroft guardian of Joseph Shirly we the subscribers being appointed to appraise the sd Joseph Shirly's pt/o his decd father's estate out of John Shirly's estate do find it to be 9 pd 15 sl 10 pn accordingly have valued & appraised it (being first sworn before Matthew Quill) & we have possessed the sd guardian with it. 1 old horse, 28 lbs of new feathers, 1 old blanket & bed tick, 9 lbs of good pewter, 4 ¼ lbs old pewter, 1 chest, 1 box, 1 cow & yearling, 1 heiffer, 4 shoats, 2 large hogs, 1 ewe & lamb, 1 piece of D[?] ware, 2 stone mugs, 1 pare fire tongs, 1 iron wedge, 1 carpenter's frow?, 3 chairs, 1 kettle, frying pan, 1 table, 1 gun, 1 loom, 1 grind stone ... [rest illegible] ... . Attest: James Fontaine clerk. (Pg 176)

An inventory of Tarkle Tarkleson's estate which we Wm Jones, Andrew Shelton & Saml Gaskins appraised according to an order of court. 4 cows & calves, 3 heifers, 1 cowhide, 1 old gun, 1 white servant man, 1 bed & furniture, 1 old 60 gall cask, 1 old tub, 1 old bed, 2 old rugs, a sheet & bolster, 5 yds broad cloath, 1 drum gigg, 1 large table, & form, 1 piggin full of salt, 1 old trunk, 1 small table, 2 old ropes, 1 old wheel, 1 violin, 1 small Bible, 1 small prayer book, 1 platter, 1 large old chest, 1 small looking glass, 1 small pocket bottle & drinking glass, 1/3 pt/o a fishing vessell, 1 canoe, etc. [Not totaled] This inventory was exhibited 10 May 1742 by Wm Hammond & John Cope executors & on their motion admitted to record. Attest: James Fontaine clerk. (Pg 177)

In obedience to an order of court dated 12 Apr 1742 we the subscribers did meet at the house of Mary Tolson decd & being first sworn before Cuthbert Spann gent did appraise the sd decd's estate in money. Beds, bolsters, rugs, blankets, sheets, bedsteads, pillows & cases, hide & cord, 1 large chest lock & key, 1 linnen wheel, a parcel of reeds, 2 matts, 2 old guns, a parsel of salt, 1 crosscut saw, 2 files, 1 hollow adz, coopers adz, a parcel of carpenter's tools … [illegible] … glass bottles, 2 sifters, 1 pare of seales & weights, 1 pare of small willards, 1 old chest, old box, 1 large trunk lock & key, 1 old cupboard, 1 Indian basket, 4 baskets, 1 old tub, 1 iron pestle, 1 pot & hooks, spinning wheel, 1 side saddle, 1 meale bag, parcel of earthen ware, parcel of corn, etc. Negroes: fellow Tom, woman Janey, child Isaac, girl Pleasant. [Rest illegible]. (Pg 177)

Pursuant to an order of court dated 12 Apr 1742 we Wm Harding, Richd Claughton & John Claughton being first sworn before Traves Colston gent justice have valued & appraised the estate of Daniel Beachum decd which was brought to our view in money. 7 cows, yearlings, 8 young cattle, calves, 2 mares & colts, 1 horse, 13 sheep, beds, bedsteads & furniture, 1 rug, 2 blankets, 1 sheet, 6 leather chairs, 9 chairs, 1 table & cloth, 1 chest, 1 box, 1 mans sadle & bridle, 1 worn sadle cloath & bridle, 1 loom & all ye gear, earthen ware, botles, 7 sickles, box iron & heaters, glasses & spectacles, parcel baskets, pickt cotton, some wool, 3 baskets, 1 pare stillards, some books, 1 looking glass, 1 pare shears, a plough., croscut saw, file, a lot of wedges, 1 Negro woman, 2 spinning wheels & 5 pare cards, etc. [Not totaled] This inventory was exhibited 10 May 1742 by Rebecka Beachum & Wm Hartly executors & on their motion admitted to record. Attest: James Fontaine clerk. (Pg 179)

In obedience to an order of court dated 12 Apr 1742 we Saml Nelms, Saml Downing & John Hudnall being appointed & sworn by Saml Blackwell did meet & value the estate of Robt Anderson decd in money. 7 cows & calf, 2 heifers, 1 sow shoat, 1 sorrel ram, 2 ewes & lamb, 12 lbs good pewter, 16 lbs old pewter, 5 chairs, beds, bedsteads, bolsters, pillows, sheets, blankets, matt, cord, 1 old chest, 2 butter pots, 1 old looking glass, 1 heifers hide, 1 old spinning wheel, old sifter, 3 old hows, 1 old ax, 1 box iron & heaters, Taylors goos, parcel of old knives & forks, 1 old saus pan, 2 old brass candlesticks, 1 old coon leged table & cloth, parcel of wooden ware, 2 old cider casks, 1 old tub, 1 earthen pan, 3 glass bottles, 3 old baskets, 1 frying pan, old how, 59 lbs pot iron. [Not totaled] This inventory was exhibited 10 May 1742 by Edward Ryan adminr with the will annexed & on his motion admitted to record. Attest: James Fontaine clerk. (Pg 179)

Pursuant to an order of court we John West, Richd Claughton, Wm Garner & James Lewis have appraised the estate of John Turner decd. … [illegible] … 1 frying pan, old tub, 3 cows & calf, 1 cart & wheels, beds & furniture, bedsteads, 1 case 3 bottles, 5 old chests, 1 cupbord, 1 pare spoon molds & butter mold, 1 candlestick, 1 oval table, old silver, 1 pare scales, razors, 1 looking glass, 1 hat, 1 pare shoes, 1 chest, 8 old chairs, 2 pare fire tongs, 2 tables, 1 gun, 1 wheel & cards, 5 reap hooks, 2 lines, fish hooks, coopers & carpenters tools, wedge, earthen ware & books, etc. Negro lad called Sam, Negro girl called Lucy. [Not totaled] This inventory was exhibited 10 May 1742 by Febbe Turner & John Turner executors & on their motion admitted to record. Attest: James Fontaine clerk. (Pg 180)

In obedience to an order of court dated 13 Apr 1742 we Thomas Winter, Henry Miller & John Waddy have met & appraised all the estate of Judith Jones decd as was shewn to us by the adminrs. 1 large ovall table, 1 bed & furniture, 1 VA curtains, 1 rug, 5 leather chairs ... [illegible] ... 1 old cupboard, books, Sunday books, Doctor Sherlock's works, 1 old small Bible, a large common prayer book, 1 old Chronicles of England, 1 old lattin book, 1 old law book, 1 old Roman history, a parsel of books of medicine, 1 horse, 1 old side sadle & bridle, 3 old hogs, 3 young hogs, 4 pigs, 5 earthen pans, 1 earthen butter pot, 5 earthen plates, 1 earthen dish, a parsel of earthen ware, 1 glass salt, 1 teapot, etc. Negro man Jack, Negro man Jacob. This inventory was exhibited 10 May 1742 by Spencer Ball gent adminr on whose motion the same is admitted to record. Attest: James Fontaine clerk. (Pg 180)

At a court held in Mar 1741 it was ordered that we Thomas Pittman, John Basye & Edwin Smith would meet & appraise the estate of Hannah Hill decd. In obedience there unto we have valued the same on inventory. 3 heifers, 1 cow, feather beds & furniture, 1 chest, 13 ½ lbs peuter, 1 spit, 1 pare stillards, 6 flag chairs, 1/3 pt/o a bound servant boy sold, 2 cow hides, 1 cupboard, 1/3 of the hogs, 1 young mare, 1 old table, small box, brass candlestick, a parcel of wearing cloths, 2 chest, 1 grindstone ... [illegible] ... 5 quart bottles, 1 gound, petticoat, 1 new porringer, 1 old trunk, 1 Bible, etc. [Not totaled] This ivory was exhibited 10 May 1742 by Ambrose Fielding executor & on his motion admitted to record. Attest: James Fontaine clerk. (Pg 182)

In obedience to an order of court dated 12 Apr 1742 we Wm Harding, Jno Claughton & Wm Gardner being appointed to appraise the estate of Thomas Hall decd being first sworn before Traves Colston gent have met & appraised the sd estate. A parcel of carpenters tools, 3 cider cask, 1 old tub, tannd leather, 1 iron wedge, some lumber, 1 canneo, 2 axes, 1 pare fire tongs, parcel of hoes, 6 gees, 6 fowls, a turkey, 1 spinning wheel & cards, beds & furniture, cord, hide, pot hooks, 1 box iron heaters, 1 gridiron, 1 table, 1 chest, 1 bag, 4 chairs, 1 cart & wheels, 1 cow & yearling, 2 year old bull, 1 trunk, 1 vest, 1 pare breeches, 1 silk handkerchief, 4 baskets, etc. [Not totaled] This inventory was exhibited 10 May 1742 by John Hall executor & on his motion admitted to record. Attest: James Fontaine clerk. (Pg 183)

... [illegible] ... Beds, bedsteads, sheets, blankets, bolsters, pillows, hide, 1 box, 1 sword, cartouch & belts, 1 chest, 1 hammer, 1 jack plain & saw, 1 spinning wheel & wool cards, 1 spice morter & pestle, 2 large hogs, 9 lbs of good pewter, 3 ¼ lbs old pewter, pot iron, 1 flesh fork, 1 iron spoon, candlestick, 1 pare sheep shears & file, parcel of old earthen ware, 2 stone mugs, 4 pieces Deef ware, glass & cream pot, 1 looking glass, 1 piging awl, parcel of old books, 4 working hows, 3 ewes & lambs, 2 old chairs, etc. [Not totaled] Robt Clark Junr, Edward Barnes, Elias Edmonds Junr auditors. This inventory of the estate of Elias Edmonds Junr was exhibited by Betty Shirly & Aejalon? Shirly executors & on their motion admitted to record. Attest: James Fontaine clerk. (Pg 184)

In obedience to an order of court held 13 Apr 1742 we Richard Hull, Edward Rogers & Abner Neale the appointed appraisers have met & have appraised the estate of Charles Wilkins decd in money. 5 old sheep, 3 lambs, 5 cows, calves, 4 stears, 1 heiffer, 2 horses, 1 spinning wheel, 1 pare wool cards, 1 pare cotton cards, 1 box iron & heaters, 1 old sword, belt & cartouch box, some pouder & bullets, 7 old hows, 2 narrow axes, 2 wedges, a pestle, spit & tongs, 1 drawing knife, 1 old plow & gear, 1 saddle & cloath, bridle, beds, bolsters, bedsteads, some furniture, 7 old chairs, 1 great table, etc. [Not totaled] This inventory was exhibited 10 May 1742 by Janey Wilkins executrix & on her motion admitted to record. Attest: James Fontaine clerk. (Pg 184)

3 May 1742. According to the will proved in court this is a just & perfect inventory of the estate of Joseph Hudnall decd: 1 pare large old oxen, 5 cows, 4 yearlings, 2 stears, 2 bulls, 13 ewes, 2 rams, 10 lambs, 11 hogs, 9 pigs, 1 sow, 5 shoats, 2 old horses, beds, bolsters, blankets, sheets, bedsteads, 2 saddles, 2 old bridles, 1 new womans saddle, 1 old one, 1 new disstill of 52 gallons & worm & tub, 1 copper kettle of 21 gallon, 2 old barrils, 5 poudering tubs, 6 bushels of salt, 1 cold still, 140 qt bottles, parcel of carpenters & coopers tools, 2 pare sheep shears, 21 midlings of bacon, some dry beef, 30 gall of brandy, 31 barrils of Indian corn, 2 bushels of wheat, 2 old croscut saws, 1 handsaw, 2 files, 2 spinning wheels, etc. Negroes: man Jack, woman Bess, girl Lucy, woman Cate, girl Hannah, girl Grace, boy Jacob, man Cuffy, woman Doll, girl Nan, boy Mark, woman Jenny, boy George, woman Rose, child Sam. This inventory was exhibited 10 May 1742 by Sarah Hudnall executrix & on her motion admitted to record. Attest: James Fontaine clerk. (Pg 185)

In obedience to an order of court dated 12 Apr 1742 we Winder Kenner, Richd Kenner & John Conway did meet at the house of Mary Parker being first sworn by Capt Spann & did appraise Wm Parker decd's estate in money. Beds & furniture, bedsteads, chest lock & key, 2 trunks, 2 flag chairs, a large chest lock & key, 2 boxes, a croscut saw, an adds & some other tools, some earthen ware & other lumber, some fishing hooks & lines, 8 hoggs, 51 lbs of peuter, 1 gun, 1 old side saddle & bridle, an old skillet, 72 lbs of pot iron, 3 pailes, some woodware, 2 washing tubs, a spring wheel, cow, heiffer, 6 shoats, a barrow, an old mare, 6 ewes & lambs, etc. [Not totaled] This inventory was exhibited 10 May 1742 by Mary Parker adminr & on her motion admitted to record. Attest: James Fontaine clerk. (Pg 186)

In obedience to an order of court dated 12 Apr 1742 we Bennet Bogges, Vincent Garner & Wm Taylor have met at the house of Griffin Fantleroy this 5 May 1742 & have appraised the estate of Mary Palfry decd. 7 yards of Bladding?, 2 yds linnen, 4 shifts, 2 [?], 1 wastcoat, 8 aprons, 5 petticoats, 4 gounds, a pare bodices & a hat, parcel of lumber, a book, parcel of wearing linnen, 1 old hat. 5 lbs 4 sl 7 pn. This inventory was exhibited 10 May 1742 by Griffin Fantleroy gent executor & on his motion is admitted to record. Attest: James Fontaine clerk. (Pg 186)

… [illegible] … -- lbs beef, parcel of lard, parcel of pork, 13 lbs of tallow, tobacco from inspectors book. This additional inventory of the estate of Wm Downing decd was exhibited 10 May 1742 by Winifrid Downing & Saml Nelms executors & on their motion admitted to record. Attest: James Fontaine clerk. (Pg 187)

In obedience to an order of court dated 12 Apr 1742 I David Lattimore have exposed to sale at outcry all the estate of John Hawkins as come to my hands & has sold it all but one bedstead to the several persons hereafter mentioned, to wit, George Tillery, Nicholas Cary, Jno Tillery, George Conway, John Oldham. 286 lbs tobacco. This inventory & sale of the estate of John Hawkins decd was exhibited 11 May 1792 by the sheriff & recorded. Attest: James Fontaine clerk. (Pg 187)

14 Jun 1742. Deed. Mary Pope of Wicocomoco Parish, Northumberland Co for 15 pd sold to George Oldham of same place ¼ pt/o a water mill upon the s br of Scotland Mill Cr which sd mill by the will of Bartholomew Schrever late decd is become vested in the sd Pope & his (sic) three sisters as coheirs to their father Saml Heath decd & is called Schrevers Mill … . Wit: Henry Miller, Joseph Webb. Ackn 19 Jun 1742 & admitted to record. Attest: James Fontaine clerk. (Pg 187)

12 May 1742. Deed. Saml Downing of St. Stephens Parish, Northumberland Co for 20 pd sold to John Mew of same parish a 40 a. tr of land on the n side of Great Wicocomoco River bounded by John Bearcroft, land formerly Richd Nelms' & the river … . Wit: John Donaway, James Pew. Ackn 14 Jun 1742 & admitted to record. Attest: James Fontaine clerk. (2nd Pg 187)

15 Jun 1742. Deed. Saml Downing of St. Stephens Parish, Northumberland Co for 20 pd sold to Aron Nelms of same parish a 65 a. tr of land on the n side of

Great Wicocomoco River bounded by Alexander Moorhead, sd Downing & land formerly John Rider's ... . Wit: Thomas Pew, John Donaway. Ackn 15 Jun 1742 & admitted to record. Attest: James Fontaine clerk. (Pg 188)

We Lindsey Opie, Jno Kennedy & Richd Claughton met at ye house of George ... [illegible] ... Lampkin his pt/o his decd father's estate did allot Lewis Lamken guardian with the same. 5 old sheep, 4 young sheep, 1 pare sheep shears, 2 guns, 1 set pistols & holsters, 1 chest & small chais, 1 table, 1 bed & furniture, 1 poudering tubb, 1 hide & tubb, 2 small cask, 1 great cask, 1 spice mortar & pestle, 2 chairs, 1 pare stockins, 1 wheel & hackle, 1 bedstead, 1 pare pumps, 1 boy Wm Standly, 1 ax, drawing knife, chisel & marking irons, handsaw & cock, 1 rack & silver spoon, 1 case & bottles, 12 lbs puter, 1 cask, a spade, 1 stear, 1 bull, 1 young bull, etc. 15 pd 2 sl 11 pn. This report & division of the estate of James Lamkin was exhibited 15 Jun 1742 by the auditors & recorded. Attest: James Fontaine clerk. (Pg 189)

In obedience to an order of court dated 10 May 1742 we Argail Taylor, Wm James & Thos Everitt have met & settled accounts between Saml Smith's executors & Robert Palmer & allotted the sd Robert Palmer's estate & has also possessed Saml Snow guardian to the sd Robert Palmer with it. 1 old feather bed, bestead, hide, cord, 2 old blankets, 1 cowhide, some tanned leather, 1 sheep, 1 old table & form, 1 tub, 1 old craht iron pot, 1 earthen pot, 1 pare horse fleams, 1 small cask, 1 chisel, 4 ¼ lbs good peuter, 1 plaine stock & iron, 4 ½ lbs powder, cash, 597 lbs of tobacco, 400 lbs tobacco recd by Saml Snow of Oldham for rent. [Not totaled] This report was exhibited 14 Jun 1742 by the auditors & recorded. Attest: James Fontaine clerk. (Pg 189)

20 May 1742. In obedience to an order of court dated 11 May 1742 we William Haynie, Edward Rogers & Silvester Welsh did meet at the house of Morely Mott & appraised one Negro man named Sam to 30 pd. This report was returned 15 Jun 1742 by the auditors & recorded. Attest: James Fontaine clerk. (Pg 189)

Pursuant to an order of court held 9 Jan 1737/8 we Thomas Winter, Josias Gaskins & Christopher Dameron did meet at the dwelling house of Charles Jones being first sworn by Capt Eustace & appraised all the estate as was brought to our view in money. 1 wallnut desk, 1 ovall wallnut table, 8 flag chairs, 1 bed, 4 pillows, 1 rug, 1 blanket, 1 pare of sheets, 1 bedsted & cord, 1 rug & blanket, 1 small chest, 1 padlock, 1 small looking glass, 1 small punch boul, 1 box iron & heaters, 1 stone jug, tablecloth, 2 napkins, 1 soop plate, 1 flat plate, 4 good dishes, 2 peuter porringers, 1 gray horse, 2 bay horses, 1 copper kettle, 2 pots, 1 earthen pot, 2 mugs, 1 pare pot hooks, 4 pailes, parsel wooden ware, 1 iron skillet, 1 large butter pot, etc.

Sundry goods valued by George Ball, Matthew Quill gent & Benjamin

Waddy by order of court & allotted Mrs. Elizabeth Jones for her pt/o her decd
father Saml Heath's estate report dated 9 Jan 1737/8. A parcel of old books.,
Doctor Wm Beverige's Works 2 volumes, Rules of Holy Living by Jeremiah
Taylor, The Careless World by Josia Woodward, His Golden Ass? 2 vol., 1
Whole Duty of Man, 1 spelling book, The Ladys Calling Quincey &
Dispensatory. Negroes: Tom, York, Hanniball, Beck, Sarah, Gridger, Nanny a
girl, a parsel of old pewter, 6 silver spoons, 1 pare sheets, 1 brass candlestick, 1
small spitt, 1 old iron ladle, 1 spade, 1 tailors goos, 7 sickles, 2 old brass cocks,
4 window curtains & vallins, etc. [Not totaled] ... [illegible] .... Elizabeth
Jones adminr. This inventory & additionall inventory of the estate of Charles
Jones decd was exhibited 14 Jun 1742 by Henry Miller & Elizabeth his wife
relict & adminr of the sd decd & on their motion admitted to record. Attest:
James Fontaine clerk. [Pg 189]

10 Jun 1742. In obedience to an order of court dated 10 May 1742 appointing
Wm Lattimore, Richd Hudnall & John Berry to appraise the estate of John
Sutton decd being first sworn before George Ball Junr have appraised the afsd
estate. 1 sow, 4 shoats, 1 sow & 3 pigs, 5 ewes & lambs, 2 feather beds &
furniture, 1 looking glass, 29 ½ lbs pewter, 1 old table, some lumber, 2 stone
jugs, 1 earthen jug, some old iron, 1 spit, 1 pestle, 1 pare sheep shears, a parsel
of old iron, 1 table, parsel of old books, parcel of old wool & cotton cards, parsel
of fishing line & hooks, 2 sugar potts?, 1 peuter plate, parcel of earthen ware,
etc. Corn & meat not appraised but for ye use of ye children. [Not totaled] This
inventory was exhibited 14 Jun 1742 by Mary Sutton adminr & on her motion
admitted to record. Attest: James Fontaine clerk. (Pg 190)

In obedience to an order of court dated 11 May 1742 we Wm Ball, Yarret
Hughlet & Thos Dameron Junr appointed to appraise the estate of John Power
decd mett & have appraised the sd estate. 3 cows, yearling, calf, 3 heiffers, 1
stear, 8 sheep, 5 lambs, 11 small hogs, 1 shoat, 2 feather beds, boulsters, pillow,
sheets, rugs, standing bedsteads & cords, 1 chest, 4 flag chairs, 1 iron spit, 1 iron
pestle, 1 pare fire tongs, 6 glass bottles, 3 stone jugs, some yellow ware, parcel
earthen pots, 6 milk pans ... [illegible] ... some tannd leather, 1 washing tub,
paile & pigin, flower tub, some wearing cloaths, earthenware pot, some corn,
etc. [Not totaled] This inventory was exhibited 15 Jun 1742 by Joseph Power
adminr on whose motion the same is admitted to record. Attest: James Fontaine
clerk. (Pg 190)

In obedience to an order of court dated 10 May 1742 we Richd Hull, Edward
Rogers & Jos Lancaster have mett & appraised the estate of John Wilkins decd
in money. Beds, bedsteads & furniture, parcel of earthenware, 2 broad hows, 4
old axes, 4 wedges, 1 old saddle & bridle, 1 new bridle, 2 chests, 1 old cupboard,
1 old table & trunk & box, 1 good blanket, linnen, 4 felt hats, 1 fine hat, a bunch

of tape, 3 butchers knives, 1 pr womens shoes, 1 lb pouder, 6 lbs shot, 4 lbs
bullets, 1 sword & cartouch box, 1 old gun, 8 chairs, 17 bottles, some oyl, 1
funnel, a pocket bottle, 1 box iron & heaters ... [illegible] ... 1 pot rack, 4 pare
pot hooks, 7 lbs new feathers, etc. This inventory was exhibited 14 Jun 1742 by
Jane Wilkins adminr & on her motion admitted to record. Attest: James
Fontaine clerk. [Not totaled]

[Page numbers illegible]

Pursuant to an order of court we William Garner, Pemberton Claughton & John
West have met & appraised the estate of Mary Bell decd. 1 old saddle, lumber,
1 old sow, 3 shoats, 6 ewes, 5 lambs, 1 spinning wheel, iron wedges, 1 pare of
stillards, 1 sword & belt, 1 mare, 2 beds, 1 spitt, 2 old iron pots, 1 frying pan, 1
iron pot & hooks, 1 salter, 2 bed cords, 2 old boxes, 1 chest, parcel of old books,
1 old coat, 2 gounes, 1 pare shoes & trifles, 1 cow bell, fire tongs, 1 old gun, 2
cows big with calf, 2 yearlings, 1 young horse, 1 tub & pigin, old paile, 5 old
chairs, 1 old table & bench, etc. [Not totaled] This inventory was exhibited 14
Jun 1742 by Francis Self adminr on whose motion the same is admitted to
record. Attest: James Fontaine clerk.

In obedience to an order of court dated 10 May 1742 we John Kennedy, James
Farned & Lewis Lamkin mett at the house of Thomas Robertson & appraised the
estate of Richd Northcut decd to a parcel of old cloaths & 1 how 15 pd, tobacco
715 weight. This inventory was exhibited 14 Jun 1742 by Thomas Robertson
adminr & admitted to record. Attest: James Fontaine clerk.

Deed. ... [illegible] ... doth sell to the sd William Hughlet a messuage & 268 a.
tr of land in the parish afsd bounded by land formerly Richard Thompson's, land
formerly Hennery Massey's now John Lewis's & Claughtons Cr ... . Wit: John
Lewis, Parish Garner, Robt Clark Junr, Wm Taylor. Ackn 12 Jul 1742 by
Rodham Kenner unto William Hughlett & Susanna Kinner w/o the sd Kenner
being privately examined by John Foushee gent relinquished her right of dower
in ye lands & admitted to record. Attest: James Fontaine clerk.

6 Jan 1741. Deed. William Hughlet of St. Stephens Parish, Northumberland Co
for 50 pd sold to Morris Gibbons of same co ... [illegible] ... to the head of the
river adj Thomas Hughlet formerly the land of Ephraim Hughlet, Richard D[?],
Robert Alexander, land now held by Cavan Dulany formerly held by Richard
Smith, land formerly held by William Humphrys now held by John Humphrys
containing 150 a. which sd tr of land was devised to the sd Wm Hughlet by the
will of William Hughlet dated 28 Jun 1716 & is pt/o a pattent of land granted to
John Hughlet for [blank] a. ... . Wit: William Thomas, Moses Oldham, George
Oldham. Ackn 12 Jul 1742 by William Hughlet & Mary his wife she being

privately examined by John Foushee gent relinquished her right of dower & admitted to record. Attest: James Fontaine clerk.

20 Feb 1741. Deed. John Lewis of Northumberland Co gent & Mary his wife for 4 pd sold to John Kennedy of same co gent a 1 a. parcel of land & an old mill & the dam that belongs to the sd mill adj to the sd parcel of land the afsd mill formerly held & kept by the sd John ... [illegible] ... . Wit: Rodham Kenner, Edward Mason, David Straughan, Richd Booth. Ackn [?] by John & Mary Lewis the sd Mary being privately examined by John Foushee gent relinquished her right of dower & admitted to record. Attest: James Fontaine clerk.

Will. William Willdy of St. Stephens Parish, Northumberland Co. 11 Apr 1742. I give my land whereon I now live being near 500 a. to be divided between my four daus Jane, Sinah?, Hannah & Leanna, & all my slaves & personal estate to be delivered to them at the age of 21 or the day of marriage. I leave my wife & Elles Gill my executors. Wit: James Adair, George Kesterson, Thomas Gill, John Robinson, Elles Gill. Proved 12 Jul 1742 by the oaths of James Adair & John Robinson wits thereto & Winifrid Wildly & Elles Gill executors made oath to ye sd will on whose motion the same is admitted to record. Attest: James Fontaine clerk. (Pg 194)

In obedience to an order of court dated 13 8br 1740 we William Taite, John Lewis, Parish Garner & Lindsey Opie did meet at the late dwelling house of John Keen (Keene) decd & after being sworn before John Waughop gent justice of the peace did proceed to value & appraise the estate of the sd John Keene decd in money. Beds, bolsters, pillows, sheets, bedsteads, quilt, blanket, rug ... [illegible] ... 1 large table, 1 old trunk, 16 tubs & casks, 6 bushels salt, 12 cider cask, 46 pare Negro shoes, 1 saddle & bridle, 1 looking glass, parsel of old books, etc. Negroes: Harry, James, Kesler, Kate, Sara, Hannah, Juda, Boson, Jesse, Sharper?, Moll, Robin, Wh[?], young Bob, old Harry, Banjo Harvy, Philian, Phillis, Mor[?], Doll, Charity, Barbell, Suckey, George, Dick. Sterling money in England: James Bochannan in London, Neale Bochannan in London, George Buck in Biddeford, Robt Beveridge in Lime, John & Richd Tucker in Waymouth, Andrew Ramsey in Glasgow. [Not totaled] This inventory was exhibited by Edward Wiatt & Edgcomb Sugget executors on whose motion the same is admitted to record. Attest: James Fontaine clerk. (Pg 194)

... [illegible] ... earthen pan, 1 old earthen pot, 1 qt bottle, 1 old bench, briches, shirt, 1 pare buckles. John Hack adminr ... [illegible] ... .

... [illegible] ... paid Swanson Pritchard, William Fallin, John Davis, Doctor [?] Thornton, Doctor [?] Taylor, [?] Dodson, Richd Hudnall, Wm [?], Thomas Edwards, Wm Eustace, Isaac Bane for a coffin, Wm Barret, Wm Jones on acct of the estate of Charles Jones decd. 5810 ½ lbs tobacco. Balance due the estate of Capt Leonard Hanson 621 lbs of tobacco. Received sums of Abner Neale under sheriff, Wm Hughlet under sheriff, Moses Champion, John Berry, David Lattimore under sheriff. Total 6421 ½ lbs of tobacco.

The estate of Capt Leonard Howson in cash. Paid David Lattimore, 2 lawsuits Archibald Johnson, Lawrence Parrot, Abner Neale, Col Presly, Mr. Edwards, Capt Eustace, Francis Anberry (Auberry?), Thos Smith. 14 pd 11 sl 9 ½ pn. ... [illegible] ... .

In obedience to an order of court dated 11 Jan 1741/2 it was ordered that we Christopher Garlington, Thos Winter & Wm Garlington should meet & divide the estate of Benjamin Waddy decd & allot James Waddy & Charles Ingram their filial parts of sd estate accordingly we have met & allotted Mrs. Jane Waddy her part being also a filial part which she freely chose of her own accord the amounts of the estate to 346 pd 5 sl 8 pn in goods & chattels first the Negroes is to be divided amongst seven persons who has only a right to them & ye goods & chattels amongst 8 persons the reason of which is that Charles Ingram had his Negroes from Mr. Waddy in his life time therefore Jane Waddy & James Waddy's part is 46 pd 17 sl 5 pn ½ penny cash & Charles Ingram's part is 18 pd 3 sl 6 pn paid them as follows: [?] Waddy's lott: 1 Negro man named Tony, cow, steer, sow, shoat, warming pan, earthen[?] pan 46 pd 17 sl 6 pn. James Waddy's lott: 1 Negro named Will, steer, shott, table, fiddle, desk, sword, pistols & holsters, leather chairs, widling pewter, ewe, young weather. 46 pd 17 sl 6 pn. Charles Ingram's lott: bed, boat? & tailes, cow, steer, sow, shott, sheep, case books, brass kettle, large table, old Bible, box iron & heaters. 18 pd 3 sl 4 pn. This report was exhibited 12 Jul 1742 by the auditors & recorded. Attest: James Fontaine clerk.

In obedience to an order of court dated 14 Jun 1742 on ye prayer of Elizabeth Lee orphan of Charles Lee gent decd for her pt/o her decd father's estate in the hands of Mrs. Elizabeth Brent her guardian we Thomas Winter, Henry Miller & John Waddey have met & set apart her pt/o her decd father's estate. Negroes: Toney, Robbin, [?] & her child, Nell. Bed, bolster, pillows, rug, blanket, pare sheets, a parcel of old goon?, 1 old chair, 2 new chairs, 1 large bull, 1 60 gallon cask, 2 rundlets, 1 horse Star, 4 lbs 3 penny wt old silver, 1 large pot, 1 pare hooks, 2 dictionarys, her pt/o sheep, 6 new flat plates, 3 cows, 1 calf, 3 young heifers, 1 young stear, 1 yearling, part of ye hogs. 99 pd 4 sl 4 ½ pn. This report & division was returned 12 Jul 1742 y the auditors & recorded. Attest: James Fontaine clerk.

In obedience to an order of court dated 12 Apr 1742 we the subscribers did meet on the land mentioned in the sd order & did divide the sd land in four parts & did allot unto the persons mentioned in the sd order their parts as follows:

William Edwards & Mary Gaskins & Jane Wilkins had the two n lotts
containing the swamp with some pt/o the upper part of the plantation & also the
w part of the plantation including … [illegible] … .

5 Jul 1742. In pursuance to an order of court dated 18 Jun 1742 John Hack, Wm
Betts & Elles Gill mett at the house of [?] & have carefully perused & examined
the acct [?] & find the def Absolom Williams indebted to the estate of William
Parker the sum of 13 pd 2 sl 1 penny & no more. This report was exhibited 12
Jul 1742 by the auditors & recorded. Attest: James Fontaine clerk.

6 Jul 1742. In pursuance to an order of court dated 13 Apr 1742 we Wm Taite,
Parish Garner & Wm Taylor met at the plantation belonging to the orphans of
James Straughan decd & after perusing all the accts [?] to us as likewise the
inventory paid Thomas Fallin? his part. This report was exhibited 12 Jul 1742
by the auditors & recorded. Attest: James Fontaine clerk.
7 Apr 1742. Deed. John Bearcroft of St. Stephens Parish, Northumberland Co
for (140 a. of land on n side of Wicocomoco to the sd John Bearcroft from [?]
Downing?) sold to Saml Nelms Junr of same place a 194 a. tr of land in
Mattapony in the afsd parish which was formerly called William Hill's pattent
being bounded by Anthony Linton, Broad Cr, Yocomoco River & the line
dividing this from the residue of the afsd Wm Hill's pattent which after was
made with the mutual consent of both partys the sd Wm Hill & Saml Churchwell
by vertue of a deed made by the sd William Hill to Saml Churchwell dated 12
Jun 1679 … . Wit: Wm Harding, John Harper. Ackn 9 Aug 1742 & admitted
to record. Attest: James Fontaine clerk.

Deed. … [illegible] … Malachi Burberry sold to Thos Yerby 100 a. of land
Wit: Dale Carter, David Fluker, Minthon Morgan. Ackn 9 Aug 1742 &
admitted to record. Attest: James Fontaine clerk.

9 Aug 1742. Bond. I Malachi Burberry of Wicocomoco Parish,
Northumberland Co am firmly bound unto Thos Yerby of Christ Church Parish,
Lancaster Co for 100 pd … the condition of this obligation is such that whereas
the afsd Malachi Burberry hath by a deed of sale dated this date sold &
conveyed unto the afsd Thos Yerby a 100 a. parcel of land in Wicocomoco
Parish, now if the sd Malchi Burberry shall save harmless & keep in the
peaceable & quiet possession of the afsd 100 a. of land the afsd Thos Yerby
without the molestation or disturbance of him the sd Malachi Burberry or any
person then this obligation to be void … . Wit: Dale Carter, David Fluker,
Minthon Morgin. Ackn 9 Aug 1742 & admitted to record. Attest: James
Fontaine clerk.

9 Aug 1742. Deed. Saml Downing of St. Stephens Parish, Northumberland Co

for 10 pd sold to Saml Blackwell of same parish a 30 a. tr of land ... [illegible] ...
. Wit: John Mayes, James Waller, John Sullivan. Ackn 9 Aug 1742 & admitted
to record. Attest: James Fontaine clerk.

9 Aug 1742. Bond. I Saml Nelms Junr of Northumberland Co am firmly bound
unto Saml Blackwell of same co for 20 pd ... the condition of this obligation is
such that whereas Samuel Downing by deed of feoffment with livery seizin
dated with these presents hath made over & conveyed to the sd Saml Blackwell
30 a. of land in St. Stephens Parish which land the sd Saml Downing had lately
conveyed & made over to him by the sd Saml Nelms Junr the title of which the
sd Saml Nelms Junr agrees to warrant unto him the sd Saml Blackwell, if the sd
Saml Nelms Junr shall save, defend & indemnify & keep harmless the sd Saml
Blackwell & to the quiet & peaceable possession & occupation of the afsd 30 a.
of land & premises & that free & clear & freely & clearly exonerate acquited &
discharged from any manner of incumbrances whatsoever then this obligation to
be void ... . Wit: John Ladford, John Nutt, Joseph Nutt. Ackn 9 Aug 1742 &
admitted to record. Attest: James Fontaine clerk.

... [illegible] ... Wit: Aron Nelms, Phenly Morrison. Memorandum that quiet &
peaceable possession of the within land & premises was this day given &
delivered by the within named Saml Downing unto the within named John
Bearcroft by the delivery of turf & twig upon pt/o the land. Ackn 9 Aug 1742
by Saml Downing unto John Bearcroft on whose motion the same is admitted to
record. Attest: James Fontaine clerk.

In obedience to an order of court dated 12 Jul 1742 we James Farned, Richd
Booth & Ormsby Haynie were sworn by John Foushee justice & then met at the
house of Elizabeth Tullos & there appraised all the goods & chattels of John
Tullos decd that was presented to our view in money. 3 cows & calves, 2 stears,
2 heiffers, 7 sheep, 1 mare, saddle & bridle, beds & furniture, set of shoemakers
tools, spinning wheel, parcel of wool cards, 1 gun & sword, cartouch box &
powder, ball & shot, 2 deer skins, 1 razor & hone, 2 chests, parcel of carpenters
tools, 1 table, 3 boxes, 2 chests, 2 cuting knives, doz bottles, 14 lbs of wool, 7
lbs of good peuter, 16 lbs of old peuter, cotton, 33 lbs of old iron ... [illegible] ...
parcel of old books, country cloth, parcel of lumber, etc. [Not totaled] This
inventory was exhibited 9 Aug 1742 & admitted to record. Attest: James
Fontaine clerk.

In obedience to an order of court dated 12 Jul 1742 we Richd Smith, Abner
Neale & George Berry did meet at the house of William Wildy decd & being
first sworn before Saml Blackwell did appraise the sd decd's estate in money. 11
sheep, 3 barrows, 11 hogs, 3 stears, 3 heiffers, 9 cows & calves, 1 mare & colt,
10 gees, 1 old silver tankard, 2 old table cloths, 1 meale sifter, 2 meale bags,

beds, rug, blankets, bolsters, sheets, bedsteads, hides, cords, 1 camelot coat & breeches, pare shoes, buckles, 1 pare wosted stockins, old yarn, 1 old coat, etc. Negroes: man Tom, man Lindsey, wench Sarah, wench Kate, girl Hannah, girl Nan, boy James, child Grace, boy Robin, girl Judy, child Dick. [Not totaled] This inventory was exhibited 9 Aug 1742 by Winifrid Wildy & Elles Gill executors & on their motion the same is admitted to record. Attest: James Fontaine clerk.

The estate of Joseph Sullivan appraised. 1 mare & colt, 4 1/2 yds of half broads, 5 yds of shaloon, triming for a coat, 2 bed ticks, 6 yds of bolster tickin, 1 coat jacket & breeches, 1 Holland jacket & breeches, some fine cloth, 1 razor, 1 pare of stockins, 1 wig, sadlecoth, bridle, 1 old gun, 1 rundlet & snuf box, 1 large chest, 1 pen knife, pare of gloves, his crop of tobacco, his crop of corn 17 barrils. [Not totaled] Robt Robuck, Saml Mahanes, Daniel Gaines. This inventory was exhibited 9 Aug 1742 by Cornelius Sullivan adminr & on his motion admitted to record. Attest: James Fontaine clerk.

12 Mar 1732. ... [illegible] ... Peter Hack hath sent one Negro named Stephen ... [illegible] ... . Wit: James McGoune, John Shapleigh. This [?] was exhibited 9 Aug 1742 by John Tunstal gent & on his request proved by the oath of James McGoune the only surviving wit to the same & was recorded & certified. Attest: James Fontaine clerk.

In obedience to an order of court dated 12 Jul 1742 we William Haynie, Silvester Welsh & Richd Cornish did meet & being first sworn before Peter Presly esqr did appraise the estate of Presly & Susanna Cockrill orphans of Presly Cockrill decd in money & delivered it unto Charles Betts Junr guardian to the sd orphans. 1 good iron pot & hook, 1 old broad ax, 1 iron pestle, 3 old hows, 1 good half broad hoe, 1 old chest, 1 old cider cask, 1 cow & yearling, 1 good heiffer, 1 steer, 4 sows, pare of pocket stillards, 5 sheep, a spinning wheel, iron spindle, box with iron, wearing cloths, etc. Negroes: woman Judy, girl Rose, girl Jean?, child Susanna, woman Jane. [Not totaled] This report was exhibited 9 Aug 1742 by the auditors & recorded. Attest: James Fontaine clerk.

In obedience to an order of court held 12 Jul 1742 John Pinkard has taken his wifes pt/o the estate of Thomas Gaskins gent decd out of the hands of Thomas Gaskins son of the afsd Thomas Gaskins decd by the consent of Richard Hull. This report was returned 9 Aug 1742 by John Pinkard & recorded. Attest: James Fontaine clerk.

The estate of John Anderson decd: sums paid Wm Ball, James Shraitkil?, Mary Anderson. Sums received from Wm Betts. 17 pd 7 sl 5 pn. Spencer Ball gent exhibited the within acct of his administration of the estate of John Anderson decd 7 Aug 1742 & made oath to ye same which was allowed & recorded. Attest: James Fontaine clerk.

17 Aug 1742. In obedience to an order of court dated 12 Jul 1742 we Griffin Fantleroy, John Cralle & Robt Clark have been upon the land of Wm Metcalf decd & find one parcel of land called Kingsah being in Westmoreland Co to be worth 530 lbs of tobacco per year, another parcel in the sd co where Wm East has a quarter value 500 lbs of tobacco per year & where Wm Taite lives in Cherry Point at 1,000 lbs of tobacco per year all being two 2,030 lbs of tobacco per year & we allot John Graham's part being 1/3 of the sd lands comes to 676 lbs of tobacco & the 1/3 pt/o 2 lbs of tobacco his part. This report & division was exhibited 9 Aug 1742 by the auditors & recorded. Attest: James Fontaine clerk.

... [first one on page illegible] ...

In obedience to an order of court dated 12 Jul 1742 we John Corbell, Wm Nelms & Joseph Lancaster being appointed by the court have met at the house of Absolom Williams & appraised the part for the widow Parker pursuant to the sd order at 13 pd 2 sl 1 penny. 34 ½ lbs of peuter, 33 lbs old iron, 3 glas bottles, 1 cros leged table, 2 stock locks, 1 wooden chair, 5 flag chairs, 1 old saddle, 3 iron wedges, 1 old plow, 1 carpenters adz, 3 hides of leather, 1 feather bed, 1 rug, 2 blankets, 2 sheets, bedstead, hide, cord, 1 iron pot, 2 cows & yearlings, 1 stear, 2 knives & forks. 13 pd 2 sl 6 pn. This report between Absolom Williams & Mary Parker was exhibited into court 9 Aug 1742 by the auditors & recorded. Attest: James Fontaine clerk.

11 Feb MDCCXXII. Deed. Henry Gaskins & Mary his wife, William Edwards the younger & Jane Wilkins of St. Stephens Parish, Northumberland Co for 6,500 lbs of tobacco sold to Peter Presly gent of same place a 95 a. tr of land in the sd parish formerly the land & plantation of Ralph Warrington decd which descended & came to the sd Henry Gaskins & Mary his wife, Wm Edwards the younger & Jane Wilkins from the sd Ralph Warrington, bounded by a cr of Little Wicocomoco River, Giles Webb, Motly Wildy, Thomas Edwards, Francis Beatly, the orphans of John Edwards & the orphans of John Paine ... . Wit: James Daughity, Wm Wilkins, Emanuel Walker. Ackn 13 --- 1742 by Henry Gaskins & Mary his wife, William Edwards Junr & Jane Wilkins & Mary Gaskins w/o the sd Henry Gaskins being privately examined by John Foushee gent relinquished her right of dower & admitted to record. Ackn Attest: James Fontaine clerk.

-- Aug 1742. Bond. Where as there have been severall lawsuits & controversys subsisting between the subscribers of & concerning a certain warranty for land passed by John Foushee to one John Book who assigned the same to George Brown & whereas both partys are now willing amicably to put an end to all the controversys concerning the sd land. Be it know to all men by these presents that the sd John Foushee & George Brown do by these presents covenant & agree with each other in manner & form following, that the sd John Foushee at the request of the sd George Brown & with a view & desire to clear himself from all incumbrances & trouble attending lawsuits doth covenant, promise & agree to & with the sd George Brown to pay to him by the last of Mar next ensuing 1,000 lbs of tobacco in consideration whereof the sd George Brown doth covenant, promise & agree to & with the sd John Foushee that the sd John Foushee shall forever hereafter be free & clear from any lawsuits & controversys relating to the sd warranty & land from the sd George Brown & it is farther agreed upon between the sd partys that notwithstanding a judgment passed in favour of the sd Foushee for a suit brought by the sd Brown agt him in Northumberland Co court relating to the sd warranty & land he the sd Foushee pays his own charges accrued by the sd lawsuit to the performance of all which premises the partys above bind themselves in the penal sum of [?] pd …. . Wit: Cavan Delany, [?] Didne, [?] Ball. Proved 13 7br 1742 & recorded. (Pg 209)

2 7br 1742. In pursuance to an order of court dated 11 Aug 1742 we John Waughop, John Foushee, Yarret Hughlet & George Conway being appointed to settle & finally determine all matters & things layed before us relating to a judgment of the court dated 11 Aug 1741 between John Donaway petr & Ezekiel Hill, George Eves & Frances his wife adminrs of the estate of Enoch Hill defts we did accordingly meet & do find that there is in the hands of the sd adminrs of the estate of the sd Enoch Hill decd the sum of 23 pd 9 sl 4 pn ½ penny which sum we find the petr hath a just right to & no more. This report was returned 13 7br 1742 & recorded. Attest: James Fontaine clerk. (Pg 209)

Will. Elizabeth Elleston. 24 May 1742. To my son Cuthbert & my dau Elizabeth Elleston my whole estate both personall & reall to be divided between them & further do appoint my brother Richard Haynie my executor. Wit: James Daughity, Hannah Shapleigh. Proved 13 7br 1742 & recorded. Attest: James Fontaine clerk. (Pg 209)

9 Oct 1742. Deed. James Magoune & Marriam his wife of St. Stephens Parish, Northumberland Co planter for 500 lbs of tobacco sold to John Webb of same place planter a messuage & tr of land which he came into possession by the sd James Magoune intermarrying with Marriam widow & relict of Thomas Webb decd by vertue of whose death the sd Marriam had a right in equity to the 1/3 pt/o the sd Thomas Webb's land being 180 a. which sd 1/3 part being suppose to be 60 a. & after the sd Thos Webb's death the sd land being divided by order of this co court & the sd Mariam was put into possession thereof & since

intermarried with James Magoune which sd land is on the s side of Little
Wicocomoco River bounded by the land of the sd Thomas Webb decd, Jacksun
Swamp, land formerly John Webb's, Giles Webb & Beverley Keeve ... during
the natural life of the sd Marriam ... . Wit: Joseph Weldy, Wm Webb, Beverley
Keeve. Ackn 11 8br 1742 by James Magoune & Marriam his wife she being
privately examined by John Foushee gent relinquished her right of dower &
admitted to record. Attest: James Fontaine clerk. (Pg 210)

In obedience to an order of court dated 13 7br 1742 we James Daughity, Abner
Neale & Joseph Lancaster having met at the plantation of Elizabeth Elleston
decd & being first sworn by Saml Blackwell gent have appraised the estate of
the sd Elizabeth Elleston in money. 4 heifers, 1 mare & colt, 2 cows & calf, 1
sow & 4 young pigs, 7 gees, feather beds, bedsteads, rugs, 1 sheet, bolster, cord,
1 old chest, 1 chest lock & key, 1 table cloth, 6 napkins, 1 towel, 1 old barrel,
old box, 6 chairs, 1 croscut saw, 2 raw hides, 3 sides of tannd leather, etc.
Negroes: woman named Sarah, girl named Hannah, boy named Philip, boy
named James, boy named Joe. [Not totaled] This inventory was exhibited 11
8br 1742 by Charles Betts Junr executor [adminr crossed out] with the will
annexed & admitted to record. Attest: James Fontaine clerk. (Pg 210)

In obedience to an order of court dated 14 7br 1742 we Richd Haynie, Benjamin
Haynie & Thos Harding have met & appraised the estate of Thomas Burnet decd
in money. Some old cloaths 10 sl, a hone 10 sl, some tobacco & corn growing 1
pd. This inventory was exhibited 12 8br 1742 by George Ball gent adminr &
admitted to record. Attest: James Fontaine clerk. (Pg 211)

Pursuant to an order of court dated 13 7br 1742 we John Foushee & Yarret
Hughlett being appointed to settle & determine the difference between James
Waller petr & William Short deft we did accordingly meet & do find that the sd
William Short is justly indebted unto the sd James Waller the sum of 13 pd 12 sl
& costs. This report was exhibited 12 8br 1742 by John Foushee gent & Yarret
Hughlet & recorded. Attest: James Fontaine clerk. (Pg 211)

In obedience to an order of court dated 11 May 1742 wherein it was ordered that
we Robt Jones, Thos Berry & Christopher Garlington should meet & settle the
accts of Mrs. Judith Jones decd & allot John Jones infant of Swan Jones decd his
pt/o his fathers estate also his filial pt/o Mrs. Judith Jones' estate both in the
hands of Capt Spencer Ball the same we are ordered to possess Zacharia Taylor
with who has now the care of the sd infant accordingly we have met &
proceeded as here underneath.
    John Jones's pt/o his fathers estate paid in goods & chattels: sum due
for crops from Mrs. Jones' estate, 72 lbs pot iron, 1 pare grid irons, 26 lbs old
brass, 1 frying pan, 24 head of neat cattle, 24 head of sheep, 22 ½ lbs good

midling pewter, 3 ½ lbs new pewter, 1 close stool pan, 7 sides tannd leather, 2 pare pot hooks, 1 great basket, 1 oval table, 1 form, 1 old chest, quilting frame, 1 old large tub, etc. 69 pd 19 sl 3 ½ pn. John Jones overpaid 3 pd. (Pg 211)

    ... [illegible] ... pt/o Mrs. Jones' estate: ... [illegible] ... parcel of books, [?] which Swan Jones had of his mother, [?] of ye Negroes, pare fire tongs, 1 pot iron, 5 pans, 1 broad & 1 narrow hoe, etc.

    Capt Spencer Ball's pt/o Mrs. Jones' estate which amounts to 55 pd 3 pn: 1 bed & furniture, 1 cold still, 1 driping pan, 2 pot racks, old puter, 1 pestle, 4 doz bottles, 1 spit, 2 spades, a churn, 2 framing chisels, pint pot, 1 large iron wedge, 1 horse, 1 saddle & bridle, 1 coopers nimble, 1 round shave, old chissel, parcel of old table linnen, 2 remnants of VA cloth, his pt/o the Negroes after John Jones is paid 15 pd 9 sl 4 pn for crops as per acct, etc. As Mr. Taylor keeps the Negroes for John Jones he is to pay Mr. Ball his part in cash.

    Whole amount of Mrs. Jones' estate is 179 pd 8 sl 3 pn. This report between Spencer Ball gent & Zachary Taylor gent concerning the estate of Mrs. Judith Jones decd was returned 11 8br 1742 by the auditors & recorded. Attest: James Fontaine clerk.(Pg 212)

In pursuance to an order of court dated 12 Jul 1742 being appointed by the sd court to sell ye estate of Wm Bently decd did on 29 Jul year afsd expose the same to sale at publick outcry & sold it to the several persons hereafter mentioned, to wit: George Ball Junr, Wm Lunsford, Wm Dameron, Ann Harrison, Andrew Chilton, James Waddy, Wm Barret, Charles Dameron, Onesiphorus Dameron, John Porter, Moses James, Joshua James. David Lattimore sheriff.

    A true & perfect inventory of the estate of Wm Bently decd taken 29 Jul 1742: 1 old horse, 8 gees, 1 razor, 1 set of iron wedges, a parsel of old foose?, 2 old beds & some feathers, 1 basket, a parsel of old puter, 1 earthen pot, 1 old box, 1 drinking glass, 8 old chairs, 1 table, 1 iron pestle, 2 iron pots, 1 old spining wheel, 1 old table, 3 stools, 8 bottles, old lumber, 2 chairs, 1 handsaw & frow, 3 cows, 1 ewe. David Lattimore sheriff.

    This inventory & sale of the estate of William Bently decd was returned to court 12 8br 1742 by the sheriff & recorded. Attest: James Fontaine clerk. (Pg 212)

... [illegible] ... between the sd Philip Smith ... 148 a. where the sd Hannah Shapleigh now dwells also his title & estate in 180 a. of land in St. Stephens Parish, part whereof was given by the will of Ralph Warrington decd to Philip Shapleigh gent father of the sd Hannah Shapleigh & the other part granted to the sd Philip Shapleigh by deed from the proprietors office, 23 Negro slaves namely Will, Tom, Bennedict, Dick, Frank, Mark, Peter, Abraham, Jacob, George, Ned, Isaac, Nanny, Rose, Beck, Lucy, James, Doll, Grace, Judith, Sarah, Winny & Letty, & also all the stocks of horses, mares, cattle, sheep, hogs or any other kind

& the utenciles & household furniture & other estate of the sd Hannah
Shapleigh. Now it is covenanted, concluded & agreed by & between the sd
partys & the sd Philip Smith doth covenant, conclude, grant & agree that the
afsd estate belonging to the afsd Hannah Shapleigh when the sd marriage shall
be had & solemnized shall be remain to the [?] of him & the sd Hannah during
their sd intermarriage & from thence or thereafter is the use of the issue of the sd
Philip & Hannah if any such & for want of such issue to the use & purpose
mentioned & comprised in the will of the sd Hannah, & the sd Philip Smith doth
further covenant, grant, conclude & agree that after the sd marriage between the
sd Philip & Hannah he the sd Philip will quietly permit & suffer the sd Hannah
(if she fortune to decease before the sd Philip without issue living) to declare &
make her will in writing & in the same to give, will & bequeath or otherwise to
assign & dispose of at her free will & pleasure to & amongst her kindred, friends
& acquaintance or to any of them or to any other person as to her shall be
thought convenient all or any pt/o the afsd estate as she shall think fit & further
that he the sd Philip Smith upon reasonable request to him will well & truly pay
or cause to be paid all & every of the sd legacys, bequests, gifts & requests to be
given & bequeathed by the sd Hannah & in such manner as shall be by her
appointed ... & after the marriage the sd Hannah Shapleigh doth covenant, grant
& agree that if after the sd marriage shall take effect (the fortunes to survive the
sd Philip Smith) she will be content with & receive & take her afsd estate in full
for her challenges, claim & demand (of) dower or portion of the estate of the sd
Philip other than what legacy he shall think fit to bequeath her in his will & doth
agree to remit, release & quit all claim & demand whatsoever which she may,
might, should or of right ought to have in or to all or any of the lands or other
estate of the sd Philip Smith for or by reason of her dower or any other right,
title or means whatsoever ... . Wit: Richard Kenner, Ephraim Waller, Thos
Edwards. Proved 9 9br 1742 & also ackn in open court by the sd Hannah to be
her act & deed & admitted to record. Attest: James Fontaine clerk. (Pg 213)

XVI Sep MDCCXLII. Bond. I Philip Smith of Wicocomoco Parish,
Northumberland Co gent am firmly bound to Thomas Edwards of Christ Church
Parish, Lancaster Co gent for 2,000 pd ... the condition of this obligation is such
that if the afsd Philip Smith shall well & truly fulfill, perform, accomplish &
keep all & singular the articles, covenants, clauses, conclusions & agreements
mentioned & comprised in an indenture of articles of agreement [see above]
between the sd Philip Smith & Hannah Shapleigh then this obligation to be voyd
... . Wit: Joshua Nelson, Richd Kenner, Ephraim Waller. Proved 9 9br 1742 &
admitted to record. Attest: James Fontaine clerk. (Pg 214)

6 Nov 1742. Deed. Yarret Hughlet of St. Stephens Parish, Northumberland Co
for 10 pd sold to John Webb of same place a 200 a. tr of land in the parish afsd
at the head of Coan River on the se side of Coan Mill the land being pt/o a patent

118

granted to Richd Eaton & Adam Yarret dated 1662, bounded by the land of Capt John Hack which was formerly Capt Motram's, land of Francis Eves called Gaines, Coan Mill Swamp, Cabbin Br & Yarret Hughlet's line which was formerly Capt John Motrom's … . Wit: Wm Cooke, Enoch Hill, Morris Gibons. Ackn 8 9br 1742& admitted to record. Attest: James Fontaine clerk. (Pg 214)

8 Nov 1742. Deed. Saml Downing of St. Stephens Parish, Northumberland Co for 2,000 lbs of tobacco sold to William Trussel of same place a 40 a. tr of land on the n side of Great Wicocomoco River bounded by Saml Downing's Mill & a cr formerly called Moses Nelms' Cr … . Wit: Peter Lewis, James Lewis. Ackn 8 9br 1742 & admitted to record. Attest: James Fontaine clerk. (Pg 215)

8 9br 1742. Deed. Daniel Gaines of Wicocomoco Parish, Northumberland Co planter for 170 pd sold to Saml Mahane of same parish planter … [illegible] … . Wit: Francis Timberlake, Dennis Sullivan, Amos Love, Cornelius Sullivan. Peaceable possession & seisen of the sd tr of land & plantation & premises was given by the delivery of turf & twigg. Wit: T. Edwards, James Fontaine. I Sarah Gaines w/o the sd Daniel Gaines do hereby freely & voluntarily release & relinquish all my right of dower of & in the lands unto the within named Saml Mahane. Ackn 8 9br 1742 & admitted to record. Attest: James Fontaine clerk. (Pg 215)

Will. Richard Rice of St. Stephens Parish, Northumberland Co. To my son William the plantation whereon my grandfather formerly lived being pt/o a parcel of land formerly patented by Richd Rice & Thos Adams the sd land is adj to the land of Warrick & the land of Hannah Higgins where Peter Ashburn now lives. To my son George the plantation whereon my father formerly lived bounded by the land that John Rice now lives on. My will is that if my afsd son George should die before he attaines the age of 21 that his land should fall to my son Richard. To my son Richard my now dwelling plantation with all the residue of my land, but if my sd son Richd should die before he attaines to the age of 21 years it is then my desire that his land shall fall to my son George. To my son being now about 3 weeks old & not christened a Negro boy named Harry & if my sd son should die before he attaines to the age of 21 years it is then my desire that the afsd Negro boy should fall into my estate again. It is my will that my wife Elizabeth Rice should have the use of all the rest of my estate during her naturall life or widdowhood & after the decease of my sd wife or marriage I do then give all my afsd estate to be divided between my nine children, viz, Elizabeth, William, Lictery?, Richard, George, Judith, Sarah & my son & dau (twins) that are now about three weeks old & not christened. I appoint my wife Elizabeth Rice & my son William executors. Wit: George Conway, John Routt (Rout). Proved 8 9br 1742 & admitted to record. Attest: James Fontaine clerk.

(Pg 216)

4 9br 1742. In obedience to an order of court dated 11 8br 1742 Argail Taylor,
John Taylor & Edwin Fielding being first sworn by George Ball Senr gent have
appraised the estate of Lazarus Smith: 1 fial & books, 1 pare fire tongs &
shovel, 1 pare of spoon molds, 1 old spining wheel, 1 rundlet, 1 young heiffer, 1
young stear, 1 gun, some trifles. [Not totaled] This inventory of pt/o the estate
of Lazarus Smith of Westmoreland Co lying in this co was exhibited into court
by John Smith executor & on his motion admitted to record. Attest: James
Fontaine clerk.

In obedience to an order of court dated 11 8br 1742 we William Haynie &
Silvester Welsh did meet & settled the accts of the estate of Presly Cockrill
decd: Thomas Hayes & the executors of Wm Wildy decd debts to the sd decd
Cockrill's estate, to what was appraised in the inventory besides Negroes &
stock. To crop of tobacco made in years 1735-1741. To Indian corn Hayes had
23 bushels. ... [illegible] ... Sums paid Thos Hayes, executors of William
Wildy decd, Charles Betts Junr guardian to Sarah & Presly Cockrill orphans of
Presly Cockrill decd, Willoughby Cockril's widdow for nursing, the orphans as
was allowed her by Charles Fallin & Richard Smith, finding the boy Presly diet
& clothing & lodging 6 years, the girl the same for 6 years, 2 years schooling the
boy, 1 year schooling the girl, Col Presly for a bushell of salt, Mrs. Fontaine
note, James Daughity judgment, Mr. Fignor judgment, George Curtis, Sarah
Fogg judgment, Wm Betts Junr judgment, Wm Hill, James Thralkill, Mr. Neale,
Mr. Hudnall, Mr. Moorhead for carting tobacco, Sarah Wilkins midwife 2 times,
Joshua Nelms, Janey Welsh wages, John Condoe, Mr. Welsh. 67 pd 12 sl 9 ½
pn. This report & settlement of the estate of the orphans of Presly Cockrill decd
was returned by Wm Haynie & Silvester Welsh & recorded. Attest: James
Fontaine clerk.

Pursuant to an order of court dated ... [illegible] ... acre of land more for the ...
division where the house & Mr. John ... to make the division of equal value ...
clearly appear by the plat given ... is guardian to & in behalf of the orphan ... &
John Kennedy in behalf of Sarah Dollings ... on the 8th day of this instant on the
sd land & mutually agreed without [?] viz Col Presly in behalf of the sd orphan
to taken the lower division where the houses now stand & Mr. Kennedy on
behalf of Sarah Dollins made choice of the upper part or division & we put them
in possession of their several parts accordingly given under our hands 8 9 br
1742. Spencer Ball, Matthew Quill, Traves Colston, John Foushee. This report
& division of the lands of Richard Fullor decd was returned into court by the
auditors & recorded. Attest: James Fontaine clerk.

At a court held 8 Nov 1742 Thomas Dameron, Yaret Hughlet & John

120

Christopher appointed to appraise the estate of Richard Rice decd in obedience have met & were first sworn before Mr. Quil & appraised as follows: 1 Negro woman, 1 Negro man, 1 Negro boy, 1 Negro boy, 1 Negro girl, 1 Negro child. 58 lbs of pot iron & pot hook, 27 of indefrant pot iron & 2 hooks, 48 lbs of good pewter, 42 lbs of sorry pewter, 2 iron spits, 1 frying pan, 6 cows with calf, 3 cows & calves, 37 heifers, 8 sheep, 1 large horse, feather beds, boulsters, pillows, rugs, blanketts, bedsteads, cord, hides, 2 guns, gun rod, 1 sadle & bridle, 1 case of pistol, holsters, 2 swords & catoch box, etc. [Not totaled] This inventory was exhibited 10 --- 1742 by Elizabeth Rice executor & admitted to record. Attest: James Fontaine clerk.

25 Jan 1741. Bond. I William Ball of St. Stephens Parish, Northumberland Co gent am firmly bound unto Rodham Kenner of same place gent for 1500 pd ... whereas there is a marriage intended to be solemnized between the afsd William Ball & Hannah Kenner by the special consent of Rodham Kenner brother & guardian of the sd Hannah now the condition of this obligation is such that in case the sd William Ball should die without issue from the sd Hannah Kenner that then the sd Hannah shall be entitled to & have an absolute property in the whole estate she brought to the sd William Ball together with the increase of the same & also the use & right of 1/3 pt/o the sd William Ball's lands during her natural life all which is hereby declared to be in lieu & full satisfaction of her dower & in case that the sd Hannah Kenner shall die without issue in the lifetime of the sd William Ball then in that case the sd William Ball shall have the use & benefit of the whole estate with the increase of the sd Hannah during his natural life & after his death it is hereby declared that the sd estate shall revert & go to the above named Rodham Kenner & his heirs & if it should so happen that the sd Hannah dies leaving issue & that issue dies before attaining to the age of 21 then the sd estate shall go as before with the sd Rodham & his heirs. Wit: Matthew Quill, John Waughop, Richard Hull, Lindsy Opie. This bond was exhibited 10 Jan 1742/3 by Rodham Kenner gent & on his motion recorded & certified. Attest: James Fontaine clerk.

Will. Thomas Wornom. 28 Dec 1741. To my wife Jean Wornom all my lands on the mouth of Potomac River in Northumberland Co to her & her heirs forever. To Nathan Hudnall one feather bed & furniture, one horse colt named Derie to be given at or when my wife shall think fit to deliver the same. Further more I leave the sd Nathan Hudnall fully possessed with his plantations & lands at 14 years of age. To my wife Jean Wornom all my moveable estate during widdowhood & if the sd ... [illegible] ... . Wit: Abner Neal (Neale), Ann Curtice. Proved 10 Jan 1743/3 & admitted to record. Attest: James Fontaine clerk.

Winnefred Rider decd. Debits: [?], 1 caddo, 1 pare shoes, 1 pare of hoes, credit to Mr. Quill, making a coffin, ½ gall brandy, sugar, sheet?, gallon molasses. 433 lbs tobacco. Credit: George Conway 550 lbs tobacco. Due to balance: 117 lbs tobacco. Errors excepted per James Lewis. 13 7br 1742 this acct of the guardianship of Winafred Rider decd was returned by James Lewis her guardian & recorded. Attest: James Fontaine clerk.

May 1742. Debits: 2 yds Ell silk?, 1 pr womans silk shoes, 1 pr stays, 1 womans laced hatt, 1 fran?, 2 yds muslin, a gloun?, Irish Holland, 1 pr womans stockins, blue thread, 5 yds linen, thread & cotton laces, thread stockings, ribbon brocaded. 4 pd 13 sl 1 pn. Credit: by tobacco 827 lbs. Errors excepted per Richard Jackson. To order guarding Jane Lewis. To order guarding John, Peter & Hannah Lamkin. This account of the guardianship of Jane Lewis & John, Peter & Hannah Lamkin was returned to the court 11 Oct 1742 by Jane Lamkin their guardian & recorded. Attest: James Fontaine clerk.

Debits: 1 covering, 32 foot tobacco house, finding boards & nails, covering a 20 foot dwelling house, keeping Bradshaw Bradley from 24 Oct 1739 to 13 Apr following & finding him a vest & britches, pair of shoes & stockings & shirts, burying of Bradshaw Bradley, quit rents of Bradley's land, paid sum to Mr. Dulany 15 sl. 1721 lbs tobacco. ... [illegible] ... pt/o a plantation of James Bradley's 1738-174. 1700 lbs tobacco. Due to balance 78 lbs tobacco. Errors excepted per Thomas Myars. This acct of the guardianship of James Bradley was returned to court 11 8br 1742 by Thomas Myars his guardian & recorded. Attest: James Fontaine clerk.

1740 Debits: ozinbrigs?, [?], 2 cadoes, 8 yds of Negroes cotton, 1 bushell of salt, 1 calling? Joe, order of court, ribbon, garls gloves, 10 pr callico, garland, wide chex, 2 slips of white & brown, pins. 4 pd 15 sl 9 pn. Credits: crop made by George Gibson, her pt/o the crop, her estate sold by way of outcry, some cattle not sould 3 cows, 2 heifers, 3 calves. 1314 ½ lbs tobacco. This acct of guardianship of Mary Waddy was exhibited 8 9br 1742 by John Waddy her guardian which is ordered to be certified. Attest: James Fontaine clerk.

Debits: 1738: cotton for Negroes, Irish Holland, thread, 5 7/8 yds tartin, pins?, 10 yds of playd, 1 felt hatt, mans cloath, mozlin, garlic, pins, [?] spread, 4 yds cloath, [?], hat & band, womans white washt gloves, lineing for Negroes, roles, chex, 1 pare shoes, credit to Ann Harrison for bringing a Negro wench to bed. 1740: 1 ax, 1 handkerchief, 1 oz of thread, pare of fine shoes, 1 yd of portion, Irish linnen, Holland, chex, course linnen, thread stockins, thread, silk lace, striped Holland, plad, muzlin. 1741: course linnen, fine linnen, Irish linnen, 1 basket of salt, fine ribbon, course linen for Negroes, chex cotton 1 pare of shoes, cotton for Negroes, callico, thread. Sundry goods Robert Osbourn took up for Jemima Waddy, John Eustace's store, linen, pins, thread, tape, chex, silk lace,

122

etc. 32 pd 14 sl 20 pn. ... [illegible] ... . Errors excepted by John Waddy. This account of the guardianship of Jemima Waddey was exhibited 8 9br 1742 by John Waddy her guardian & is ordered to be certified. Attest: James Fontaine clerk.

Debits: 1740-1742: bobs had from my wife's coat, feathers put in your bed, replacing? the house where Mr. Jones was guardian, meat when you all lived together, your levies & quit rents, George Warwick for 2 hoes, Simon Pritchard for smiths work, Ann Barnet for laying 2 Negro wenches, rum & sugar for Negro Judy, leavies by desire of Mr. Pope, Jos Nut for 8 leavies, quit rents of 400 a. of land, the clerk for registering 2 children, John Coleman's crop of tobacco, James Gordon for goods, Thomas Berry for goods, John Eustace for linnen, Coleman's share of tobacco, Wm Hunt for VA cloth, Wm Sears for shoes, lace at York, Henry Young for goods, Jno Hammond for smiths work, Wm James for 6 pair of shoes, sheriff for leavies & quit rent, Thomas Berry for goods, your board for a year, 3 pr Negroes shoes, John Webb for [?], 1 pr stockins, gloves, Ann Benet for laying Negro wenches, James Gordon for goods. 7 pd 6 sl 7 ½ pn. 6722 lbs tobacco. Credit: crop of tobacco made per Jno Coleman. 2864 lbs tobacco. Cash her part from Thos Gill 5 pd, cash ¼ of a mill sold 3 pd 12 sl 9 pn. From Jean Waddey for 8 barrels of corn, rent from Jno Hammond, tobacco MD for 2 years rent sold, corn. 10 pd 17 sl 3 pn. This acct of the guardianship of Mrs. Judith Heath was returned to the court 11 7br 1742 by Henry Miller her guardian & recorded. Attest: James Fontaine clerk.

The estate of Thomas Bonum. Sums paid to Alexander Anderson for making britches, Capt Richard Pearcey, Travers Colston, John Fowshee church warden, William Taite for making shoes, James Daughitey, Matthew Quell, Christopher Neele for your pt/o a runaway Negro, Spencer Corbell for schooling you, Alexr Anderson for tailoring, Thos Toben for finishing the crop, horse bought for you of Sam Bonum, saddle & bridle, your Negro child allowance & 2 barrels corn, your mother for 2 hhds, your bord with me, John Littrel for dressing a dear skin ... [illegible] ... acct Marget Stranghan ... . 5348 lbs tobacco. Received sums for hire of one Negro man to Wm Taylor, hire of Negro woman to James Booth, 4864 lbs tobacco. Balance 484 lbs tobacco. Errors excepted per Lindsy Opie. Tobacco inspected for Mrs. Elizabeth Stranghan. Lindsey Opie guardian of Thomas Bonum returned this acct of his guardianship to court 13 7br 1742 which was recorded. Attest: James Fontaine clerk.

11 Feb 1742. Deed. John Webb of St. Stephens Parish, Northumberland Co planter for 10 pd & 2 young Negroes 4' in height sold to Griffin Fauntleroy Junr of same parish a 2 a. parcel of land with a mill & dam with all manner of runing gere & also all manner of utencels & impliments used with the sd mill now in the possession of the sd John Webb the sd land & mill lying upon the head of

Coan River in the sd parish the mill called Coan Mill ... . Wit: Joseph McAdams, Edward Mason. Ackn --- 1742/3 & admitted to record. Attest: James Fontaine clerk.

9 Nov 1742. Bond. I John Webb of St. Stephens Parish, Northumberland Co planter am firmly bound unto Griffin Fauntleroy Junr of same place gent for 100 pd ... the condition of this obligation is such that whereas the sd John Webb has sold to the sd Griffin Fauntleroy a dam & appurtenances [see above] for the consideration of two young Negroes 4' in height at the least 10 pd mony, now if the sd John Webb shall at the request, cost & charges of the sd Griffin Fauntleroy make over or convey & confirm unto the sd Griffin Fauntleroy the sd water corn mill with its dam & 2 a. of land, utensils, houses & appurtenances in fee simple without fraud then this obligation to be void ... . Wit: Yarret Hughlett, John Hughlett. Ackn 14 Feb 1742/3 & admitted to record. Attest: James Fontaine clerk.

10 Feb 1742. Deed. William Hughlett of St. Stephens Parish, Northumberland Co for 40 pd 10 sl sold to Peter Presly gent of same place an 81 a. tr of landing in the sd parish bounded by Thos Wornham Junr, land of Thos Wornham formerly belonging to Benjamin & Jean Foster, Limekiln Cr, John Blundle & Joseph Robinson, which parcel of land the sd Hughlet bought of Benj Foster & Jean his wife, also that tr of land which the sd Hughlet bought of Richard Dudly & Winifrid his wife bounded afsd ... . Wit: Jas Daughity, William Blundall, Joseph Robinson, John Lancaster. Ackn 14 Feb 1742/3 by Wm Hughlet & Mary his wife she being privately examined by John Foushee gent & relinquished her right of dower & admitted to record. Attest: James Fontaine clerk.

... [illegible] ... a 56 a. tr of land adj Thos Wornham Junr, Wm Hughlet & John Layland, is the ½ pt/o that tr of land devised to the sd Joseph & Benjamin Robinson by the will of their decd father Jno Robinson & is distinguished from the sd Benjamin by a line of division concluded & agreed upon by the sd Joseph & Benjamin Robinson ... Joseph Robinson unto the sd Peter Presley ... . Wit: Jas Daughity, William Hughlet, Wm Blundall, John Lancaster. Ackn in court 14 Feb 1742/3 by Joseph Robinson unto Col Peter Presley & Frances w/o the sd Joseph Robinson being privately examined by John Foushee gent came into court & relinquished her right of dower in the land & the same is admitted to record. Attest: James Fontaine clerk.

14 Feb 1742. Deed. John Lewis of St. Stephens Parish, Northumberland Co planter for the thirds held by Hughlet's wife of her decd husband's lands, the mill only excepted, sold to the sd William Hughlet of same place planter a 25 a. tr of land in the parish afsd pt/o which sd land was purch of James Thompson & part of Edwd Lawrence bounded by one of the brs of Coan River, land now the

sd Hughlet's, land of sd Lewis formerly Allen's?, Richd Thomas & Stoney Br
.... Wit: Jno Oldham Junr, Nathaniel Barnet, Ackn 14 Feb 1742/3 by John
Lewis & Mary his wife she being privately examined by Jno Foushee gent &
relinquished her right of dower & the same is admitted to record. Attest: James
Fontaine clerk.

27 Jan 1742/3. In pursuant to an order of court dated 10 Jan 1742/3 we John
Routt, Wm Thomas & Jno Christopher being appointed to appraise the estate of
Jno Donaway decd did meet & have appraised the same in money. 3 cows,
yearlings, hogs, 12 piggs, beds & furniture, yarn, spun cotton, 4 lbs of good
pewter, 3 lbs of old pewter, 2 barrells of corn, pork, old iron, 1 box iron &
heaters, 2 lbs old brass, 2 pair old cards, 1 spinning wheel, 3 pecks of beans, 2
old tubs, 1 Testament Comon Prayer Book, 1 old looking glass, pair of sizers,
etc. A servant man 3 years to serve so distempered with sore legs that we think
him to be worth nothing. [Not totaled] This inventory was exhibited 14 Feb
1742/3 by Joseph Humphris adminr & admitted to record. Attest: James
Fontaine clerk.

Pursuant to an order of court dated 13 Dec 1742 we John Foushee, John Lewis
& Lindsy Opie did meet on the lands of Peter Neal decd & divided the sd land
into three parts. We have allotted Elias Edmunds the plantation that was Daniel
Neal's & the plantation where Benjn Bussell now lives & the sd Edmunds is to
have 300 lbs to tobacco yearly rent paid him by the orphant Rodham Neal & to
be lead by the mane road of the s side that leads to Coan Warehouse of the upper
tr to Shurley's line & the beginning as the road is from Lewis' ordinary & the
main County Road & further we agree that Mr. Edmunds shall pay the quit rents
of what land we have allotted him which was agreed to be 1/3 of the whole
lands. This report was exhibited 14 Feb 1742/3 by the auditors & recorded.
Attest: James Fontaine clerk.

16 Jan 1742/3. In obedience to an order of court dated 10 Jan 1742/3 we
Matthew Quill, Jas Kennedy & John Lewis mett at the house of Opmobie
Haynie & settled the accts of the decd Matthew Neal's estate & possessed
Christopher Neal orphan of the sd Matthew with his pt/o the personall estate
being 23 pd 10 sl 8 pn ½ penny also we delivered & possessed him with his
share of the decd Christopher Neal's estate in the hands of the sd Ormbie Hayne
amounting to 47 sl 4 pn. We likewise deliver'd & possess'd him with two
young Negro boys named James & Sam his pt/o his father's Negroes & settled
all accts between him & Ormbie Hayne to this day & saw them discharged. This
report was exhibited 14 Feb 1742/3 & admitted to record. Attest: James
Fontaine clerk.

... [illegible] ... for love & affection which he hath for the sd Baldwin Mathew

Smith who is the eldest son & heir apparent of the sd Philip Smith he the sd
Philip Smith hath given granted & confirmed unto the sd Baldwin Mathew
Smith all that 250 a. parcel of land in Wicocomico Parish bounded by Bernards
Cr & Squires Cr ... . Wit: J. Edwards, James Fontaine. This deed of gift was
ackn 14 Mar 1742/3 in court by Philip Smith gent unto his son Baldwin Mathew
Smith gent on whose motion the same is admitted to record. Attest: James
Fontaine clerk.

14 Mar 1742/3. Indenture. John Neal son of Matthew Neal by the consent of
Ormsby Haynie & Sarah his wife mother of the sd John Neal doth put himself
apprentice to Francis Brown joyner to learn his art of a joiner & chair maker &
with him after the manner of an apprentice to serve from this day during the term
of 5 years next ensuing ... . Signed & sealed in presence of the court. Ackn 14
Mar 1742/3 & admitted to record. Attest: James Fontaine clerk.

8 Dec 1742. Pursuant to an order of court granted to Leroy Griffin, Traves
Colston & John Foushee gent adminrs of the estate of Francis Peart decd we
Wm Taite, G. Fauntleroy & Robert Clarke Junr being first sworn before Mathew
Quill have mett & appraised the sd decd's estate in money. ... [illegible] ... 7
cows & yearlings, 3 heifers, 16 barrow calves & heifers, 1 bull, 38 sheep, beds,
bedsteads, rugs, blankets, sheets, pillows, counterpin curtins, vallins, 1 close
stool, 1 box of wareing apparel, 1 warming pan, parcel of books, 1 chest, pr
saddlebags, 2 curb bridle belts, 1 calf skin, 1 bag, 22 lbs of twine, 1 lock, some
brass nails, 1 table, 1 chest, old brown linnen sheets, 1 slate, 1 slay, parcel of
table linnen, 1 watering pan, some lumber, trunks, felt hats, womans stays, some
spices, parcel of glass & earthen ware, sugar scales & weights, etc. Negroes:
man named Arthur, man named Richmond, man named Oxford, man named
Cupit, man named Worscester, man named Crownly, man named Ralph, man
named Davy, Rose & her child Jenny, Maria & her child Jacob, Dinah & her
child Rose, child Nan, child George, Belindoe & her child Susannah, Patty &
her child Sarah. [Not totaled] This inventory was exhibited 14 Mar 1742/3 by
Leroy Griffin, Travers Colston & John Foushee gent adminrs & on their motion
the same is admitted to record. Attest: James Fontaine clerk.

2 Feb 1742/3. A just & true inventory of the estate of Thomas Wornom decd: 4
feather beds & furniture, 3 chests, 1 ovel table, 1 square table, 1 case of pistols
& holsters, 1 warming pan, 1 pewter bed pan, 1 walking can, pewter plates, 3
pewter dishes, pewter basons, 2 iron pots, 1 pr pot hooks, 9 fagg chairs, 1 set
shoemakers tools, some carpenters tooles, some joiners tools, some coopers
tools, a parcel of books, a parcel of earthen ware, 50 qt bottles, 3 guns, 1 iron
spit, 12 cyder casks, 3 powdering tubs, 1 hand mill, 3 canoes, 2 pr iron tongs, 3
iron candlesticks, 1 pewter candlestick, 1 small box, 1 box iron & heaters, 2
looking glasses, a parcel of doctors means & instruments, parcel of wareing

clothes, 1 old sword, 1 cubbard, 1 chest of drawers, 2 pewter tankards, etc. This inventory was exhibited into court 14 Mar 1742/3 by Jean Wornom executrix & on her motion admitted to record. Attest: James Fontaine clerk.

An obedient to an order of court dated 14 Feb 1742/3 we Saml Nelms, John Hudnall & Samll Downing did meet & did appraise the estate of James Pew decd. 3 cows & yearling, 5 ewes & lambs, parcel of corn, 4 old chairs, 1 stool, 1 bench, 2 iron wedges, 1 iron pestle, a parcel of old hoes, 1 old washing tub, 5 piggins, 11 glass bottles, 4 baskets & some cotton & wool, parcel of coopers & carpenters tools, 2 tables, 62 lbs of pot iron, 17 lbs of pewter, 1 old box iron &heaters ... [illegible] ... feather beds, bedsteads, cords, hides, old rug, some feathers in a canvas case, 2 old bolsters, 6 geese, 1 mare, 1 old side saddle, etc. [Not totaled] This inventory was exhibited 14 Mar 1742/3 by Thomas Pew adminr on whose motion the same is admitted to record. Attest: James Fontaine clerk.

In obedience to an order of court held 14 Feb 1742/3 we Saml Winsted, John Allgood & Wm Thomas being first sworn before Mr. Quill justice have appraised the estate of Thomas Penly decd in money. 3 cows, 2 yearlings, 3 heifers, bed & furniture, 3 lbs of old pewter, 1 tin pan, 1 old iron pot & pan, 1 old chest, some lumber, 1 old ax, grubbing hoes, 1 spinning wheel, 5 & 6 pn cash. [Not totaled] This inventory was exhibited 14 Mar 1742/3 by John King adminr & on his motion admitted to record. Attest: James Fontaine clerk.

Will. Thomas Pitman Senr of Northumberland Co. 19 Nov 1742. To my son John Pittman all the land that lies the other side of the old Houses? Br. To my son Thomas Pitman my plantation where I dwell & all the land this side of the sd br. To my son Elizamond Pitman that land that I bought of John Copre. My will is if my son John Pitman should die without heir that his pt/o the land shall fall to my son Benjamin Pitman. My will is that if my son Thomas Pitman should die without heir that his pt/o the sd land shall fall to my son Isaac Pitman. To my dau Elizabeth Edwards one Negro garl named Hager that she has now in possession in lieu of any other pt/o of my estate. To my son John Pitman all my wearing cloths. To my son Thomas Pitman my pistols & holsters & sword. To my son George Pitman my gun. My will is that all my younger sons shall live together upon my plantation & be brought up to moderate labour at the decresion of my executors & be schooled out of the profits of my estate before any division be made & that they shall be at their own desposing at the age of 18. My will is that there shall be no division in my estate before my youngest son Isaac Pitman comes of the age of 18. My will is that my wife Sarah Pitman shall have the use of my plantation & my whole estate except the legacy during her living my widdow. I make my wife Sarah Pitman & my son Thomas Pitman executors. Wit: Stephen Mullis, Elizmond Basye. Proved 14 Mar 1742/3 by admitted to record. Attest: James Fontaine clerk.

Will. Mary Bogges of Cherry Point, St. Stephens Parish, Northumberland Co.
11 Feb 1742/3. To my dau Elizabeth Anderson my ryding horse & side sadle,
bridle & sadle cloth with one cow & calf & three ewes & lambs to be wholy at
her disposall. To my son Thomas Bogges six ewes & lambs. To my son Bennet
Bogges 1 sl. To my son Robert Bogges 1 sl. To my son Henry Bogges 1 sl. I
give my mare to my dau Ruth & I give the horse Jolly to my son Jno Bogges.
All the rest of my estate to my son John Bogges & my dau Ruth Bogges. I
appoint Wm Hughlet, Wm Taite & my son John Bogges executors. Wit:
Rebecka Crute, Barbra Jones. Proved 18 Mar 1742/3 & admitted to record.
Attest: James Fontaine clerk.

11 Feb 1742/3. Deed of Lease. Rachel Miller of Cherry Point, St. Stephens
Parish, Northumberland Co spinster for 5 sl leased to William Gill of same place
all her right, title & intrest to a 174 a. tr of land in Cherry Point whereon the sd
Wm Gill now liveth formerly granted by patent to Henry Rock dated 13 Oct
1661 & by his son John Rock sold to Thos Miller decd grandfather to the sd
Rachel Miller & is bounded by Lindsey Opie's landing & land of Abraham
Joyce (Joice) now in possession of Lindsey Opie, the 74 a. being the residue adj
Abraham Joyce, land of Frances Simons (Symonds) now Capt Kenner's, path
that leads to Philip Carpenter's, land of George Courtnell now John Lewis's, sd
Lindsey Opie, land of Henry Rock now Rachel Miller's ... for 6 months ... .
Wit: Thos Taylor, Thos Myars, Elizabeth Myars. Proved 11 Apr ---- &
admitted to record. Attest: James Fontaine clerk.

12 Feb 1742/3. Deed of Release. Rachel Miller of Cherry Point, St. Stephens
Parish, Northumberland Co spinster for 100 pd released unto William Gill of
same place a 174 a. tr of land ... [same as above] ... . Wit: Thos Taylor, Thos
Myars, Elizabeth Myars. Proved 11 Apr 1743 & admitted to record. Attest:
James Fontaine clerk.
12 Feb 1742/3. Bond. I Rachel Miller of St. Stephens Parish, Northumberland
Co spinster am firmly bound unto William Gill of same place planter in the
penal sum of 600 pd ... the condition of this obligation is such that if the afsd
Rachel Miller do perform, fullfill, acknowledge, without fraud or delay when
required thereunto by the afsd William Gill deeds of lease & release [see above]
& further do & execute all & every such further act, thing, devises &
conveyances for the conveying the sd land unto the sd William Gill then this
obligation to be void ... . Wit: Thomas Taylor, Thomas Myars, Elizabeth
Myars. Proved 11 Apr 1743 & admitted to record. Attest: James Fontaine
clerk.

9 Apr 1743. Deed. Thomas Berry of Wicocomico Parish, Northumberland Co

for 350 lbs of tobacco sold to John & William Berry of same place a 300 a. tr of land on the s side of Wicocomoco River in the afsd parish (only the sd Thomas Berry to have the full propriety of 150 a. of the sd land during his natural life & his wife's widdowhood according to the directions of his father's will) bounded by David Lattimore & land of the late John Sutter, is the land late of Thomas Berry Senr, together with all his right & property of a tr of land the n side of the Wicocomoco River sold by Thos Berry Senr decd to Thomas Gill decd & now in possession of Ellis Gill ... . Wit: George Mills, Lecannah Badger, David Lattimore. Proved 11 Apr 1743 & admitted to record. Attest: James Fontaine clerk.

9 Apr 1743. Bond. I Thomas Berry of Wicocomoco Parish, Northumberland Co am firmly bound unto John & William Berry of same place for 500 pd ... the condition of this obligation is such that if the afsd Thomas Berry do well & truly stand & perform all the articles, agreements, covenants & contracts specified in a deed [see above] then this obligation to be void ... . Wit: George Mills, Lecannah Badger, David Lattimore. Proved 11 Apr 1743 & admitted to record. Attest: James Fontaine clerk.

Will. William Barrett of Northumberland Co. To my wife Elizabeth Barrot all my estate during her widowhood. It is my desire that all my daus shall live on my land during their maiden lives & not to be disturbed. To my son John Barrot 100 a. of land at the upper end of my land in lieu of the estate that John Wood left him. To my son George Bennot 100 a. of land next adj to my son John Barrot's land. To my son Will Barrot the plantation whereon I now live with all the rest of my land not before given. To my five daus each of them a young Negro.
David Lattimore maketh oath that the above written will of William Barrot was dictated to him by the sd Barrot & after it was written so far as the last bequest the sd decd expressed himself well satisfied & contented with the same & sd it was as he would have it & then directed the gift afsd to his daus of a young Negro a piece but died whilst that bequest was writing. Sd Lattimore further saith that no other person was present to the sd William at this time. This will was proved 11 Apr 1743 to be the last will of William Barrot decd by the oath of David Lattimore wit thereto & exhibited. Elizabeth Barrot adminr with the will annexed made oath thereto & on her motion the sd will is admitted to record. Attest: James Fontaine clerk.

... [illegible] ... 1 spinning wheel, 1 linning wheel, 1 old chest, 1 old razor & hoane, 2 iron wedges, 2 old axes, 2 old hoes, 1 iron spit, 1 iron pestle, 1 old hand saw, 1 old drawing haspe, 1 old stock lock, 1 old pad lock, 1 basket, old lumber, some wool, old sheers, parcel of tannd leather, 1 old Bible, 1 old common prayer book, 2 old frying pans, old landle stick, old shovel, table, old pewter, 19 lbs of old iron, 1 old box iron & heaters, 1 old tankard, 11 lbs pewter, 2 glass bottles, 1 old water paile, 1 iron pot & hooks, 2 sheep, etc. [Not totaled] Charles Coppedge, Lawrence Parrote, Thos Everitt. This inventory of the estate of Robert Lowry decd was exhibited 4 Apr 1743 by Henry Mays adminr of the sd decd & admitted to record. Attest: James Fontaine clerk.

7 Apr 1743. In obedience to an order of court held 14 Mar 1742/3 we John Hill, Ambrose Fielding & John Basye have met & appraised the estate of Thomas Pitman decd. 10 sheep, 6 hogs, 1 black mare, 1 gray horse, 5 cows & calfes, 1 yearling, 2 heifers, 4 young cattle, 8 geese, 1 cubard, beds, bedsteads & furniture, parcel of carpenter tools, parcel of coopers tools, parcel of money scales, 1 pair of small stillards, 1 pair of great stillards, 1 chest, 9 flag chairs, 1 oval table, 1 small table, 1 old small trunk, lumber, parcel of books, 1 old trunk, 1 gun, 1 case of pistols, 1 great chest, some old tubs, 2 old sadles & bridles, 6 knives & forks, etc. 108 pd 15 sl 1 pn. This inventory was exhibited by Sarah Pitman & Thos Pitman executors & admitted to record. Attest: James Fontaine clerk.

In obedience to an order of court dated 15 Mar 1742/3 we Griffin Fauntleroy, Paris Garner & John Lewis mett on the plantation of the decd Mary Bogges being first sworn by Capt Matthew Kenner gent & appraised the estate of the decd which was brought to our view. 2 horses, 1 young mare, 12 sheep, 1 shoat, 16 lambs, 8 other sheep, 4 cows & calves, yearling, 1 heiffer, 1 sow & 8 pigs, 6 shoats, 2 hives of bees ... [illegible] ... 1 large chest, 1 small box, 1 large Bible, some other small books, parcel of old books, 1 large looking glass, 1 multiplying glass, 1 little glass, carpenters & coopers tooles, 3 pr sheep shears, etc. Negroes: woman Dinah, woman Nan, garl Lettis, [?] Frank. [Not totaled] This inventory was exhibited 11 Apr 1743 by William Hughlet, Wm Taite & John Bogges executors & admitted to record. Attest: James Fontaine clerk.

An exact acct of the late Rev. Mr. Pearl's estate sold at auction Nov 1742 by the adminr. At Cherry Point Glebe: to John Cralle 1 tumbler, 20 sheep, [?], 1 close stool, [?]. To Robt Clark Junr 3 pot hooks, 1 chain, 1 bedstead, 1 box & brown sugar. To Griffin Fauntleroy Junr 1 box chain, 40 hogs, 6 [?] leather, stear. To Jno Sebrey 2 shoats, 2 cows, 1 steer, 1 black mare & colt, 2 hones. To James Lampkin 2 cows & calves, 6 boys folt?. To Daniel Sturlock 2 cows. To Thos Vallandigam 2 cows. To Travers Colston 1 cow & calf & baron colt, 1 horse. ... [illegible] ... To John King 1 sadle. To Edward Mason 1 bay chare & colt, 1 table, 1 bed, old table, a tub, beans. To Jas Taptor 1 goose, mare. To Stokely To[?] Negro Rose & child. To Allen Hunter Negro Murreah & child. To Yarret Hughlet Negro Dinah & child, gail (girl) Nanny & a boy. To Elias Edmonds Negro Belinda & child, 6 chairs, 1 skillet, wedges, brass kettle. To John Foushee Negro Pattie & child, parcel of twister, parcel of nails. To Capt John

Bale Negro man Cromly. To John McCave 1 yoke of oxen. To Rodham Kenner 1 bull & stear, pr oxen, old iron, sugar, 22 swine, table linnen, 6 pewter. To Jno Cral 6 cows, sugar. To Richd Rogers 2 stears, 1 bed, &c. To George Hunt 22 cattle. To Linsey Opie 2 fother stacks, sugar, 1 sugar box, knives, leather, 13 baskets. To Major Waugh [?]. To Nichs Hood 1 gilt trunk, [?], sadle baggs, chocks, killard & stills, brush, broom, old hose. To Matthew Quill sugar, 1 large trunk, woman's hatt & stays, ring of pans. To Francis Brown sugar, 1 chair whip, 1 sadle, harness, salt, [?], barrel soap, nails, tacks, powter. To Wm Taite sugar, 1 ring, medicines?. To Joshua James sugar. To Richd Tomson chairs, lumber. To Edgcomb Suggett large table. To Edwd Noles butter. ... [illegible] ... To Wm Blackerby 11 broad hoes. To Geo Gillson cross cut saw, whip. To George Oldham sugar, sheets. To Johanna Wig[?] cloths, To Thos Cammet? parcel cloths. To Francis Tarpley 1 [?]. To Isaac Clark 1 [?]. To Edwd Barns old lumber. To Jno Swillivant beds &c, chairs, pewter, table. To Jno Shadock wool. To Wm Balto [?]. To John Tayloe 150 [?]. 543 pd 7 sl.

The Lower Glebe: To Francis Brown corn. To [?] Gill corn. To Saml Nelms 5 cider casks. To Jas Berry 5 casks, 1 spade. To Geo Humphris 1 still. To Jos Robinson 1 cask of cider. To Daniell Cotterel 1 pot, 1 tub. To Thos Hurst 2 cows. To Mr. Ledford 2 cows. To Shapleigh Neal 3 cows, 2 yearlings. To Wm Ellitt 1 cow & yearling. To Thos Harding 1 bull, earthen ware. To Thos Allison 1 bull. To Wm Fallin fother. To Jno Graham 10 sheep. To Charles Pritchett a tub, beans. To Richd Read a box with wool. To David Lattimore 1 sive. To Geo Gibson 6 bar corn. To Jno Conway parcel of lumber. To Willm Harcum old hoes. 55 pd 1 sl.

Charles Dodson 1 gray mare in Richmond. 1 pd 15 sl.

Sale of the cargoe goods at Mr. Berrys in lots: To Benja Taylor, David Lattimore, Leroy Griffin, Moses Webb, Richd Hudnall, Jos Chattin, Jno Stott, Jno Adams, Capt Geo Bell, Peter Miller, Willm Hughlet, Jno Hazard, Geo Paine, Jos Gaskins, Travers Colston. ... [illegible] ... . Leroy Griffin, Tras Colston, John Foushee.

This acct was exhibited 11 Apr 1743 by the auditors & admitted to record. Attest: James Fontaine clerk.

4 Apr 1743. In pursuant to an order of court dated 12 Mar 1743 we John Foushee, Yarret Hughlet & George Conway being appointed to settled & determine the difference between John Ashburn petr & William Booz executor of the will of John Lancaster decd deft we did meet & upon hearing both partys it is considered that the deft hath no estate of the petrs in his hands. This report was exhibited 11 Apr 1743 by the auditors & recorded. Attest: James Fontaine clerk.

In obedience to an order of court dated 14 Feb 1742/3 the former order of court made 14 Dec last not being complied with, we David Lattimore, John Berry,

Moses Champion, John Ingram & Edm Barratt being ordered by the court to meet some time before next court & settle the accounts relating to the estate of William Thrift decd & also to appraise & possess Abraham Stears executor of the sd decd's estate with the orphans pt/o sd decd's estate in the hands of Robt Reddin which on 28 Feb year afsd did meet at the house of Robt Redding's & settled all accts relating to the sd decd's estate & after the accts is all fairly settled we find there is due to the orphans for their parts 22 pd 3 sl & we have praised as much of the sd decd's estate as amounts to the above 22 pd 3 sl & have possessed sd Abraham Stears executor of the sd decd's estate with the same. This report was exhibited 28 Feb 1742/3 ... [illegible] ... .

... [illegible] ... sd Pain ... . Wm Barret, Joshua James, David Fluker. This report was exhibited 11 Apr 1743 by William Barratt, Joshua James & David Flucker & admitted to record. Attest: James Fontaine clerk.

9 May 1743. Deed. Edmund Northern of Lunenburg Parish, Richmond Co planter for 160 pd sold to Joshua Nelms of St. Stephens Parish, Northumberland Co planter a parcel of land whereon the sd Joshua Nelms liveth bounded by ... [illegible] ... . Wit: William Nelms, Joseph Lancaster, Hezekiah Haynie. Ackn 9 May 1743 by Edmond Northern & Elizabeth his wife she being privately examined by John Foushee gent relinquished her right of dower & the same is admitted to record. Attest: James Fontaine clerk.

... [illegible] ... 25 a. adj Richard Cornish, land which formerly belonged to [?] Haynie, William Hughlet, [?] Holland ... from the sd Uriah Haynie to the only proper use & behoof of the sd Charles Betts ... . Wit: W. Betts Junr, J.L. Daughity, Thomas Bridgman, Samuel Aires, Richard Cornish. Proved 9 Mary 1743 & admitted to record. Attest: James Fontaine clerk.

... [illegible] ... unto the sd William Thomas a 100 a. parcel of land in St. Stephens Parish bounded by the Main Swamp ... survey of Capt John Haynie ... the sd Clement Alridge for himself & his heirs doth covenant, grant & agree to & with the sd William Thomas ... . Wit: Henry Tapscott, James Blackerby. Ackn 9 May 1743 by Clement Alridge & Ann his now wife she being privately examined by John Foushee gent relinquished her right of dower in the land & the same is admitted to record. Attest: James Fontaine clerk.

... [illegible] ... unto the sd George Hunt for & during & until the sd apprentice shall arrive to the full age of 22 ... the sd George Hunt doth hereby covenant, grant & agree to & with the sd Mathew Neal to learn him the trade he the sd Hunt now follows of a joiner & house carpenter ... . The sd Matthew Neal was 19 years old 20 Feb last. Signed, sealed & delivered in the presence of the court. This indenture between Matthew Neal & George Hunt was ackn in court by both parties 9 May 1743 & on their motion admitted to record. Attest: James Fontaine clerk.

14 Mar 1742. Deed. William Hughlet of St. Stephens Parish, Northumberland Co planter for 27 pd sold to James Self of same place a 93 a. tr of land in the parish afsd bounded by the sd Hughlet's mill, the road that leads from Mr. Rutter's to the sd Hughlet's mill pond & the Main Swamp ... . Wit: Adam Booth, John Basye, John Beacham, Mary Whiteing. Ackn 9 May 1743 by William Hughlet & Mary his wife she being privately examined by John Foushee gent ackn her right of dower in the land & the same is admitted to record. Attest: James Fontaine clerk.

Bond. I Uriah Haynie am firmly bound unto Charles Betts Junr in the penal sum of 20 pd ... the condition of this obligation is such that ... [illegible] ... if the sd Uriah Haynie by an indenture bearing date with these presents according to the true intent & meaning of the sd deed then this obligation to be void ... . Wit: W. Betts Junr, James Daughity, Thomas Bridgman, Samuel Aires, Richard Cornish. Proved 9 May 1743 & admitted to record. Attest: James Fontaine clerk.

In obedience to an order of court dated 11 Apr 1743 we Moses Champion, Joseph Hester & John Ledford being first sworn by Capt George Ball mett at the dwelling house of Randolph Mott decd & appraised the estate. Beds & furniture, 3 small trunks, 1 square table, bullet moulds, pr sole, earthen ware, 3 glasses, 1 spice morter & pestle, pepper box, 1 mans hat, pr mens stockings, pr bretches, 2 coats, 1 gun, parcel of old books, 1 old gun, 9 cheares, 1 looking glass, 1 chest, 1 box iron & heaters, 1 old fiddle, 1 side sadle, old trunk, 1 box, 1 case of bottles, 3 juggs, 2 ½ lbs cotton, 1 plow, 1 spinning wheel, 1 spit, etc. Negro man Dick, Negro man Charles. 113 pd 11 sl 9 ½ pn. This inventory was exhibited by Frances Mott adminx & admitted to record. Attest: James Fontaine clerk.

... [illegible] ... earthen ware, pot iron, pot hooks, 1 frying pan, 1 iron spit, 1 iron pestle, 1 shovel, 1 old bridle & sadle, 1 spinning wheel & cards, 1 duz rattels & a vial, 4 old chair frames, 1 chest, 1 large book, 1 Bible & prayer book, parcel of old books, 1 old looking glass, 2 worn hats, 2 ½ yds of linen, 1 sute of thick cloths, mettle buttons, 2 shirts, 2 pr old shoes, stockings, 22 spoones, 4 basons, 10 new plates, salt seller, 3 dishes, parcel of old gloves, old trunk, bed, bedstead & furniture, 6 flag chaires, 1 pistole, etc. 23 pd 13 sl 11 ½ pn. Aron Taylor, John Hill, Richard Nutt. This inventory of the estate of William Short decd was exhibited to the court 9 May 1743 by James Waller adminr & on his motion admitted to record. Attest: James Fontaine clerk.

10 Jun 1743. Deed of Lease. John Beacham of St. Stephens Parish, Northumberland Co planter for 5 sl leased to Rebecka Beacham of same place widdow a 30 a. parcel of land in the sd parish formerly given by Daniel Beacham by his will dated 9 Jan 1741 to his son Jacob (Joab?) Beacham & by the death of Jacob Beacham descended to come to the sd John Beacham ... for 1 year paying one ear of Indian corn yearly if demanded ... . Wit: William Hartley, Benedict Shortt, Ann Short. Ackn 13 Jun 1743 by John Beacham unto Rebecka Beacham on whose motion the same is admitted to record. Attest: James Fontaine clerk.

11 Jun 1743. Deed of Release. John Beacham of St. Stephens Parish, Northumberland Co planter for 800 lbs of tobacco released to Rebecka Beacham of same place a 30 a. tr of land ... [same as above] ... . Wit: William Hartley, Benedict Shortt, Ann Shortt. Ackn 11 Jun 1743 & admitted to record. Attest: James Fontaine clerk.

20 Jan 1742. Deed of Lease. Richard Kenner of St. Stephens Parish, Northumberland Co & Hannah his wife for 5 sl leased to Robert Vanlx of Washington Parish, Westmoreland Co gent a 700 a. tr of land in St. Stephens Parish in Writons Neck including that plantation whereon the sd Richard Kenner now lives it being all the remainder of the sd Richard Kenner's lands in the sd neck which sd land was formerly gave to the sd Richard Kenner by the will of Elizabeth Winder & by a deed of gift past from the sd Elizabeth Winder some time before her death to the sd Richard Kenner ... for the term of 1 year paying the rent of one ear of Indian corn on the last day of the sd term if demanded ... . Wit: Winder Kenner, John Throp, Dority Throp. Ackn 13 Jun 1743 by Richard Kenner & admitted to record. Attest: James Fontaine clerk.

21 Jan 1742. Deed of Release. Richard Kenner of St. Stephens Parish, Northumberland Co gent & Hannah his wife for 300 pd sold to Robert Vaulx of Washington Parish, Westmoreland Co a 700 a. tr of land ... . Wit: Winder Kenner, John Throp, Dority Throp. Ackn 13 Jun 1743 by Richard Kenner & admitted to record. Attest: James Fontaine clerk.

21 Jan 1742. Bond. I Richard Kenner of St. Stephens Parish, Northumberland Co gent am firmly bound unto Robert Vaulx of Washington Parish, Westmoreland Co for ... [illegible] ... the condition of this obligation is such that if the afsd Richard Kenner shall well & truly perform, fulfill, accomplish & keep all the grants, articles, clauses & agreements which are mentioned in a deed [see above] of the sale of 700 a. of land then this obligation to be void ... . Wit: Winder Kenner, John Throp, Dority Throp. Ackn 13 Jun 1743 & admitted to record. Attest: James Fontaine clerk.

27 May 1742. Power of Attorney. I Andrew Allen gent of Ackamack Co, VA have constituted in my stead Sarah Ann Hobson of Northumberland Co my atty to ackn an instrument of writing in Northumberland Co court which bond dated 6 Dec 1742 for the payment of 200 pd to Elizabeth Allen wife to the sd Andrew Allen gent of Ackamack Co to the use of her & her heirs … . Wit: Giles Webb, John Leach. Proved 13 Jun 1743 & admitted to record. Attest: James Fontaine clerk.

26 Dec 1742. Bond. I Andrew Allen of Ackamack Co, VA gent am firmly bound unto Elizabeth Hobson of St. Stephens Parish, Northumberland Co for 200 pd … the condition of this obligation is such that whereas a marriage is shortly by God's grace intended to be had & solemnized between the afsd Andrew Allen & Elizabeth Hobson, if after the sd marriage be solemnized its agreed by the afsd Andrew Allen that the sd Elizabeth Hobson shall have a right to the dispose of all of the sundry Negroes hereafter mentioned either by way of device at her death or any other firm piece of writing, Negroes, viz, two women called Judith & Lucy & there future increase with three boys called James, Killy & one to be named or called Joseph to be disposed of by her the sd Elizabeth Hobson at her pleasure without any claim, challenge, suit, trouble, damage, molestation or interruption of the sd Andrew Allen … . Wit: James Adair, Henry Christall. Proved 13 Jun 1743 & admitted to record. Attest: James Fontaine clerk.

Pursuant to an order of court dated 10 May 1743 to us directed we Saml Blackwell, Argail Tayler & Christopher Dameron being appointed by the sd court to finally settle & determine a difference which was brought by Thomas Williams & Jean his wife in Chancery agt Thomas Mahane (Mahanes), we do find that the sd Thomas Williams & Jean his wife plts has had no cause of complaint agt Thomas Mahane deft for not settling the bounds of their land left them by the will of Samuel Mahane (Mahanes) lately decd for that there has been a line made between the sd plts & deft by the consent of both partys this 3 years. We also do find that the sd line is right & justly made between the sd petrs & deft according to the true intent & meaning of the will of the sd Samuel Mahane late decd who gave the sd land to the sd Thomas Williams's wife Jane & Thomas Mahane. We likewise find that there is a balance of the moveable estate of Saml Mahane late decd still remaining in the hands of Thomas Mahane his executor 119 lbs tobacco & that Thomas Williams is intitled to 1/6 pt/o it & of this we make our report. This report was exhibited 14 Jun 1743 by the auditors & admitted to record. Attest: James Fontaine clerk.

In obedience to an order of court dated 9 Mar 1742/3 we Joseph Wildy (Willdy), John Downing & Thomas Wornom did meet & settle & appraise the estate of Elenor Wallis Junr to the securitys William Hughlett & Ellis Gill. 3 muggs, 30 lbs pewter, 1 table, 2 flag chairs, 1 iron pot & hooks, 1 frying pan, 16 hogs, 1 cow & yearling, 2 bulls, 1 bed, bolster, 1 hamer, tongs, 1 pale, saw, shears, etc. 12 pd 17 sl 1 pn. This report between Ellis Gill & William Hughlet petrs & Elenor Wallis deft was exhibited into court by the auditors & recorded. Attest: James Fontaine clerk.

30 Jan 1737/8. I John Humphris of St. Stephens Parish, Northumberland Co in consideration that a Negro boy named Tom to me delivered in hand & the thirds of the land ackn according to the bond by Winnefrid Humphris of same parish whereof I do hereby ackn my pt/o the Negro woman named Lucy & also my pt/o my brother William Humphris decd's estate was to have & to hold the sd Negro woman & all her increase & all other bargained premises unto the sd Winnefrid Humphris to the only proper use & behoof of her the sd Winnefrid Humphris forever … . Wit: John Alexander, Joseph Humphris, George Humphris. Proved 13 Jun 1743 & admitted to record. Attest: James Fontaine clerk.

In obedience to an order of court dated 11 Apr 1743 we Thomas Hurst, John Berry & John Ledford being first sworn by Capt George [?] met at the dwelling house of William Barratt decd & appraised the estate. Negroes: Dick, Moll, Jane, Tom, Knor, [?], Doll. 2 draft stears, 6 cows & calves, 1 cow with calf, 4 young cattle, cart & wheels, ring & bolt, plow & chain, beds & furniture, blankets, rugs, 3 hides, table, bottels, pewter, 4 juggs, 2 warming pans, 2 candlesticks, garlic, 1 remnant of linnen, parcel of earthen ware, 2 chests, 2 trunks, 1 box, 1 pr stillards, 1 side sadle & bridle, shoemaker tools, 2 leather aprons, 1 runlet, 1 horse & mare, 1 gun, etc. 268 pd 4 ½ pn. This inventory was exhibited 13 Jun 1743 by Elizabeth Barrat (Barratt) executrix & on her motion admitted to record. Attest: James Fontaine clerk.

Will. Hannah Smith of Northumberland Co. 18 Apr 1743. To my cuzin Susannah Nellams five Negroes, viz, Ned, Frank, Abraham, Judey, Whinney. To my cuzin Richard Neaill all the rest of the Negroes that I am now possessed with. To my cuzin Susannah Nellams all my waring clothes, rings & jewels. All the rest of my estate to be divided between my cuzin Richard Neaill & William Nellams Junr after the debts being paid. I appoint my good friend Winder Kenner executor. Wit: George Begbee, Junifred Bluford. Proved … [illegible] … & admitted to record. Attest: James Fontaine clerk.

11 Jul 1743. Deed. John Christopher of Saint Stephens Parish, Northumberland Co for 6,500 lbs of tobacco sold to George Christopher of same place a 119 a. tr of land in the sd parish between the two main brs of Coan River being a parcel of land which belonged to Thos Adams & conveyed by the sd Adams by deed dated 1695 to Robert Reeves & the sd Robert Reeves conveyed to his son John Reeves & by the sd John Reeves sold to John Christopher & he being first party

to this indenture, bounded by John Ward, Thos Towers, Thos Dyer, Wm Taylor & Thos Timmens ... . Wit: Massey Woolridge, Yarrat Hughlett. Ackn 11 Jul 1743 by John Christopher & Susanna his wife she being privately examined by John Foushee gent relinquished her right of dower & admitted to record. Attest: James Fontaine clerk.

11 Jul 1743. Bond. I John Christopher of St. Stephens Parish, Northumberland Co am firmly bound unto George Christopher of same parish in the penal sum of 13,000 lbs of tobacco ... the condition of this obligation is such ... [illegible] ... if the sd John Christopher shall perform, fulfill, & keep all & every clause, articles, conditions & agreements mentioned in the sd deed [see above] then this obligation to be void ... . Wit: Massey Woolridge, Yarrat Hughlett. Ackn 11 Jul 1743 & admitted to record. Attest: James Fontaine clerk.

Will. Philip Smith of Wiccocomico Parish, Northumberland Co gent. XXV May 1743. I desire that all my just debts be paid & satisfied as soon as may be after my decease. To my dau Mary w/o Jesse Ball gent 5 pd. I do declare this legacy to be in full for her part or portion which she can or may claim of my estate having heretofore given her a sufficient fortune. To my five daus Mildred, Elizabeth, Sarah, Jane & Susannah each of them 200 pd & one feather bed & plain furniture to be paid them as they attain the age of 21 or day of marriage. I do declare it to be my true intent & meaning that in case either of them die before she attains the sd age or marries her legacy shall be vested in & belong to the survivors of them my sd daus Mildred, Elizabeth, Sarah, Jane & Susanna & be paid to them as afsd. It is my will that my sd five daus last mentioned be provided for & maintained by my son Baldwin Mathews Smith till they become intitled to their fortunes suitable to their estate & degree without any deduction or abatement out of their afsd legacies for the same. I have given my son a letter to Mrs. Dickey to let her know that I would make my son worth more than 2,000 pd with his estate at York which on acct of having Mrs. Fany Burgis he will be intitled at my decease & my true intent & meaning is that my son pays my afsd daus the afsd mentioned legacy according to my will before mentioned, & that my wench Peg be set free. All the rest of my estate of what nature or quality soever whether real, personal or mixt, I give to my son Baldwin Mathews Smith. I desire that my estate may not be appraised. I appoint my brother Augustine Smith, my nephew John Smith & my son Baldwin Mathews Smith executors. I do desire my son in law Jesse Ball & my friend Thos Edwards to be my trustees to be aiding & assisting to my sd executors. To each of the sd executors & trustees I give a mourning ring. Wit: Charles Copedge Junr, Thos Clement, Samuel Hamilton, Thomas Sullivant (Selevent). Proved 11 Jul 1743 & admitted to record. Attest: James Fontaine clerk.

Will. James Thomson of Saint Stephens Parish, Northumberland Co. 22 Dec

1742. To my grandsons James Thomson (son of?) Richd Thomson one young cow. To my granddau Jane Thomson (dau of?) my son James Thomson one heifer with calf. To Willm Hughlet of the afsd parish all that tr or dividend of land whereon I now live being 50 a. it being in consideration of a (piece?) gave by the sd Hughlett to my son James Thomson where my son now lives. After the death of my wife Barberry all & singular the rest of my estate of moveables whatsoever to my son Madcalf Thomson but if my son Madcalf dyes without issue then to be divided amongst my grandchildren. I appoint my wife Barberry & my son Madcalf executors. Wit: Willm Hughlett, Saml Pattridg (Partridge), Mary Coleman. Proved 11 Jul 1743 & admitted to record. Attest: James Fontaine clerk.

Will. John Dameron of Northumberland Co. 18 Dec 1742. To my son Joseph Dameron all that tr or dividend of land I now live on which my father Barther Dameron gave me, to him & his male heirs, & for want of male heirs then to my son Thos Dameron & his male heirs & for want of such male heirs then to my son John Dameron & his male heirs. But if it should so happen that neither of my three sons Joseph, Thomas & John Dameron have any male heirs then my will is that my son Joseph Dameron's female heirs enjoy the sd land in the same manner as the male heirs & for want of such females to descent to the females in the same manner as is before directed. To my son Thos Dameron one Negro woman Hannah & her increase. To my son Bartholomew Dameron 3,000 lbs of tobacco to be paid by son Joseph Dameron. I give all my Negroes & personal estate of what nature or kind forever to be divided between my wife Elizabeth Dameron & my four sons Joseph, John, Thomas & Bartholomew Dameron when they obtain to the age of 18. Farther my will is that my wife Elizabeth Dameron have my Negro woman named Judy in her pt/o my Negroes & her future increase. I appoint Thos Taylor & my wife executors. Wit: Josias Gaskins, John Ingram, Christopher Dameron. Proved 11 Jul 1743 & admitted to record. Attest: James Fontaine clerk.

A true & perfect inventory of sundry debts received (due to the estate of John Keene decd) by us his executors to be added to the former inventory returned to court. Received sums of Wm Hughlett, Lindsey Opie, Geo Conway, John Lewis, Jas Blackeby. 28 pd 7 sl. This additional inventory was exhibited 11 Jul 1743 by Edwd Wiatt & Edgcomb Suggitt executors & on their motion admitted to record. Attest: James Fontaine clerk.

In obedience to an order of court dated 13 Jun ---- we Richard Hull, Elles Gill & Edward Rogers did meet at the house of Mrs. Hannah Smith & appraised her goods & chattels. Some old lumber in the old house, old brick molds, 2 hand saws, some old tools, 1 spice morter, 4 candlesticks, pare button moulds, 1 pair of dogs, fire tongs, pair of old iron racks, 1 stand, tooth drawers, a parcel of old books, a large looking glass, 1 desk, 1 chest of drawers, 1 decanter, 1 ovel wallnut table, 6 old chairs, 1 old safe, 1 chest, 2 old trunks, 2 doz pully's, beds, steads & furniture, 1 small crane, 2 sises wire, 1 old close stool, 7 basons, 2 tin pans, 6 good plates, 5 old plates, bed & furniture at Wm Nelms, etc. Negroes: men Tom, Benedick, Dick, George, Jacob, Abraham, Ned, Will, Peter, Mack, women Rose, Nan, girls Judey, Letty, Sarah, Winney, 1 old Negro Frank. This inventory of the estate of Mrs. Hannah Smith decd was exhibited 11 Jul 1743 by Winder Kenner executor & on his motion admitted to record. Attest: James Fontaine clerk. (Pg 256)

5 May 1743. Power of Attorney. John Tunstall & Spencer Hack, of Summerset Co, MD gent heirs of Spencer Hack decd appoint our trusty & well beloved friend John Flack of this co gent to be our atty to ask, demand & receive of the heirs of John Shapleigh late of this sd of Northumberland gent decd or of any other person whatsoever, all debts, dues & demands whatsoever due from the estate of the afsd John Shapleigh unto the heirs of Spencer Hack of Northumberland Co decd ... . Wit: Jonathan Betts, William Hunt. Proved 14 Jun 1743 & further proved 11 Jul 1743 & admitted to record.

In obedience to an order of court dated 14 Mar 1742/3 we have mett & set apart the estate of George James from the estate of Swanson Prichard decd's & has allso possest Thomas James petitioner with the sd George James' estate as follows: 1 cow & calf, 1 old heifer, 1 cubbard, 1 small feather bed & furniture, 1 old gun, 1 old spice morter, 1 old spinning wheel & cards, 1 old chest, some old tubs, 2 sheep, 3 old charrs, 1 large chest, 1 old table, 1 iron spit, 1 cross cut saw & file, earthen ware, 2 juggs, 2 sider casks, 100 ½ lbs pewter, 1 old box iron & heaters, candle stick, 1 small stone jug, iron hook. 12 pd 18 sl. This report & division of the estate of George James decd from the estate of Swanson Prichard decd in the hands of Thos Harrison was exhibited by Argail Taylor, John Coppedge & Robert Boyd & recorded. Attest: James Fontaine clerk.

Pursuant to an order of court dated 14 Mar 1742/3 we Argail Taylor, John Coppedge & Robert Boyd have met being first sworn by George Ball Junr & valued all the estate of Swanson Pritchard decd in the hands of Thomas Harrison that was brought to our view the sd Harrison & his wife was upon oath to tender the same & also have allotted & possessed Joshua James guardian of Judith, Betty & Margaret Pritchard orphans of the afsd decd their pts/o the sd estate to our knowledge & settled ye accounts on each party his proportionable part the including inventory (with the debts due out of the estate to sundry persons). 1 Negro man named Dick, 1 Negro woman named Jane. 3 cows, yearling, calf, heifer, stear, mare, 1 old horse, 5 new casks, 2 tubs, old barrels, feather beds, bolsters, pillows, sheets, quilt, bedsteads, curtains, vallins, cord, rug, blanket, 3 chairs, 5 old chairs, 1 old gun, 1 old table cloth, 1 case of bottles, 1 small box, 1 small chest, 1 small looking glass, 2 old axes, 1 carpenter's adze, 1 coopers, 1 hand saw, 1 grubbing ax, 3 iron wedges, etc. [Not totaled] This report & division was exhibited 11 Jul 1743 & recorded. Attest: James Fontaine clerk.

I James Adair of Northumberland Co have constituted Major Robert Tucker of the City of Norfolk my atty to ask, demand, sue, recover & receive of Edward Masee of same City of Norfolk the sum of 8 pd due to me by vertue of one note of bond or writing obligatory from the sd Edward Masee to me the sd James Adair dated ever since Nov 1740 .... Wit: Argail Taylor, Lawrence Parrot, John Nutt. Proved 8 Aug 1743 & recorded & certified. Attest: James Fontaine clerk.

8 Aug 1743. Deed. Vincent Garner of St. Stephens Parish, Northumberland Co for 20 pd sold to John Donaway of same place an 84 a. tr of land in the parish afsd upon the head of Coan River being pt/o a pattent granted to Thomas Tenions? dated 1666 & now belonging to the sd Vincent Garner bounded by the Main Road, John Christopher, William Gounstout & George Brown .... Wit: Edward Mason, James Garner, John Dollins. Ackn 8 Aug 1743 by Vincent Garner & Winiford his wife she being privately examined by John Foushee gent ackn her right of dower & the same is admitted to record. Attest: James Fontaine clerk.

8 Aug 1743. Bond. I Vincent Garner of St. Stephens Parish, Northumberland Co am firmly bound & indebted unto John Donaway of same place in the penal sum of 40 pd ... the condition of this obligation is such that whereas the afsd Vincent Garner by one deed [see above] sold an 84 a. tr of land unto the sd John Donaway, now if the sd Vincent Garner shall observe, perform, fulfill, accomplish & keep all & every clause, articles & conditions mentioned in the sd deed then this obligation to be void .... Wit: Edward Mason, James Garner, John Dollins. Ackn 8 Aug 1743 & admitted to record. Attest: James Fontaine clerk.

In obedience to an order of court dated 11 Jul 1743 for the inventorying & appraising the estate of Abraham Low, we David Fluker, Wm Barret & Pitts Curtis have valued & appraised as followeth: 1 mare, bridle & saddle, 4 cows, calves, heiffer, 2 bulls, beds & furniture, sheets, rugs, blankets, bedsteads, cord, 1 old chest, wheel & cards, 1 old box, 6 chairs, 2 old tables, 1 gun & sword, powder, 1 barril of a gun, old lock ... [illegible] ... earthen ware, sows, a meale bag, meale sifter, table cloth, 2 tubs, pans, funnel, parcel new wearing cloaths, parcel cider cask, a washing tub, water paile, skillet, frying pan, 1 old brass skillet, 1 iron pot, parcel of leather & baskets, 1 hide & calf skin, 1 canneo, 11 lbs old peuter, 5 gees, tobacco, etc. [Not totaled] This inventory was exhibited 8 Aug 1743 & by Martha Low adminr & on her motion admitted to record.

Attest: James Fontaine clerk.

In obedience to an order of court dated 11 Jul 1743 we John Lewis, John Kennedy & James Farned mett at the house of James Tomson decd & valued the estate of the sd decd. Beds & furniture, rug, 1 large Japand table, 1 looking glass, 2 best chests, 1 small trunk & box, 17 1/2 lbs best peuter, 22 lbs old peuter, 1 iron pestle, 1 spitt, 1 pare flesh forks & skimmer, 2 pare fire tongs, 1 spice mortar, some wooden ware, ½ doz books, parcel of old earthen ware, 3 old tubs, 1 small cask, 1 frying pan, 1 old broad ax, 1 old table & chair, 91 ½ lbs pot iron, 1 old Bible, 1 old cupboard, 1 rolling pin, coopers compas, 3 cows & calves, 2 steers, 1 horse, 1 sow & 9 piggs, etc. [Not totaled] This inventory was exhibited 8 Aug 1743 by Barbary Thomson executrix & on her motion admitted to record. Attest: James Fontaine clerk.

11 7br 1743. Deed of Lease. Richard Way of St. Stephens Parish, Northumberland Co planter for 5 sl leased to Peter Mason of same place planter a 27 a. parcel of land in the afsd parish near to Wicocomoco River bounded by the sd Richd Way, William Harcum, Wooldridge Smith & Fignors Cr or Ways Cr, which sd parcel of land did formerly belong to John Way father of the sd Richard Way & is now legally vested in the sd Richard Way ... for the term of 1 year paying yearly the rent of one ear of Indian corn if demanded ... . Wit: Wm Taite, Thos Edwards. Ackn 12 7br 1743 & admitted to record.

12 7br 1743. Deed of Release. Richard Way of St. Stephens Parish, Northumberland Co planter for 2,120 lbs of tobacco sold to Peter Mason of same place planter a 27 a. tr of land ... [same as above] ... . Wit: Thos Edwards, Wm Taite. Ackn 12 7br 1743 & admitted to record. Attest: James Fontaine clerk.

Will. Rodham Kenner of St. Stephens Parish, Northumberland Co. 1 Mar 1742/3. To my wife Susanna Kenner my chair & horses & servant boy James. To my wife 1/3 pt/o of all my land, Negroes & personal estate after my just debts & funerall expences are paid for & during her natural life & after her decease the sd Negroes with their increase to be divided between my two sons Richard & Rodham Kenner. To my son Richd Kenner all that tr of land called Old Rodoms Land?. To my sd son Richd 1/3 pt/o all my Negroes & personal estate after my just debts & funerall expenses are paid. To my son Rodham Kenner all that tr of land called Old Sutell's (Sutche's?) Land. If my son Richard Kenner or his heirs shall offer to sue for & recover the land from my son Rodham or his heirs then my will is that my sd son Rodham shall have all the Negroes with their increase before bequeathed to my sd son Richard. To my sd son Rodham Kenner 1/3 pt/o all my Negroes & personall estate after my debts & funeral expences are paid. I appoint my wife Susanna Kenner & my brother in law Lindsey Opie, Major John Waughop & John Kennedy executors. Wit:

Joseph Adam, David Morgan. Codicil 4 Mar 1742/3. I doeth desire & impower my executors to carry on my lawsuit which I have already commenced agt Jesse Ball of Lancaster Co for a tr of land & a water grist mill formerly one Fox's & further that my sd executors shall act & do as they shall think most proper in that affair & desire that this codicill may be fulfilled & performed & stand in as much force & vertue as any pt/o my above written will. Wit: Joseph Adam, David Morgan. This will & codicill proved 8 Aug 1743 & admitted to record. Attest: James Fontaine clerk.

10 Sep 1743. Deed. Charles Betts Junr of St. Stephens Parish, Northumberland Co for 20 pd sold to William Haynie of same place a 25 a. parcel of land in Newmans Neck in the sd parish bounded by a small marsh belonging to Chingohan Cr, Richard Cornish, land which formerly belonged to Maximillion Haynie & William Haynie ... . Wit: Thos Dameron Junr, Silvester Welsh, Thos Harding, Richd Cornish. Ackn 12 7br 1743 by Charles Betts Junr & Vido Betts his wife she being privately examined by George Ball Junr gent relinquished her right of dower & the same is admitted to record. Attest: James Fontaine clerk.

10 Sep 1743. Bond. I Charles Betts Junr of Northumberland Co am firmly bound & indebted unto William Haynie of same place in the penal sum of 40 pd ... the condition of this obligation is such that if the afsd Charles Betts shall ... [illegible] ... to the tenor of a deed [see above] then this obligation to be void ... . Wit: Silvester Welsh, Thos Harding, Richd Cornish. Ackn 12 7br 1743 & admitted to record. Attest: James Fontaine clerk.

12 Sep ----. Deed. John Hack of St. Stephens Parish, Northumberland Co gent for 2,500 lbs of tobacco sold to Peter Presly of same place gent a 125 a. tr of land in the sd parish formerly the land of William Norman decd by pattent granted from the Proprietor's Office dated 7 Apr 1716 which sd land is now legally descended & come to William Norman who sold it to John Hack party to these presents adj William McNatt, Mr. Ingram, John Million, Wats's Cr by Norman's Landing & Quiff's? line ... . Wit: Jonathan Betts, Beverly Keeve, John Beekley. Ackn 12 7br & admitted to record. Attest: James Fontaine clerk.

In obedience to an order of court dated 8 Aug 1743 we John Lewis, Parish Garner & Wm Hughlet the appraisers appointed in the sd order being first sworn before Traves Colston justice met 13 Aug at the house of Rodham Kenner decd & did value & appraise the sd estate into current money & inventory of the same is as followeth: 1 large Bible, 1 desk, 1 watch, 4 small books, 2 pare money scales, 1 looking glass, 1 large table, 1 midling table, 20 flag chairs, 3 children's chairs, 1 old fiddle, 1 tea kettle, chafing dish, 1 large sugar box, 1 speaking trumpet, 1 gunn best, 1 old gunn, 1 case pistols, 5 china cups, 8 sausers, 2 large punch boules, 2 small punch boules, snuffers, glasses, earthen ware, twine, 1 small table & old chair, white cordage, 1 pare of scales & weights, 1 parsel table linnen, 1 old box, etc. Negroes: man named Peter, man named Lieutenant, man named Tom, man named Demeny, man named Ambrose, woman named Judy, woman named Hannah ... [illegible] ... child Ammy?, child Nan, Phillis & her child Simon, boy Ned, Kinark & her child James, boy Sollomon, girl Hannah, Great Rose & her child James, Winne, boy George, girl Dewcey, boy Natt, boy Sam, girl Bell, woman Mary & child Dick, woman Mattapony Kate, girl Silla, girl young Kate, woman young with child, woman Sarah, woman Lucy & Sharper & Benn, boy Joseph, boy Will, boy Adam, girl Siah, woman Kate, woman old Moll. [Not totaled] This inventory was exhibited 12 7br 1743 by Mrs. Susanna Colson, Lindsey Opie & John Kennedy executors & on their motion admitted to record. Attest: James Fontaine clerk.

In obedience to an order of court dated 11 Jul ---- granted to Thomas Taylor executor of the decd John Dameron for the appraisement of the decd's estate, we Thos Winter, Henry Miller & John Waddy the appraisers being first sworn have met & appraised the afsd estate in money. Negroes: Will, Dick, George, James, Robin, Hannah, Jude, Jim a boy, Mime a girl. Beds, bolsters, pillows, sheets, blankets, curtains & valins, bedsteads, hides, cords, 1 chest of drawers, 1 crosleged black wallnut table, 1 iron bound painted chest, 1 new chest, 1 old chest, 1 square pine table, 1 new spinning wheel, 1 old side saddle, 2 snaffle bridles, new mans saddle & howsing, 1 mill pad, 1 old chest, 1 old leather trunk, 1 gun, 1 old gun, 1 case bottles, 1 old safe, 8 flag chairs, 1 small leather trunk, 39 ½ lbs old pewter, 9 lbs new pewter, 2 pewter porringers, 1 pewter spoon, 2 pewter chamber pots, etc. [Not totaled] This inventory was exhibited 12 7br 1743 by Thomas Taylor executor & admitted to record. Attest: James Fontaine clerk.

In pursuance to an order of court dated 9 May 1743 we being appointed to appraise the estate of Peter Dawkins decd did meet & have appraised the same in money. 5 cows, 3 lambs, 1 heiffer, 1 bell & buckle, 1 old handsaw, cards & trowel, 4 flag chairs, 1 leather chair, 1 currying knife, 2 pare of kniting needles, 1 broad ax, persel of old iron, 1 meale sifter, a parcel of ware & rope, parsel of old puter, 1 chest, a table, box, 1 old wheel, a low bed head, 1 mare, feather bed & furniture, bedstead, linnen, 1 earthen pot, 2 sows, etc. Negroes: wench named Frank, girl named Nann, boy named Jack, boy named Anthony. This inventory was exhibited [?] by Winifield Wright adminr & admitted to record. Attest: James Fontaine clerk. [Auditors names illegible].

INDEX

ACKAMACK COUNTY, 134
ADAIR, Doctor, 77; James, 74, 82,
    108, 134, 139
ADAM, Joseph, 141
ADAMS, John, 130; Thomas, 118,
    135
AIRES, Samuel, 131, 132
ALDERSON, Richard, 27, 30
ALDRIDGE, Mathew, 12
ALEXANDER, John, 89, 90, 135;
    Robert, 40, 41, 88, 107
ALGOOD, John, 5; Mary, 5
ALLEN, Andrew, 134; Elizabeth, 134
ALLEN'S LAND, 124
ALLENS QUARTER, 79
ALLGOOD, John, 88, 90, 126
ALLIN, Elizabeth, 54
ALLISON, Thomas, 130
ALLISTON, Elizabeth, 64
ALRIDGE, Ann, 131; Clement, 131
ALVINSON, Elinor, 11
AMSTERDAM, 48
ANBERRY, Francis, 109
ANDERSON, Alexander, 26, 72,
    122; Elizabeth, 96, 127; John, 81,
    87, 96, 112; Mary, 112; Robert,
    40, 96, 101; Thomas, 86;
    William, 96
ANGEL, Robert, 74; Uriah, 89, 91
ANGELL, Robert, 35, 42, 45, 74, 89,
    90, 93, 98
ARMSTRONG, Adam, 62
ASHBURN, John, 97, 130; Peter, 118
ASHTON, James, 91
ATKINS, Elizabeth, 60; John, 60;
    William, 60
AUBERRY, Francis, 109
BACKER, John, 42
BADGER, Lecannah, 128; William,
    40

BAIR, George, 90
BAKER, John, 89, 90
BALE, John, 130
BALES, John, 33
BALEY, Timothy, 96
BALL, Colonel, 21; George, 7, 8, 11,
    15, 21, 22, 23, 25, 41, 59, 63, 73,
    78, 85, 90, 98, 105, 106, 115,
    116, 119, 132, 138, 141; James,
    11; Jesse, 136, 141; John, 41, 98;
    Joseph, 15; Mary, 136; Mr., 116;
    Spencer, 18, 55, 81, 84, 87, 102,
    112, 115, 116, 119; William, 21,
    73, 81, 84, 90, 106, 112, 120
BALLE, James, 64
BALLENGER, Francis, 74
BALLINGER, Francis, 74
BALTO, William, 130
BANE, Edmond, 75; Isaac, 108;
    John, 75
BARCROFT, Peter, 5
BARECROFT, Thomas, 31
BARNES, Edward, 14, 32, 90, 103
BARNET, Ann, 122; Nathaniel, 124
BARNETT, John, 94
BARNS, Edward, 130
BARRAT, Elizabeth, 135
BARRATT, Edmund, 131; Elizabeth,
    135; William, 131, 135
BARRET, George, 36, 56, 57; John,
    29; Nathaniel, 28; William, 22,
    29, 32, 43, 67, 73, 74, 77, 88, 89,
    108, 116, 131, 139
BARRETT, William, 2, 67, 128
BARROT, Elizabeth, 128; George,
    128; John, 128; William, 128
BASEY, Edmond, 88, 89; Elizabeth,
    31; Elizamond, 91; Isaac, 12, 28,
    31; John, 88; William, 28, 31

BASHFORD, Elizabeth, 59; Judith, 59
BASIE, Elizamond, 89; Jares, 66; Jesse, 88; John, 89; Josia, 89; Josias, 23, 91; William, 89, 90
BASY, George, 93
BASYE, Edmond, 28, 29, 66; Elizabeth, 29; Elizmond, 126; Gene, 29; Isaac, 28; Jene, 28; John, 29, 64, 102, 129, 132; Josias, 66; Judith, 29; William, 28, 29; Winefort, 29
BAYLEY, Thomas, 89
BEACHAM, Daniel, 133; Jacob, 133; John, 132, 133; Rebecka, 133
BEACHUM, Abraham, 94, 95, 99; Ann, 95; Daniel, 89, 90, 94, 95, 99, 101; Isaac, 94, 95; Joab, 95; John, 89, 90, 94; Mary, 95; Mary Magdaline, 95; Rebecca, 95; Rebecka, 101; William, 94, 95; Winifred, 95
BEARCRAFT, Peter, 95
BEARCROFT, John, 88, 89, 104, 110, 111; Peter, 66, 88, 89, 99, 100; Simon Peter, 76; Thomas, 12, 89
BEATLY, Francis, 88, 113
BEE, Sarah Keene, 53, 54
BEEKLEY, John, 141
BEGBEE, George, 135
BELFIELD, Mrs., 94
BELFIELD'S QUARTER, 94
BELL, Andrew, 72; Elizabeth, 64, 65; George, 43, 130; John, 65; Mary, 107
BENATT, Robert, 72
BEND, William, 29
BENET, Ann, 122
BENNET, John, 72
BENTLY, William, 11, 116
BERNARDS CREEK, 125

BERRY, George, 3, 4, 46, 50, 75, 77, 88, 90, 111; James, 130; John, 3, 36, 43, 67, 90, 106, 109, 130, 135; Mr., 130; Patience, 3, 49; Sarah, 25, 59, 83; Thomas, 2, 3, 8, 17, 23, 49, 90, 92, 115, 122, 127, 128; William, 13, 92, 128
BERRY'S CORNER, 24
BETTS, Bostin, 77; Charles, 40, 48, 50, 67, 68, 91, 112, 115, 119, 131, 132, 141; Jonathan, 66, 77, 88, 90, 93, 138, 141; Vido, 141; W., 10, 71, 131, 132; William, 25, 48, 80, 87, 88, 91, 110, 112, 119
BEUMER, James, 76
BEVERIDGE, Robert, 108
BEVERIGE, William, 106
BICKREN, William, 18
BIDDEFORD, 108
BIVEN, William, 84
BLACKEBY, James, 137
BLACKERBY, James, 9, 21, 131; William, 130
BLACKWELL, Samuel, 18, 25, 34, 36, 38, 42, 45, 58, 59, 60, 73, 76, 77, 78, 85, 88, 93, 101, 111, 115, 134; Samuell, 17, 27, 50
BLAINE, Archibald, 76
BLARCK, James, 23
BLEDVAN, John, 11
BLINCO, Susanna, 6
BLINKER, James, 89
BLUFORD, Junifred, 135
BLUNDALL, William, 123
BLUNDLE, John, 123
BOAZ, William, 1
BOCHANNAN, James, 108; Neale, 108
BOCKING, Thomas, 13
BOGER, Bennet, 21

BOGGES, Ann, 65; Barrnit, 72;
Bennet, 21, 72, 88, 89, 104, 127;
Hennery, 65; Henry, 127; John,
72, 127, 129; Mary, 65, 127, 129;
Robert, 127; Ruth, 127; Thomas,
72, 127
BOGGESS, Bennet, 49; Bennit, 7;
Mrs., 52
BOGGUS, Bennet, 21; John, 21
BOIANT, Robert, 88
BOICKETT, Banon, 61
BOIERT, Thomas, 72
BOLEY, Simon, 10
BONDLEY, Henry, 60
BONUM, Samuel, 39, 63, 122;
Samuell, 19; Thomas, 19, 63, 122
BOOK, John, 114
BOOR, John, 14
BOOTH, Adam, 31, 132; James, 31,
72, 89, 122; John, 31, 72;
Martha, 31; Richard, 31, 32, 69,
89, 90, 95, 108, 111; William, 31
BOOZ, William, 130
BOWEN, Edward, 24, 32, 89, 90;
John, 24, 32; William, 67
BOWEN'S LINE, 24
BOWINS CREEK, 49
BOWLEY, Sarah, 7; Simon, 8;
William, 8
BOWLY, Sarah, 7, 10; Sarah Ann, 7;
Simon, 8; William, 8, 89
BOWMAN, Richard, 61
BOYD, George, 79; John, 21, 22, 79,
80, 82, 99; Robert, 46, 80, 83,
138; Winifrid, 80, 99
BOYER, Andrew, 74; Edward, 83
BRADFORT'S LAND, 60
BRADLEY, Bradshaw, 121; James,
121
BRANSDELL, John, 88
BRANSDON, John, 56
BREARTONS CREEK, 57

BRENNAN, James, 5
BRENT, Elizabeth, 70, 109; William,
14
BRERETON'S NECK, 15
BRIDGE CREEK, 26
BRIDGE SWAMP, 30
BRIDGMAN, Thomas, 88, 90, 131,
132
BRIGHT, Thomas, 66
BROAD CREEK, 12, 110
BROADY, John, 81; Spry, 81
BROTH, Richard, 72
BROWN, Benjamin, 41; Corbett, 25;
Ellinor, 7; Footman, 6; Francis,
65, 72, 125, 130; George, 72, 89,
90, 114, 139; John, 41; Mandly,
61; Manly, 61; Thomas, 6, 7
BROWNTOWN, 37
BRYAN, Robert, 89
BUCK, George, 108
BUDGAR, William, 75
BULGAR, John, 72
BULL RUN, 29
BURBERRY, Malachi, 110
BURBER'S LINE, 84
BURBURY, Mallachy, 89
BUREL, Matthew, 27
BURGIS, Fany, 136
BURN, Grace, 59; John, 59; Thomas,
17, 59, 63, 78
BURNET, Thomas, 115
BURREL, Farned, 72; Matthew, 72
BURRELL, John, 72; Matthew, 28,
61
BURTAN, Gilbert, 91; John, 91;
Sarah, 91
BURTON, Gilbert, 91; John, 91;
Sarah, 91
BUSSELL, Benjamin, 124
BUSTLE, Benjamin, 8
BUTCHER, Thomas, 23
BUTLER, John, 46, 89, 90

CABBIN BRANCH, 118
CABIN NECK, 36
CALLEY, William, 7
CAMMET, Thomas, 130
CAMPBELL, Collin, 85, 88, 90;
    Mary, 85; Thomas, 72; William,
    78
CARLILE, John, 46
CARLYLE, John, 46
CARPENTER, Christopher, 43, 67;
    Philip, 127
CARR, Joseph, 78
CARTER, Colonel, 58; Dale, 110;
    Landon, 89; Robert, 3, 41, 73;
    Secretary, 44
CARTWRIGHT, Thomas, 13
CARY, Nicholas, 104
CASIBER, Joseph, 61
CEDAR COVE, 24
CHAMPION, Joshan, 43, 67; Joshen,
    67; Moses, 24, 32, 40, 42, 89, 90,
    109, 131, 132
CHAMPION'S LINE, 24
CHANDLER, Daniel, 25; John, 25
CHARLES COUNTY, MD, 58
CHATTIN, Joseph, 130
CHERRY POINT, 5, 6, 8, 9, 13, 35,
    86, 113, 127
CHERRY POINT GLEBE, 129
CHERRY POINT NECK, 28
CHERRY POINT ROAD, 8
CHICHAHAN CREEK, 49
CHICKCONE RIVER, 25
CHICKESTER, Richard, 53
CHILTON, Andrew, 41, 81, 88, 90,
    116; Benjamin, 42
CHINGOHAN CREEK, 141
CHRIST CHURCH PARISH, 15, 34,
    35, 110, 117
CHRISTALL, Henry, 134
CHRISTOPHER, George, 135, 136;
    John, 9, 10, 21, 30, 60, 83, 88,

89, 120, 124, 135, 136, 139;
    Susanna, 136
CHURCH SPRING SWAMP, 54
CHURCHILL, Emery, 45; Joseph,
    45; Rance, 84; Samuell, 12;
    Willoughby, 84, 88, 90
CHURCHWELL, Samuel, 110
CLAPSHOO'S OLD FIELD, 76
CLARK, Daniel, 12, 13, 50, 88;
    George, 72, 99; Isaac, 130;
    Robert, 1, 14, 17, 28, 32, 66, 72,
    81, 90, 95, 103, 107, 113, 129
CLARKE, Robert, 14, 60, 125
CLAUGHTON, John, 6, 11, 13, 58,
    69, 78, 86, 88, 90, 100, 101, 102;
    Pemberton, 69, 84, 88, 90, 107;
    Reinbevton, 38; Richard, 6, 11,
    12, 13, 14, 38, 58, 69, 72, 78, 84,
    86, 88, 90, 100, 101, 105
CLAUGHTONS CREEK, 2, 107
CLAYTON, Richard, 44
CLEMENT, Thomas, 136
CLONERE, Josias, 7
COACH ROAD, 3, 41
COAN MILL, 117, 123
COAN MILL SWAMP, 118
COAN RIVER, 5, 28, 117, 123, 135,
    139
COAN WAREHOUSE, 124
COANE, James, 90
COCKRIL, Richard, 90; Willoughby,
    119
COCKRILL, Presly, 112, 119; Sarah,
    119; Susanna, 112
COLE, Edmond, 72; John, 35, 46, 77,
    90
COLEMAN, John, 122; Mary, 137
COLES, Edward, 34, 35, 87, 88;
    John, 1, 3, 16, 34, 35, 40, 50, 62,
    67, 82
COLE'S ORPHANS, 10
COLSON, Susanna, 142

COLSTON, Mr., 61; Tavers, 130; Travers, 25, 122, 129; Traves, 19, 27, 32, 38, 61, 62, 71, 79, 89, 98, 100, 101, 102, 119, 125, 141
COLTON, John, 48
COMPTON, Thomas, 13
CONDOE, John, 119
CONDRA, John, 25
CONDRE, John, 62
CONNELY, John, 72
CONTANUEAN, Ann, 26; Peter, 25, 26
CONWAY, Ann, 98; Denis, 41, 89; Dennis, 21, 22, 80, 88; Edmond, 20, 67; Edwin, 15; George, 22, 54, 72, 73, 82, 86, 88, 89, 90, 98, 99, 104, 114, 118, 121, 130, 137; John, 27, 34, 35, 41, 88, 89, 103, 130; Peter, 29, 51
CONWAY'S OLD FIELD, 30
COOK, P., 42; Platt, 81
COOKE, William, 118
COOPER, George, 46
COPE, John, 100
COPEDGE, Charles, 136
COPIDGE, Charles, 84; John, 84
COPLE PARISH, 26, 57
COPPEDG, John, 50
COPPEDGE, Charles, 23, 35, 52, 65, 66, 76, 129; James, 76; John, 21, 35, 37, 52, 55, 65, 66, 138
COPPIDG, John, 68
COPPIDGE, Charles, 30, 44, 71, 78, 88; James, 71; John, 34, 44, 69, 88, 89; Moses, 71
COPRE, John, 126
CORBELL, John, 13, 50, 88, 91, 113; Spencer, 72, 89, 122
CORBETT, Clement, 5; John, 25, 56; Mary, 5
CORBILL'S LAND, 91
CORBIN, Spencer, 89

CORNISH, Richard, 88, 89, 91, 112, 131, 132, 141; William, 91
CORNWELL, Dennis, 99
COSTANS, Charles, 86; William, 86
COTRELL, Daniel, 45; Lucretia, 96; Thomas, 45
COTTEREL, Daniell, 130
COTTRELL, Daniel, 91; Lucretia, 96; Thomas, 96
COULTON, Doctor, 77; J., 16
COUNTY ROAD, 124
COUTA, Richard, 72
COUTNELL, George, 127
COX, John, 97
CRABB, John, 46
CRAFFORD, Winiford, 20
CRAIG, William, 5, 6
CRAL, John, 130
CRALLE, Hannah, 60; John, 7, 35, 36, 51, 55, 60, 69, 72, 88, 90, 113, 129; Mary, 60
CRANE, James, 89
CRAVEN, Betty, 65; Charles, 16, 65, 69; Francine, 65; Lucy, 65; Mary, 65; Rebecca, 65; Rebecka, 65, 69; Rhoda, 65
CROCKET, John, 72
CROW, James, 72
CRUIT, Richard, 88, 89
CRUMP, Adam, 61
CRUPPER, James, 84
CRUTE, Rebecka, 127
CUMBERLAND COUNTY, 20
CURRIE, David, 58
CURTICE, Ann, 120
CURTIS, Benjamin, 89; Elizabeth, 22, 42; George, 77, 119; John, 69, 72; Pitts, 89, 90, 139; Sarah, 13
DAMERON, Barther, 137; Bartholomew, 137; Charles, 88, 90, 116; Christopher, 18, 88, 90,

105, 134, 137; Elizabeth, 137;
John, 137, 142; Joseph, 137;
Onesiphorus, 116; Thomas, 4, 9,
10, 60, 61, 76, 88, 90, 97, 106,
119, 137, 141; William, 69, 88,
90, 116

DAMESON, Thomas, 76

DAMIRON, Christopher, 43, 47

DANKINS, William, 72

DANON, Mary, 41

DARE, William, 8

DASQUET, Mary, 65; William, 65

DAUGHITEY, James, 122

DAUGHITY, J.L., 131; James, 13,
23, 24, 25, 39, 49, 75, 77, 82, 88,
89, 91, 97, 113, 114, 115, 119,
123, 132; John, 23, 24, 88, 89

DAVENPORT, William, 9

DAVIS, Elizabeth, 28; James, 72, 89,
90; John, 17, 27, 28, 108; Robert,
5, 10, 45, 72, 90; Sarah, 44;
Thomas, 3, 41, 44, 88, 89;
William, 44

DAVISON, James, 74, 87, 98

DAWKINS, Benly, 89; George, 41,
72, 86, 88, 89; Penly, 88; Peter,
142; William, 88, 89

DAWSON, Anne, 86; Benjamin, 61;
Henry, 86, 89, 90; John, 86

DELANY, Cavan, 114

DEMACK, Mary, 26

DENERY, Richard, 90

DENNE, Richard, 12, 41

DENNEE, John, 41; Richard, 41

DENNY, John, 90; Richard, 89

DICKEY, Mrs., 136

DICKIN, John, 30

DINKARD, John, 97; Thomas, 97

DINNEE, John, 41; Richard, 41

DODSON, Bartholomew Richard, 20,
33; Charles, 130; Richard, 72

DOEDEN, Robert, 67

DOGED, Richard, 68

DOGGED, Richard, 68

DOGGET, John, 38, 69; Mary, 38;
William, 99

DOLLINGS, Sarah, 119

DOLLINS, John, 22, 72, 139; Sarah,
119

DONAWAY, Catherine, 97; John,
72, 104, 105, 114, 124, 139

DONLY, Sarah, 62

DOUGHERTY, John, 12

DOUGHITY, John, 23

DOWLY, William, 88

DOWNING, Charles, 48, 87;
Edward, 27, 77, 78; Frances, 77;
Francis, 27; Hannah, 87; John,
18, 49, 60, 77, 78, 87, 88, 90,
134; Samuel, 31, 40, 77, 81, 88,
101, 104, 110, 111, 118;
Samuell, 4, 17, 126; William, 1,
3, 16, 58, 59, 62, 81, 82, 104;
Winifrid, 81, 82, 104

DREDDON, Robert, 67

DRIDON, Robert, 43

DUCHER, John, 72

DUDLY, Richard, 92, 123; Winifrid,
123

DUGGINS, Daniel, 12; Daniell, 9

DUGINS, Daniel, 72

DUKE, George, 31

DULANY, Cavan, 36, 107; Mr., 61,
77, 121

DUNLOP, William, 6

DURSLEY, John, 65

DURUM PARISH, 58

DYER, Thomas, 136

EAST, William, 113

EATON, Richard, 118

ECONOMIC CHURCH, 61

EDMONDS, Elias, 4, 5, 90, 103, 129

EDMUNDS, Elias, 124; Mr., 124

EDWARD, Thomas, 17

EDWARDS, Elizabeth, 126; Grace, 35, 66; Grice, 31; Hannah, 49; Isaac, 31, 40, 88, 89; J., 125; John, 40, 66, 88, 89, 92, 96, 113; Mr., 109; T., 22, 118; Thomas, 15, 38, 72, 99, 108, 113, 117, 136, 140; William, 34, 74, 75, 110, 113

EDWARDS CREEK, 49

EIAS, Denis, 41

ELDRIDGE, Elizabeth, 80

ELIAS, Davis, 41

ELINORE, Jonas, 72

ELISTONE, Jervis, 50

ELLERTON, Gervace, 25

ELLESTON, Cuthbert, 114; Elizabeth, 114, 115

ELLET, William, 43, 67

ELLIS, William, 90

ELLISTONE, Cuthbert, 48; Elizabeth, 48; Jarvise, 48

ELLITT, William, 130

ELMORE, George, 72

ENGLAND, 38, 48, 108

ESKRIDGE, George, 26; Robert, 66

ESSEX COUNTY, 18, 55

EUSTACE, Ann, 36, 37, 43; Anne, 37; Captain, 14, 77, 105, 109; Elizabeth, 37; Hancock, 37, 38; Isaac, 37; J., 92; John, 37, 38, 43, 67, 121, 122; Sarah, 37; William, 8, 11, 19, 20, 23, 24, 31, 36, 37, 43, 108

EVANS, John, 72, 89

EVANS & DAVIS, 61

EVENS, Elizabeth, 28; Jane, 28; John, 28

EVERIT, Hannah, 2; Thomas, 1, 2

EVERITT, Thomas, 2, 105, 129

EVES, Frances, 114; Francis, 118; George, 114

EVINS, Jane, 27, 28; John, 17, 27, 28, 89

EVRITT, Rauleigh, 74; Rawleigh, 89; Rawligh, 90; Thomas, 89

EWELL, Bertrand, 11, 45, 62, 67

FAIRWEATHER, Patrick, 43, 67

FALLIN, Charles, 36, 61, 89, 90, 119; Fignor, 88, 89; Thomas, 110; William, 30, 33, 34, 40, 67, 68, 72, 75, 77, 78, 89, 90, 96, 108, 130

FALLING, William, 40, 68

FALMOUTH, 37

FANSBURY, Captain, 72

FANTLEROY, Ann, 79; Gress, 36; Griffin, 39, 63, 69, 72, 78, 79, 87, 90, 104, 113

FARIND, James, 38

FARNED, James, 7, 8, 14, 107, 111, 140

FARNID, James, 47

FARNIFOLD, John, 23

FAUNTLEROY, G., 125; Griffin, 7, 39, 88, 89, 122, 123, 129

FAYBE, William, 19

FEALDING, Ambrose, 59; Edwin, 59; John, 59; William, 59

FEOGING SWAMP, 1

FIELDING, Abraham, 89; Abrose, 64; Ambrose, 3, 44, 75, 92, 102, 129; Edward, 64; Edwin, 3, 41, 59, 73, 89, 119; Judith, 3, 64

FIELDING SWAMP, 96

FIELDINGS BRIDGE, 67

FIELDINGS MILL SWAMP, 73

FIGAN, John, 72

FIGNOR, Elizabeth, 11; James, 1, 77, 88; Joseph, 77; Mr., 119; William, 88

FIGNORS CREEK, 140

FINCH, Samson, 97

FLACK, John, 138

FLAKER, David, 76
FLAX POND COVE, 92
FLAXPON COVE, 3
FLETCHER, William, 89, 91
FLICKER, David, 71, 89, 90, 93
FLINT, Ann, 46; John, 36; Richard, 35; Thomas, 46
FLINTS MILL, 46
FLOWERS, Ransford, 45
FLOYD, Nathaniel, 43, 77
FLUCKER, David, 110
FLUKER, David, 110, 131, 139
FOGG, Israel, 1, 3; Leah, 1, 3; Sarah, 119
FOLSON, Benjamin, 56
FONTAINE, James, 1, 2, 3, 4, 5, 6, 7, 8, 9, 10, 11, 12, 13, 14, 15, 16, 17, 18, 19, 20, 21, 22, 23, 24, 25, 26, 27, 28, 29, 30, 31, 32, 33, 34, 35, 36, 38, 39, 40, 41, 42, 43, 44, 45, 46, 47, 48, 49, 50, 51, 52, 53, 54, 55, 56, 57, 58, 59, 60, 61, 62, 63, 64, 65, 66, 67, 68, 69, 70, 71, 72, 73, 74, 75, 76, 77, 78, 79, 80, 81, 82, 83, 84, 85, 86, 87, 88, 89, 90, 91, 92, 93, 94, 95, 96, 97, 98, 99, 100, 101, 102, 103, 104, 105, 106, 107, 108, 109, 110, 111, 112, 113, 114, 115, 116, 117, 118, 119, 120, 121, 122, 123, 124, 125, 126, 127, 128, 129, 130, 131, 132, 133, 134, 135, 136, 137, 138, 139, 140, 141, 142; Mrs., 119
FOORIED, James, 65
FOOTMAN, John, 57
FOSTER, Benjamin, 123; Jean, 123
FOUCT, William, 72
FOULSON, John, 86, 87; Mary, 86, 87; Thomas, 1, 3; William, 86
FOUSHEE, John, 1, 3, 14, 64, 68, 69, 71, 72, 74, 75, 79, 82, 83, 87, 91, 107, 108, 111, 113, 114, 115, 119, 123, 124, 125, 129, 130, 131, 132, 136, 139
FOWSHEE, John, 122
FOX'S GRIST MILL, 141
FRANCE, John, 72, 84
FRASIER, Thomas, 27
FRAZER, Thomas, 53
FRAZOR, Thomas, 52
FREDERICKSBURG, 37
FREEMAN, John, 20
FULLOR, Richard, 119
FURNAT, James, 62
GADDES, Ellenor, 62; James, 62
GAINES, 118, Daniel, 84, 88, 90, 112, 118; John, 81; Sarah, 118
GAINS, John, 7
GAMES, Vincent, 72
GANUR, John, 72
GARDNER, Edward, 91; William, 8, 90, 102
GARLINGTON, Christopher, 18, 43, 67, 109, 115; John, 59; Morris, 59; Samuel, 47, 59; Samuell, 17; William, 11, 59, 90, 91, 109
GARNER, Edward, 67, 89; Frances, 6; Hannah, 6; James, 73, 83, 89, 90, 139; John, 78; Joseph, 7, 78; Parich, 89; Paris, 129; Parish, 6, 39, 44, 49, 54, 55, 63, 72, 88, 107, 108, 110, 141; Rebecca, 1; Spelman, 6; Thomas, 78; Vincent, 73, 81, 83, 88, 104, 139; William, 14, 84, 88, 90, 100, 101, 107; Winiford, 139
GARRET, Edward, 43; William, 31
GASKIN, Isaac, 27; Leaseah, 27
GASKINS, Anna, 85; Anne, 85; Edwin, 85; Francis, 27, 29; Henry, 113; Isaac, 27; Jesse, 27; John, 85, 88, 89; Jonas, 47; Joseph, 88, 130; Josia, 90; Josias,

105, 137; Mary, 15, 19, 20, 43, 44, 110, 113; Samuel, 81, 90, 92, 100; Sarah, 85; Thomas, 15, 19, 20, 38, 43, 67, 85, 112

GASKINS' LINE, 24

GATER, Mary, 62

GENN, James, 13, 40, 41, 49, 99

GEORGE, Benjamin, 15

GERITED, Ann, 42

GIBBONS, Morris, 61, 69, 107

GIBONS, Morris, 118

GIBSON, George, 121, 130

GIL, Elles, 77

GILBERT, Mary, 91; Sarah, 91

GILBERTS CREEK, 46

GILL, Ellas, 33; Elles, 33, 34, 50, 66, 74, 75, 92, 96, 108, 110, 112, 137; Ellis, 3, 46, 88, 128, 134, 135; John, 33; Thomas, 3, 4, 10, 16, 23, 33, 46, 108, 122, 128; William, 8, 9, 12, 13, 33, 45, 61, 72, 90, 127; Winford, 13; Winiford, 12

GILLCHRIST, Archibald, 5

GILLSON, George, 130

GINN, James, 40, 41; Thomas, 88, 89

GLASGOW, 5, 61, 108

GLEBE LAND, 8

GLEBE LANE, 12

GLEEB LINE, 46

GLOCESTER COUNTY, 58

GOARD, Nan, 94

GOOCH, William, 17, 18

GOOD, Alexander, 20

GOODMAN, Jeane, 61

GORDON, James, 61, 67, 122; Robert, 43, 67

GORIDGE, Geffery, 36

GOUGE, Geffery, 36; John, 90

GOUNSTEED, Susan, 95

GOUNSTOUT, William, 139

GRAHAM, Anne, 79; John, 5, 6, 36, 58, 59, 61, 77, 79, 113, 130; Mr., 79

GRATINGTON, Christopher, 11

GREAT BRIDGE, 67

GREAT WICCOCOMOCCO PARISH, 3

GREAT WICCOCOMOCO RIVER, 9

GREAT WICCOMOCO PARISH, 1, 2

GREAT WICOCOMOCO, 21, 33

GREAT WICOCOMOCO PARISH, 28, 41, 63, 64, 79, 80

GREAT WICOCOMOCO RIVER, 34, 35, 40, 41, 44, 46, 60, 67, 68, 75, 95, 104, 105, 118

GREENSTREET, John, 53, 89; Peter, 53; William, 9, 10, 21, 88

GRIFFIN, Leroy, 73, 125, 130

GRIGS, James, 89

GRISESTEAD, William, 89

GRUGA, John, 90

HACK, John, 18, 42, 50, 62, 64, 88, 108, 110, 118, 141; Peter, 112; Spencer, 138

HACKNEY, William, 55

HADWELL, Richard, 34, 88

HAIL, Joseph, 44

HAILE, Joseph, 44; Peter, 13

HALL, Betty, 95; Hannah, 95; John, 72, 95, 100, 102; Rodham, 100; Thomas, 10, 14, 38, 72, 88, 90, 95, 100, 102

HAMBLETON, Samuel, 59

HAMILTON, Patrick, 57; Samuel, 90, 136; Samuell, 59

HAMMILTON PARISH, 40, 41

HAMMOND, Absolem, 59; George, 60; John, 122; William, 97, 100

HAMMONDS, Sarah, 46

HAMMONS, Absalom, 64

HAMMONTREE, Jonathan, 72
HANLY, John, 72
HANSON, Leonard, 109
HARCUM, Elizabeth, 13, 77;
   Thomas, 13; William, 130, 140
HARDEN, Charles, 74; Thomas, 74;
   William, 72
HARDIN, Charles, 74; Thomas, 49,
   73, 90; William, 89, 90
HARDING, Charles, 98; Judith, 42;
   Samuel, 43; Thomas, 42, 49, 74,
   76, 98, 115, 130, 141; William,
   44, 71, 86, 88, 101, 102, 110
HARK, Richard, 5, 6
HARNET, Gilbert, 72
HARPER, John, 110
HARREL, Gilbert, 90
HARRELL, Gilbert, 89
HARRIL, Gibbord, 95; Gilbert, 95
HARRISON, Ann, 116, 121; Daniel,
   58; George, 26, 89; John, 90;
   Samuel, 58; Thomas, 30, 138;
   William, 40
HARRY, John, 77
HART, John, 92
HARTGROVE, John, 71
HARTGROVES, John, 62
HARTIE, William, 60
HARTLEY, William, 133
HARTLY, Elizabeth, 27, 28; Jane,
   27; John, 17, 27, 28; Thomas, 61;
   William, 101
HARVEY, John, 24, 32, 42, 73, 88,
   90; Thomas, 49, 90, 91
HARVY, William, 23
HARWOOD, Judith, 55; Rose, 55;
   Sarah, 55; Thomas, 55, 71
HAWKINS, John, 104
HAWSON, Richard, 66
HAYDEN, Elizabeth, 96; William, 90
HAYDON, William, 90

HAYES, Peter, 40, 50, 61, 66, 74, 75,
   77, 88; Thomas, 77, 88, 90, 119
HAYLETT, Garret, 83
HAYNES, Ormsby, 7
HAYNEY, Ormsby, 38
HAYNIE, Benjamin, 90, 115;
   Bridgar, 4, 18, 54, 55, 60;
   Charles, 55; Frances, 77; Henry,
   88, 90; Hezekiah, 131; Jacob, 90;
   John, 18, 55, 131; Martha, 76,
   77; Mary, 18, 55; Maximillion,
   55, 141; Mrs., 78; Ormbie, 124;
   Ormsbe, 100; Ormsbea, 88;
   Ormsbee, 32, 90; Ormsby, 72,
   111, 125; Richard, 4, 114, 115;
   Sarah, 125; Spencer, 76; Stephen,
   88; Thomas, 42, 76; Uriah, 131,
   132; William, 5, 18, 45, 55, 77,
   78, 87, 91, 105, 112, 119, 141
HAZARD, John, 130
HEALE, Abner, 27
HEALES, Joseph, 3
HEATH, Ann, 98; Elizabeth, 106;
   Judith, 122; Samuel, 41, 98, 104,
   106; Thomas, 25; William, 25
HELMS, Samuel, 25
HENSON, Richard, 90
HERRING CREEK, 13, 55, 71, 91
HERRING POND, 91
HERST, John, 65
HERTER, Joseph, 67
HERVART, William, 5, 6
HESTER, Joseph, 43, 90, 132
HICKMAN, Thomas, 89
HIGGINS, Hannah, 118
HIGHTOWER, Thomas, 77
HILL, Britain, 89; Britan, 60;
   Elizabeth, 41; Enoch, 114, 118;
   Ezekiel, 9, 21, 97, 114; Hannah,
   59, 75, 93, 102; John, 29, 41, 64,
   86, 88, 89, 92, 93, 129, 132;

153

Mary, 86, 93; William, 12, 25,
110, 119
HILLMAN, Thomas, 40
HOBSON, Adcock, 99; Betty, 26;
Clarck, 27; Clark, 27, 29, 64;
John, 26; Judith, 26, 27, 29;
Mary Ann, 26; Sarah, 26; Sarah
Ann, 134; Thomas, 26, 91;
William, 3, 10, 25, 26, 29, 33, 97
HOBUN, Thomas, 57
HOLESON, Thomas, 57
HOLLAND, Daniel, 91
HOLT, Ann, 25; John, 92; John
Bearmonale, 91; William, 14
HOOD, Nicholas, 130
HOPKINS, Matthew, 77
HORNSBY, John, 46, 59, 66, 89, 90
HORSEHEAD SWAMP, 42
HOWEL, Ann, 75
HOWELL, Ann, 40
HOWELS CREEK, 34
HOWSON, Elizabeth, 38; Hannah,
67; Leonard, 17, 109; Richard,
31, 66, 88
HUDNAL, Sarah, 33
HUDNALL, Elizabeth, 40; John, 25,
40, 42, 56, 89, 90, 96, 101, 126;
Joseph, 25, 36, 40, 77, 95, 103;
Mr., 119; Nathaniel, 120;
Richard, 23, 74, 88, 106, 108,
130; Sarah, 95, 103; William, 56
HUDSON, Fielding, 58; Henry, 58;
Robert, 58, 90; Rodum, 58;
Thomas, 58
HUGHLET, Ephraim, 107; John, 107;
Mary, 9, 107, 123, 132; Mr., 51,
52; Thomas, 88, 89, 107;
William, 28, 31, 39, 52, 56, 66,
75, 76, 77, 88, 89, 107, 109, 123,
127, 129, 130, 131, 132, 135,
137, 141; Yaret, 119; Yarnet, 60;
Yarrat, 9, 10; Yarret, 21, 30, 61,

88, 89, 106, 114, 117, 118, 129,
130
HUGHLET'S LAND, 94
HUGHLETT, John, 62, 123; William,
9, 74, 107, 123, 134, 137; Yarrat,
136; Yarret, 115, 123
HULL, Richard, 15, 19, 20, 50, 52,
69, 85, 87, 90, 103, 106, 112,
120, 137
HUMPHRIS, George, 49, 90, 130,
135; John, 88, 90, 135; Joseph,
90, 124, 135; William, 135;
Winnefrid, 135
HUMPHRY, George, 23
HUMPHRYS, George, 88; John, 107;
William, 107
HUNT, Andrew, 72; Elizabeth, 15;
George, 21, 68, 87, 90, 130, 131;
Thomas, 87; William, 122, 138
HUNTER, Allen, 9, 72, 129; Ann, 46;
Findly, 46; John, 52; Joshan, 46;
Josken, 52; Robert, 46, 52
HURLEY, John, 14
HURST, Elizabeth, 24; Henry, 24,
32; John, 49, 89, 90; Thomas, 24,
31, 59, 90, 130, 135
HURT, Henry, 24; John, 43, 88;
Thomas, 24, 89
HURTS SPRING BRANCH, 24
HUST, John, 67
HUTSON, Robert, 11, 89
HYNES BRANCH, 57
INDIAN FIELD, 60
INGRAHAM, Abraham, 74
INGRAM, Abraham, 8; Charles, 24,
67, 68, 69, 94, 109; John, 24, 43,
67, 88, 90, 131, 137; Mr., 141;
Samuel, 54, 89, 90; Samuell, 8
IRONS, John, 21, 32, 69, 72
JACKSON, Richard, 7, 46, 121;
Samuel, 88
JACKSUN SWAMP, 115

JAMES, George, 138; John, 40, 88, 89, 95, 96; Joseph, 77; Joshan, 67; Joshua, 22, 42, 43, 54, 55, 67, 76, 89, 90, 93, 116, 130, 131, 138; Moses, 15, 54, 89, 90, 116; Parter, 83; Partin, 3, 59, 83; Thomas, 90, 138; William, 23, 35, 76, 89, 90, 105, 122
JENKINS, Ann, 15; Edwin, 15; John, 15; Jurakann, 15
JOHNSON, Archibald, 109
JOHNSTON, Archibald, 17, 28, 44, 69; Elizabeth, 6; George, 17; William, 10
JOICE, Abraham, 127
JONES, Ambrose, 11; Ann, 64, 65, 95; Barbra, 127; Captain, 77, 99; Charles, 105, 106, 109; Elizabeth, 41, 106; John, 1, 5, 7, 72, 88, 90, 115, 116; Judith, 102, 115, 116; Leeanna, 64, 65; Mary, 6; Mr., 122; Mrs., 115, 116; Owen, 88; Robert, 27, 31, 34, 43, 44, 46, 47, 51, 52, 55, 66, 67, 71, 83, 85, 88, 89, 90, 91, 99, 115; Swan, 115, 116; Thomas, 7, 89; William, 7, 64, 65, 89, 100, 108
JOYCE, Abraham, 127
KEEN, John, 66, 108; Ruth, 86; William, 39
KEENE, John, 26, 53, 54, 108, 137; Ruth, 53, 54
KEEVE, Beverley, 115; Beverly, 141
KELINS, Samuel, 18
KELLER, Henry, 88
KELLY, William, 88, 89
KENNADY, John, 89
KENNARD, Howson, 11
KENNEDAY, John, 69
KENNEDY, James, 124; John, 5, 9, 39, 49, 71, 72, 78, 84, 85, 90, 93,

105, 107, 108, 119, 140, 142; Mr., 119; Richard, 25
KENNER, Captain, 61, 127; Francis, 8; Hannah, 120, 133; Howson, 8, 17; Mathew, 2, 12; Matthew, 32, 38, 49, 54, 56, 58, 79, 87, 88, 89, 129; Richard, 15, 17, 45, 56, 57, 61, 77, 82, 89, 90, 92, 103, 117, 133, 140; Rodham, 2, 17, 27, 28, 60, 61, 72, 89, 93, 96, 99, 107, 108, 120, 130, 140, 141; Susanna, 140; Winder, 45, 56, 57, 58, 59, 62, 82, 89, 94, 103, 133, 135, 138
KENT, John, 14
KERTERSON, George, 77
KESTERSON, George, 40, 67, 89, 93, 108; William, 67
KILPATRICK, Ann, 13; Anne, 16; Elizabeth, 13; John, 13
KING, Ann, 32; John, 126, 129
KING CREEK, 99
KING GEORGE COUNTY, 64
KINGSAH, 113
KINNER, Susanna, 107
KNIGHT, Joseph, 89, 91
KNIGHTS CREEK, 58
KNOLL'S LAND, 26
KNOT, George, 99; William, 88
KUTZMAN, George, 88
LADFORD, John, 111
LAMFORD, William, 54
LAMKEN, Lewis, 105
LAMKIN, George, 44, 47, 71, 78, 88, 90; Hannah, 78, 121; James, 78, 105; Jane, 78, 85, 121; John, 78, 121; Lewis, 47, 89, 90, 107; Peter, 78, 121
LAMKINS, Jeane, 71
LAMPKIN, James, 129

LANCASTER, John, 1, 14, 77, 91, 123, 130; Joseph, 82, 88, 106, 113, 115, 131
LANCASTER COUNTY (Virginia), 2, 15, 21, 34, 35, 41, 63, 64, 67, 84, 92, 110, 117, 141
LANCE, Martha, 8; William, 8
LANE, Thomas, 74
LANKIN, George, 13
LANSDELL, Benjamin, 89; Richard, 89, 90
LARNKIN, George, 6
LATIMORE, David, 54
LATTIMER, Clement, 34, 35
LATTIMORE, David, 3, 31, 66, 88, 92, 104, 109, 116, 128, 130; William, 42, 47, 83, 88, 89, 106
LATTIMORE'S CORNER, 24
LAVENDER, William, 92
LAWRANCE, Edward, 2, 17
LAWRENCE, Edward, 2, 17, 28, 61, 69, 72, 123; Sarah, 2; Susanna, 27, 28
LAWSON, Anna, 80; Henry, 65
LAYLAND, John, 123
LEABAND, John, 38
LEACH, John, 91, 134
LEALAND, John, 88, 90; Joseph, 77
LEAZURE, Mary, 26
LEAZURE'S LAND, 26
LEDFORD, John, 132, 135; Mr., 130
LEE, Ann, 70; Charles, 65, 69, 70, 85, 109; Elizabeth, 70, 109; Hancock, 11; Henry, 57, 58; John, 37; Judith, 48, 51, 85; Major, 14; Margaret, 70; Richard, 11, 48, 51
LETHAM, John, 7
LEWIS, Corban, 56; Corben, 52; Corbin, 51, 52; Edward, 99; Elizabeth, 78; Griffin, 51, 52; Hannah, 86; J., 52; James, 88, 90, 96, 101, 118, 121; Jane, 85, 121; John, 1, 2, 6, 7, 12, 14, 27, 28, 36, 39, 45, 47, 51, 52, 54, 63, 66, 69, 71, 72, 78, 81, 84, 85, 89, 93, 107, 108, 123, 124, 127, 129, 137, 140, 141; Lewis ab Lewis, 47; Mary, 16, 108, 124; Peter, 72, 118; William, 52, 56, 90
LEWIS' LAND, 124
LEWIS' MILL, 76
LEWIS' ORDINARY, 124
LEY, Hugh, 5
LEZENBY, Thomas, 43, 67
LIME, 108
LIMEKILN CREEK, 123
LINDSAY, Robert, 72
LINKHORN, William, 21, 68, 88, 89
LINKORN, Jane, 68; William, 21, 68
LINTON, Anthony, 12, 58, 110
LITREEL, James, 99; John, 99
LITREIL, John, 94
LITTLE WICOCOMOCO, 74, 75
LITTLE WICOCOMOCO RIVER, 113, 115
LITTREL, John, 122
LITWELL, John, 99
LOCK, Richard, 37
LONDON, 13, 37, 108
LONG BRANCH, 76
LOVE, Abraham, 90; Amos, 90, 118
LOW, Abraham, 88, 139; James, 72; Martha, 139; Thomas, 72
LOWRY, Robert, 129
LUCAS, Samuel, 62
LUNENBURG PARISH, 131
LUNSFORD, Betty, 33; Charles, 55; Elizabeth, 74; John, 33, 34, 35, 74; Joseph, 88, 89; Martha, 35; Mary, 33; Moses, 35, 73, 74, 98; Richard, 33, 34, 43, 67; Samuel, 20, 33, 34; Sarah, 33; Sevenson, 67; Swanson, 31, 54, 74, 89, 90;

William, 33, 35, 43, 67, 88, 90,
116; Winefred, 55
LUTWIDGE, Thomas, 20
MCADAMS, Joseph, 123
MCCALL, Samuel, 61; William, 61
MCCARTY, Ann, 9, 21, 68;
Billington, 9, 21, 68; Captain, 55;
Daniel, 21, 55, 60
MCCAULL, William, 5; 6
MCCAVE, John, 130
MACCLANE, Thomas, 5
MCCLANE, Thomas, 5
MCGEE, William James, 96
MCGOO, William James, 55
MCGOUNE, James, 112
MACHEN, Thomas, 18, 55
MACK, James, 89; William, 88
MCKALL, William, 74
MCLEA, James, 77
MCNATT, William, 141
MAGOUNE, James, 114, 115;
Marriam, 114, 115
MAHAN, Thomas, 67
MAHANE, Dorothy, 42; Samuel, 42,
47, 69, 89, 90, 118, 134; Sarah,
42; Thomas, 42, 43, 73, 90, 134
MAHANES, Samuel, 112, 134;
Thomas, 134
MAHONE, Samuel, 42
MAIN BRANCH, 91
MAIN ROAD, 23, 42, 76, 139
MAIN SWAMP, 21, 41, 68, 73, 92,
131, 132
MAISE, John, 88
MAKAGUE, Thomas, 48
MANES, Samuel, 88; Thomas, 88
MANLY, Daniel, 72; Thomas, 72
MARON, Peter, 25
MARRINERS CREEK, 46, 50
MARROW'S OLD FIELD, 30
MARSH, Richard, 12
MARSHY SWAMP, 99

MARTIN, Elias, 15, 56, 77, 81
MARYLAND, 13, 20, 72, 122
MASEE, Edward, 139
MASH, Arthur, 41; James, 4, 88;
Sarah, 61; William, 4, 88
MASON, Edward, 27, 28, 49, 81, 83,
108, 123, 129, 139; Peter, 77,
140; Winifrid, 81
MASSEY, Hennery, 107; Henry, 2
MATTAPONY, 54, 110
MATTAPONY CREEK, 76
MATTAPONY RIVER, 35
MATTHEW, Anna, 13; John, 13;
Thomas, 13
MATTHEWS, Thomas, 39
MAYES, Elizabeth, 54; Henry, 23,
54, 86; John, 64, 111; Josias, 54
MAYS, Henry, 129
MEALEY, Ann, 46; Daniel, 46
MEALY, Ann, 46; Daniel, 46;
Patrick, 89, 90
MEATH, John, 80, 83, 84
MERATTICO CREEK, 21
MERCER, John, 37
METCALF, Ann, 6; Betty, 87;
Elizabeth, 6; Henry, 6; William,
79, 87, 113
METHAPONIA, 8, 9
MEW, John, 40, 75, 104
MICHELL, Robert, 77
MIDDLETON, Robert, 89, 90
MIFLANDIGEN, Thomas, 89
MILL ROAD, 30
MILL SWAMP, 64
MILLARD, Christopher, 36;
Elizabeth, 36; Jane, 8, 36, 38;
Jean, 8; Joseph, 8, 9, 36, 38;
Thomas, 8
MILLER, Christopher, 45; Elizabeth,
106; Henry, 90, 98, 102, 104,
106, 109, 122, 142; Hugh, 31,
36; Jane, 45, 69, 84; John, 61;

Joseph, 69; Peter, 130; Rachel,
  61, 127; Thomas, 127
MILLION, John, 141
MILLS, George, 20, 23, 33, 35, 43,
  44, 49, 54, 65, 67, 86, 88, 91, 98,
  128
MINOR, Nicholas, 94
MITCHELL, Robert, 64, 89, 91
MOON, James, 81, 83; Mary, 81;
  Sarah, 81, 83; Sarah Anne, 81
MOOR, Benjamin, 72; Case, 76;
  Judith, 55; William, 55
MOOREHEAD, Alexander, 8, 10
MOORHEAD, Alexander, 88, 90,
  105; Elec, 86; Mr., 119
MOREHEAD, Alexander, 10
MORGAN, David, 72, 141; Minthon,
  110
MORGIN, Minthon, 110
MORRICE, Thomas, 77
MORRIS, Bradshaw, 72
MORRISON, Phenly, 111
MORTON, Jóseph, 61
MOSES, Thomas, 30
MOTHER OLIVERS, 54
MOTHER OLLIVERS, 58
MOTLEY'S OLD FIELD, 3
MOTRAM, Captain, 118
MOTROM, John, 118
MOTT, Frances, 132; Moody, 88;
  Morely, 105; Morley, 69;
  Mosely, 88; Randolph, 43, 67,
  90, 91, 132
MUCKS, John, 26
MULATTO, Tom, 52
MULLIS, Stephen, 126
MURPHY, Ann, 82; Benjamin, 80;
  Daniel, 80, 83; Darby, 80; Darly,
  72; Elenor, 80; Mary, 64, 80;
  Merrimon, 80; William, 80, 81,
  83, 84

MYARS, Ann, 36; Elizabeth, 127;
  Thomas, 10, 36, 72, 121, 127
MYEARS, Thomas, 8, 9
NARROW NECK, 4
NASH, Richard, 46
NEAILL, Richard, 135
NEAL, Abner, 87, 88, 120;
  Christopher, 124; Daniel, 124;
  John, 125; Mathew, 131;
  Matthew, 124, 125; Peter, 124;
  Rodham, 124; Shapleigh, 130
NEALE, Abner, 1, 13, 30, 48, 88, 91,
  96, 103, 109, 111, 115, 120;
  Abraham, 10; Christopher, 4, 5,
  78; Hannah, 4, 5; John, 4, 5, 69;
  Lucanna, 64; Mr., 119; Prichard,
  64; Shapleigh, 57, 58, 59, 64, 82,
  88, 89
NEALES, Abner, 23, 52
NEALL, Abner, 29
NEELE, Christopher, 122
NEGRO, Abbe, 63; Abby, 93;
  Abigail, 43; Abil, 19; Abraham,
  34, 116, 135, 138; Adam, 79, 96,
  142; Ambrose, 142; Ammy, 142;
  Andrew, 33, 34; Anthony, 51, 70,
  142; Aron, 26, 29; Arthur, 43,
  125; Ax, 85; Banjo Harvy, 108;
  Barbell, 108; Beale, 87; Beck,
  106, 116; Belinda, 79, 129;
  Belindoe, 125; Bell, 142; Ben,
  34, 53, 70; Benedick, 138; Benn,
  43, 142; Bennedict, 116; Bess,
  34, 43, 103; Bett, 80, 82; Betty,
  33, 70, 79, 85; Billy, 20, 34; Bob,
  70, 108; Boson, 108; Bristol, 27;
  Bristow, 92; Caffey, 33; Cain,
  43; Cango, 52; Cate, 47, 70, 103;
  Cesar, 31, 32, 33, 34, 87;
  Charity, 29, 54, 86, 108; Charles,
  43, 63, 70, 80, 82, 85, 132;
  Charrity, 26; Congo, 51; Cromly,

130; Crownly, 125; Cuffy, 34, 103; Cupit, 125; Daniel, 20, 26, 29, 34, 99; Darby, 63, 93; Davie, 96; Davis, 34; Davy, 125; Demeny, 142; Derby, 19; Dewcey, 142; Diana, 79; Dick, 20, 31, 32, 33, 34, 38, 43, 44, 53, 64, 79, 87, 108, 112, 116, 132, 135, 138, 142; Dinah, 19, 34, 63, 85, 93, 125, 129; Doll, 33, 34, 53, 103, 108, 116, 135; Emanuel, 43; Fanny, 22; Frank, 43, 50, 51, 59, 63, 70, 94, 129, 135, 138, 142; Garet, 82; Geney, 33, 34; George, 14, 34, 43, 59, 63, 103, 108, 116, 125, 138, 142; Grace, 33, 59, 103, 112, 116; Gridger, 106; Hafford, 20; Hagar, 65; Hager, 126; Hagor, 69; Hannah, 34, 44, 53, 103, 108, 112, 115, 137, 142; Hanniball, 106; Harre, 63; Harry, 22, 53, 64, 65, 69, 70, 108, 118; Henry, 43; Humphry, 63; Isaac, 70, 82, 101, 116; Jack, 34, 51, 52, 80, 85, 94, 102, 103, 142; Jacob, 34, 52, 85, 87, 96, 102, 103, 116, 125, 138; Jade, 43; James, 16, 63, 69, 70, 79, 82, 108, 112, 115, 116, 124, 134, 140, 142; Jamie, 19, 87; Jamy, 22, 53, 59; Jane, 26, 29, 43, 44, 51, 112, 135, 138; Janey, 101; Jean, 112; Jeanne, 61; Jeffery, 59, 66; Jemmy, 50; Jenne, 34; Jenny, 50, 60, 87, 103, 125; Jeny, 33; Jesse, 34, 108; Jim, 142; Joan, 61; Joane, 60; Job, 34; Joe, 43, 50, 82, 115; John, 82; Joseph, 34, 134, 142; Joshua, 43; Juda, 108; Jude, 63, 82, 142; Judey, 135, 138; Judie, 87; Judith, 31, 70, 116, 134; Judy, 20, 27, 32, 33, 34, 43, 53, 59, 61, 70, 82, 85, 87, 112, 122, 137, 142; Jug, 95; Kate, 22, 70, 96, 108, 112, 142; Kelter, 53; Kent, 43; Kertshuch, 22; Kesler, 108; Killy, 134; Kinark, 142; Kit, 20; Knail, 65; Knor, 135; Lettis, 129; Letty, 20, 70, 80, 85, 87, 116, 138; Liddy, 85; Lieutenant, 142; Limus, 63; Lindsey, 112; London, 79; Lucey, 33; Lucia, 34; Lucy, 16, 20, 22, 31, 32, 34, 43, 64, 70, 87, 96, 102, 103, 116, 134, 135, 142; Lukee, 82; Lukey, 33, 34; Mack, 138; Mancor, 34; Maria, 125; Mark, 33, 34, 103, 116; Martha, 70; Mary, 142; Mattapony Kate, 142; Mime, 142; Moll, 34, 43, 53, 64, 70, 82, 108, 135, 142; Moses, 26, 34, 51, 85; Mous, 29; Murreah, 129; Nail, 69; Nan, 6, 14, 43, 50, 61, 63, 70, 93, 94, 103, 112, 125, 129, 138, 142; Nann, 19, 94, 142; Nanny, 106, 116, 129; Natt, 142; Ned, 33, 34, 65, 69, 116, 135, 138, 142; Nel, 70; Nell, 70, 79, 92, 94, 109; Oxford, 125; Pattie, 129; Patty, 125; Peg, 20, 26, 29, 136; Peter, 50, 64, 79, 82, 116, 138, 142; Philian, 108; Philip, 115; Phillis, 22, 68, 108, 142; Piliana, 53; Piper, 22; Pleasant, 34, 101; Poll, 50; Priscilla, 64; Prisilla, 96; Rachel, 53, 60; Rachell, 82; Ralph, 125; Richmond, 125; Robbin, 109; Robin, 34, 43, 47, 63, 70, 108, 112, 142; Rose, 34, 56, 63, 65, 69, 82, 103, 112, 116, 125, 129, 138, 142; Sain, 96; Sam, 14, 19, 34, 64, 65, 69, 70, 71, 79, 87, 102, 103, 105, 124,

142; Sambo, 76; Samson, 19; Samuell, 14; Sandle, 51; Sandy, 52; Sara, 108; Sarah, 33, 34, 43, 70, 80, 106, 112, 115, 116, 125, 138, 142; Sary, 38; Sener, 63; Sharper, 53, 108, 142; Siah, 142; Silla, 14, 80, 85, 142; Silvia, 82; Simon, 65, 69, 142; Sollomon, 142; Solomon, 20, 44, 51; Stephen, 51, 112; Suckey, 108; Suckie, 51; Suckils, 53; Sucky, 52; Sue, 34, 70, 82; Susanna, 112; Susannah, 125; Tad, 43; Thomas, 51; Toby, 80, 85; Tom, 1, 14, 20, 43, 50, 51, 63, 68, 70, 77, 80, 82, 85, 93, 94, 101, 106, 112, 116, 135, 138, 142; Toney, 64; Tony, 43, 70, 79, 82, 109; Tuck, 34; Vall, 52; Vilat, 52; Vilet, 1; Wenny, 87; Whinney, 135; Will, 1, 22, 29, 43, 51, 70, 80, 82, 85, 96, 109, 116, 138, 142; Wine, 19; Winie, 19; Winne, 142; Winney, 1, 138; Winny, 29, 116; Worcester, 125; York, 106

NELLAMS, Susannah, 135; William, 135

NELMES, William, 49

NELMS, Aron, 89, 104, 111; Joshua, 23, 119, 131; Moses, 118; Richard, 23, 104; Samuel, 29, 42, 45, 76, 81, 82, 88, 89, 90, 101, 104, 110, 111, 126, 130; Samuell, 40; William, 40, 49, 81, 88, 89, 90, 113, 131

NELSON, Joshua, 117; Richard, 18; Samuell, 49; William, 8

NEWMAN, William, 26

NEWMANS NECK, 141

NEWTON, Willoughby, 35, 36, 46, 88, 89

NEWTON'S LAND, 9

NICKENS, Elizabeth, 65

NICKLESON, John, 11

NOLAN, Samuel, 23

NOLES, Edward, 130

NORFOLK, 139

NORMAN, William, 12, 141

NORMAN'S LANDING, 141

NORTH BRITAIN, 5·

NORTH CAROLINA, 91

NORTH FARNHAM PARISH, 9, 21, 60

NORTHCUT, Richard, 107

NORTHERN, Edmund, 131; Elizabeth, 131

NORTHERN NECK, 26

NOTT, William, 90

NULEANS CREEK, 2

NULL, Joseph, 67

NULLS THICKET PLANTATION, 57

NUT, Joseph, 122

NUTT, Benjamin, 65; Farnifold, 23, 24, 89; John, 1, 2, 23, 88, 111, 139; Joseph, 43, 67, 89, 90, 111; Richard, 60, 88, 132; Sarah, 23, 24

OLD RODOMS LAND, 140

OLD SUTCHE'S LAND, 140

OLD SUTELL'S LAND, 140

OLDHAM, George, 25, 83, 88, 89, 104, 107, 130; James, 42; John, 53, 88, 89, 90, 104, 124; Moses, 88, 90, 107; Tarply, 88, 90

OLLIVER, Benjamin, 11

OPIE, Captain, 8; John, 8; Lindsay, 27, 71; Lindsey, 5, 21, 39, 47, 58, 61, 63, 69, 78, 84, 85, 89, 105, 108, 122, 127, 137, 140, 142; Lindsy, 28, 45, 120, 122, 124; Linsay, 72; Linsey, 51, 130

OPIES QUARTER, 96

ORLAND, David, 92
OSBOURN, Robert, 121
OVERWHARTON PARISH, 98
OWENS QUARTER, 79
PAINE, George, 64, 88, 130; John, 59, 113
PALFRY, Mary, 95, 104
PALMER, Alice, 30; Argail, 89; Benjamin, 23, 30; Isaac, 23, 89, 90; Robert, 30, 105; Thomas, 23, 89, 90
PARCELL, John, 40
PARKER, Mary, 94, 103, 104, 113; Tolson, 94; Widow, 113; William, 103, 110
PARROT, Lawrance, 15, 16; Lawrence, 46, 69, 88, 109, 139
PARROTE, Lawrence, 129
PARRY, Thomas, 33
PARSONS BRIDGE, 23
PART, Francis, 8
PARTRIDGE, Richard, 72, 97; Samuel, 72, 137
PARUTT, Laurence, 52
PATON, James, 20
PATTEN, James, 77
PATTRIDG, Samuel, 137
PAYN, John, 59
PAYNE, George, 63
PEARCE, Captain, 77; Margit, 42, 45; Richard, 42, 45
PEARCEY, Richard, 122
PEARL, Reverend Mr., 129
PEART, Francis, 125
PEASE, Richard, 25
PEN, James, 5
PENLY, Thomas, 126
PENNY, John, 49
PETERSON, Thomas, 12
PEW, James, 104, 126; Thomas, 4, 89, 105, 126

PHILIPS, Edward, 60; James, 40, 75, 77; Jane, 75; John, 40, 93
PICKERIN, George, 88
PICKRELL, George, 90
PIERCE, Richard, 42
PIGNUT RIDGE, 37
PINKARD, John, 80, 112; Thomas, 80
PITMAN, Benjamin, 126; Elizabeth, 126; Elizamond, 126; George, 126; Isaac, 126; John, 126; Sarah, 126, 129; Thomas, 64, 75, 90, 99, 126, 129
PITTMAN, Thomas, 102
PLATT, Peter, 57
PONDER, John, 62
POPE, John, 21, 41, 89; Joseph, 68, 80, 83, 88; Mary, 104; Mr., 122; Richard, 89, 90
PORTER, Edward, 29; John, 29, 84, 116; Samuel, 29; William, 16
POTOMAC RIVER, 120
POTOMACK RIVER, 13, 57
POTTS, Robert, 81
POWER, Catherine, 97; John, 97, 106; Joseph, 97, 106; Peter, 97
PRESLEY, Peter, 5, 23, 54, 75, 123
PRESLY, Colonel, 10, 15, 77, 91, 109, 119; Peter, 5, 40, 49, 55, 58, 71, 75, 91, 93, 112, 113, 123, 141
PRICE, David, 91, 92; Richard, 88
PRICHARD, Charles, 22, 42, 43; Margaret, 44; Margrit, 42; Swanson, 22, 34, 42, 44, 108, 138
PRIEST, Thomas, 12, 13
PRINCE WILLIAM COUNTY, 17, 29, 30, 37, 40, 41, 53, 64, 72, 73
PRINCE WILLIAM COURT, 73
PRITCHARD, Betty, 138; Charles, 54, 67, 88, 90; Judith, 138;

Margaret, 138; Simon, 122;
Swanson, 23, 35, 67
PRITCHETT, Charles, 130
PUGH, Elizabeth, 50
PURCELL, John, 40
PURSELL, Jane, 30; John, 30;
Tobias, 34
PURSLEY, John, 65, 69
QUELL, Matthew, 122
QUIFF'S LINE, 141
QUIL, Mr., 120
QUILL, Elizabeth, 71; Mathew, 2, 7,
13, 125; Matthew, 3, 14, 19, 20,
21, 23, 25, 26, 32, 38, 54, 61, 64,
71, 72, 79, 85, 86, 89, 90, 93,
100, 105, 119, 120, 124, 130;
Mr., 121, 126
RAGLEY, John, 72
RAMSEY, Andrew, 108
RANKINS, William, 34, 40
RANSDELL, Edward, 94
RAPPAHANNOCK, 64
RAPPAHANNOCK RIVER, 55
RAPPAHANNOCK ROAD, 8
REA, John, 88
READ, Judith, 7, 8; Richard, 130
REALY, Timothy, 77
REASON, Charles, 16; Thomas, 81
REAVES, Elizabeth, 50; John, 50
REDDIN, Robert, 131
REDDING, Robert, 131
REEDY BRANCH, 3, 44
REEVE, Beverley, 25, 27; John, 44
REEVES, Elizabeth, 46, 73; John, 46,
73, 89, 135; Richard, 73; Robert,
135
REEVES' LAND, 21
REITER, Joseph, 89
RESTERSON, John, 3, 4
RICE, Elizabeth, 118, 120; Enock, 9;
George, 118; John, 9, 10, 88, 89,
118; Judith, 118; Lictery, 118;

Richard, 89, 118, 120; Sarah,
118; William, 118
RICHARDSON, John, 30, 43, 67, 88,
90; Simon, 55
RICHMOND, 130
RICHMOND COUNTY, 9, 21, 58,
60, 73, 74, 75, 131
RIDER, Alexander, 40, 49; Alice, 22,
31; Elizabeth, 16; Hannah, 86;
John, 16, 17, 22, 31, 105; Sarah,
16; Winafred, 121; Wineford, 54;
Winifrid, 16, 86; Winnefred, 120
RIGENS, George, 7
RIGGINS, George, 72, 89, 90
RION, Edward, 88
ROBERTSON, Thomas, 107
ROBINSON, Benjamin, 123;
Frances, 123; Jesse, 33; John, 74,
91, 108, 123; Joseph, 74, 90, 91,
92, 123, 130; Thomas, 72
ROBISON, Edward, 80; John, 91;
Nicholas, 91
ROBUCK, George, 74; Robert, 50,
112; William, 50
ROCHE, John, 8
ROCK, Henry, 127; John, 127
RODHAM, Matthew, 5
ROGERS, Edward, 23, 25, 48, 50, 52,
88, 89, 91, 103, 105, 106, 137;
John, 78, 89, 90; Richard, 130
ROLLAND, Robert, 72
ROSE, John, 22, 68
ROUT, John, 72, 82, 86, 99, 118
ROUTT, John, 118, 124
ROWT, Richard, 88; Thomas, 88
ROYSTON, Jonathan, 91
RUST, George, 37
RUTTER, Mr., 132
RYAN, Edward, 101; Michael, 2, 5,
8, 9, 12, 13, 69; Mitchell, 72
RYON, Edward, 88
SADLER, Robert, 66

162

ST. MARYS COUNTY, MD, 9
ST. MARYS PARISH, 40, 41
ST. MARYS WHITE CHAPEL
PARISH, 63
ST. MARY'S WHITE CHAPPEL, 2
ST. MARYS WHITE CHAPPEL
PARISH, 64
ST. STEPHEN PARISH, 12, 31
ST. STEPHENS PARISH, 1, 2, 3; 4,
5, 6, 7, 8, 9, 10
SAINT STEPHENS PARISH, 15, 17
ST. STEPHENS PARISH, 21, 23, 24,
25, 26, 27, 28, 33, 34, 35, 40, 41,
42, 46, 49, 50, 53, 54, 55, 56, 57,
58, 60, 62, 67, 68, 74, 75, 76, 79,
80, 81, 86, 91, 92, 94, 95, 96, 97,
99, 104, 107, 108, 110, 111, 113,
114, 116, 117, 118, 120, 122,
123, 127, 131, 132, 133, 134,
135, 136, 139, 140, 141
SALBERRY, Thomas, 42
SAMFORD, John, 60; William, 60
SAMPSON, Ann, 80
SANDERS, Captain, 46; Edward, 34,
50
SAYLOR, James, 84
SCHOFIELD, Henry, 40
SCHREEVER, Bartholomew, 41, 98
SCHREEVERS MILL, 41, 98
SCHREVER, Bartholomew, 104
SCHREVERS MILL, , 104
SCHRIVER, Elizabeth, 15, 18, 19, 85
SCOTLAND, 74
SCOTLAND MILL CREEK, 41, 54,
104
SCOTLAND MILL SWAMP, 84
SCRNAVERS LAND, 84
SEABRE, Richard, 88
SEALE, Anthony, 30
SEARS, John, 58; William, 122
SEBAREES, James, 41
SEBREY, John, 129

SEEBRE, James, 89; Richard, 90
SEEBREE, Richard, 71
SELEVENT, Thomas, 136
SELF, Francis, 78, 107; James, 95,
132
SELFE, Stephen, 78
SHADOCK, John, 89, 90, 130
SHAPLEIGH, Captain, 77; Hannah,
64, 82, 114, 116, 117; John, 12,
13, 15, 19, 20, 23, 28, 33, 39, 45,
51, 53, 55, 56, 57, 64, 112, 138;
Philip, 116; Phillip, 57
SHAPLIGH, John, 39
SHARMAN, Nathaniel, 98
SHAUGHAN, James, 2
SHEARS, Abraham, 88, 90
SHELTON, Andrew, 100
SHERBOW LANE, 13
SHIRLY, Aejalon, 103; Archland, 95;
Betty, 95, 103; John, 95, 100;
Joseph, 100; Susanna, 95
SHORT, Benedict, 95; Elizabeth, 31;
Robert, 88, 89; Thomas, 2, 43,
67; William, 64, 89, 115, 132
SHORTT, Ann, 133; Benedict, 133
SHRAITKIL, James, 112
SHREVER, Elizabeth, 15
SHURLEY, Argaland, 3; Daniell, 3;
Elizabeth, 3; Grace, 3; John, 3,
14, 89; Joseph, 3; Richard, 3
SHURLEY'S LINE, 124
SHURLY, Daniel, 89; John, 66, 89
SIMONS, Frances, 127
SIMS, James, 90; Sarah, 82; Thomas,
82
SMALL HOPES, 53, 54
SMITH, Ann, 59, 66, 77; Augustine,
136; Baldwin Mathew, 125;
Baldwin Mathews, 136; Betty,
59; David, 78; Edwin, 44, 58, 59,
64, 73, 75, 89, 91, 102;
Elizabeth, 136; George, 3;

Hannah, 135, 137, 138; James, 88, 90; Jane, 136; Joan, 78; John, 23, 24, 45, 88, 89, 90, 119, 136; Judy, 59; Lazarus, 119; Mary, 22, 136; Mildred, 136; Philip, 88, 89, 116, 117, 125, 136; Phillip, 22, 51; Rebekah, 54; Richard, 1, 3, 16, 27, 33, 40, 45, 62, 67, 68, 77, 82, 87, 107, 111, 119; Samuel, 30, 31, 56, 59, 66, 105; Samuell, 59; Sarah, 7, 8, 59, 136; Susannah, 136; Thomas, 41, 109; William, 9, 90, 98; Winne, 59; Woldridge, 90; Wooldridge, 89, 140
SMYTH, Samuel, 50; Samuell, 57
SNELLING, Aquila, 59
SNOW, Samuel, 43, 67, 89, 105
SPAN, Grace, 1; John, 74
SPANN, Captain, 77, 103; Cuthbert, 1, 18, 71, 100; Grace, 1
SPRING BRANCH, 28
SPURLOCK, Daniell, 9
SQUIRES CREEK, 125
STAFFORD, Zachariah, 69
STAFFORD COUNTY, 13, 37, 98
STANDLY, William, 105
STANLEY, Thomas, 6
STANLY, Joseph, 78
STAUGHAN, James, 19
STEARS, Abraham, 131
STEGMAN, Thomas, 5
STEPTO, Elizabeth, 80; James, 89, 99; John, 69, 70, 80, 85; Lucy, 80; Thomas, 80; William, 80, 86
STEPTOE, William, 54
STEUART, William, 77
STEWART, William, 77
STONE, William, 62
STONEY BRANCH, 124
STOT, John, 88
STOTT, John, 2, 130

STRANGHAM, James, 5
STRANGHAN, Elizabeth, 122; Marget, 122
STRAUGHAN, David, 72, 108; Elizabeth, 63; James, 39, 47, 62, 63, 93, 110; Mr., 76; Thomas, 72, 76, 90; Winiford, 93
STUCKEY, Richard, 12
STURLOCK, Daniel, 129
SUGGET, Edgcomb, 58, 108; Edgcome, 54; Elizabeth, 53, 54, 58; John, 53, 54; Lucy, 53
SUGGETT, Edgcomb, 130
SUGGITT, Edgcomb, 137
SULLIVAN, Charles, 65; Cornelius, 112, 118; Dennis, 118; John, 111; Joseph, 112
SULLIVANT, Thomas, 136
SUMMERSET (Somerset) COUNTY, MD, 55, 138
SUTTER, John, 128
SUTTON, Ann, 98; Dorothy, 98; Elizabeth, 98; John, 88, 90, 98, 106; Lazarus, 43, 67, 89, 90; Mary, 98, 106; Richard, 98; Sarah Ann, 98; William, 46, 50, 98
SWANSON, Benjamin, 88, 90; Elizabeth, 67; John, 35, 86; Richard, 74
SWIFT, Elizabeth, 13, 16; John, 13, 16
SWILLIVANT, John, 130
SWORDS, John, 92
SYDNER, Eraphrodelris, 62
SYMONDS, Frances, 127
TAITE, Ann, 6, 25, 26, 32; Mr., 6, 61, 79; William, 6, 7, 25, 26, 32, 39, 44, 45, 51, 54, 55, 66, 79, 87, 88, 96, 108, 110, 113, 122, 125, 127, 129, 130, 140

TAPSCOTT, H., 67; Henry, 80, 86, 131
TAPTOR, James, 129
TARKELSON, Tarkle, 90
TARKLESON, Tarkle, 88, 100
TARLESON, Elizabeth, 97; Mary, 97; Sarah, 97; Tarkle, 97
TARPIT CREEK, 40, 75
TARPLEY, Francis, 130
TASKMENDERS CREEK, 15
TAYLER, Argail, 134; Mary, 76; Thomas, 76, 86; William, 44
TAYLOR, Aaron, 2, 3, 23, 31, 52; Argail, 16, 21, 22, 30, 36, 43, 44, 52, 67, 69, 78, 88, 99, 105, 119, 138, 139; Aron, 23, 30, 89, 91, 132; Benjamin, 130; Doctor, 108; Francis, 31; Jeremiah, 106; John, 2, 16, 21, 22, 35, 58, 78, 89, 91, 119; Lawrence, 34; Lazarus, 55; Mr., 116; Thomas, 8, 9, 12, 13, 66, 72, 99, 127, 137, 142; William, 5, 6, 7, 26, 52, 63, 72, 90, 104, 107, 110, 122, 136; Zacharia, 115; Zachary, 116
TEAGUE, William, 53
TEMPLE, Samuel, 89, 91
TENIONS, Thomas, 139
TEVISDALE, Samuell, 58
THOMAS, Ann, 91; Darcus, 64; Elizabeth, 15; Gilbert, 91; Hannah, 80; James, 78; John, 88, 90, 91, 92; Mary, 80; Moses, 80; Peter, 67; Richard, 22, 29, 48, 67, 72, 80, 86, 124; Robert, 80; William, 21, 43, 63, 64, 67, 80, 82, 83, 86, 88, 89, 99, 107, 124, 126, 131
THOMAS MILL, 96
THOMASES ISLAND, 92
THOMPSON, James, 88, 90, 123; Richard, 2, 89, 90, 107

THOMSON, Barbary, 140; Barberry, 137; James, 72, 136, 137; Jane, 137; Madcalf, 137; Richard, 39, 65, 69, 137
THORNTON, Doctor, 108
THRALKILL, James, 119
THRIFT, Elizabeth, 78; William, 131
THROP, Dority, 133; John, 77, 133; Robert, 77
TIERR, Jeane, 64
TILLERY, George, 104; John, 104; Maryann, 68
TILLEY, John, 9
TIMBERLAKE, Francis, 11, 90, 91, 118
TIMERLAKE, Francis, 11
TIMMENS, Thomas, 136
TOBEN, Thomas, 122
TOBIN, Michael, 23; Thomas, 93
TOBY, Thomas, 89
TOLLY, John, 67
TOLSON, Elizabeth, 16, 94; John, 15, 16, 81, 94; Mary, 16, 94, 100; William, 15, 16, 19; Winifride, 16
TOMSON, James, 12, 140; Richard, 2, 12, 28, 130
TOULSON, Benjamin, 15; Hannah, 87; John, 19; Mary, 19
TOWERS, Thomas, 136
TRUNILL, William, 58
TRUSEL, William, 90
TRUSSEL, William, 118
TRUSSELL, John, 12; Matthew, 12
TUBIN, Thomas, 72
TUBMAN, Edward, 61
TUCKER, John, 108; Richard, 108; Robert, 139
TULLOS, Elizabeth, 111; John, 89, 90, 111
TULLY, Elizabeth, 34; John, 34, 35, 69, 90

TUNSTAL, John, 112
TUNSTALL, John, 138
TURBERVILE, Major, 7
TURNER, Ann, 96; Edward, 1, 6, 7,
13, 78, 96; Edwin, 1; Elizabeth,
1; Febbe, 97, 102; Fielding, 1, 6,
7, 14, 78; George, 69, 72, 96;
Harry, 96; Henry, 96; John, 1, 6,
7, 96, 97, 99, 101, 102; Mary, 1;
Monaca, 96; Priscila, 7; William,
1
TURNSTAL, James, 5
VALANDENHAM, Thomas, 90
VALLANDIGAM, Thomas, 129
VANLANDENHAM, Elizabeth, 41,
42; Francis, 41, 90; George, 42;
Jane, 42; John, 42; Thomas, 41;
William, 90
VANLANDIGAN, Francis, 71, 88
VANLANDINGHAM, Elizabeth, 44;
Francis, 44; Michael, 5; Thomas,
72
VANLX, Robert, 133
VIRGINIA, 13, 17, 18, 20, 61, 71
VULCANS CREEK, 92
WADDEY, Benjamin, 47, 63; Jean,
122; Jemima, 122; John, 109
WADDINGTON'S LINE, 91
WADDY, Benjamin, 17, 23, 24, 43,
68, 69, 70, 93, 94, 106, 109;
James, 94, 109, 116; Jane, 94,
109; Jemima, 121; John, 90, 91,
102, 121, 122, 142; Mary, 121;
Mrs., 94; Thomas, 24
WADINGTON, Robert, 60
WADINTON, Robert, 33
WALKDEN, James, 16, 66;
Margaret, 39; Margret, 16
WALKER, Emanuel, 113; Richard,
41, 89; Samuel, 84
WALL, Lezure, 26

WALLER, Ephraim, 117; James, 111,
115, 132; Richard, 88
WALLICE, William, 43
WALLIS, Elenor, 134, 135; Ellinor,
39; Joseph, 38; William, 67
WARD, John, 136
WARRICK, Richard, 89
WARRICK'S LAND, 118
WARRINGTON, Ralph, 113, 116
WARWICK, George, 122
WASHINGTON PARISH, 133
WATS'S CREEK, 141
WATTS, John, 5, 11, 95; Mary, 97;
Thomas, 62
WAUGH, John, 3; Major, 130
WAUGHOP, John, 2, 25, 32, 39, 61,
69, 89, 108, 114, 120, 140
WAY, John, 140; Richard, 140
WAYMOUTH, 108
WAYS CREEK, 140
WEBB, Elizabeth, 25, 74; Giles, 66,
74, 75, 113, 115, 134; James, 4,
28, 58, 89, 91, 98; John, 25, 28,
43, 67, 68, 72, 88, 89, 97, 114,
115, 117, 122, 123; John Span,
74, 75; Joseph, 104; Marriam,
114; Mary, 4; Moses, 43, 67, 84,
89, 90, 130; Samuell, 4; Thomas,
23, 25, 55, 114, 115; William, 4,
25, 71, 88, 89, 90, 115; Winiford,
25
WEBSTER, Henry, 18; Thomas, 72
WELCH, Silvester, 45
WELDY, Joseph, 115
WELSH, Janey, 119; Matthew, 77;
Mr., 119; Silvester, 5, 10, 88, 90,
105, 112, 119, 141
WENSTED, Samuel, 38
WEST, John, 5, 9, 88, 90, 101, 107
WESTLY, William, 95
WESTMORELAND COUNTY, 26,
35, 46, 57, 94, 113, 119, 133

WESTMORELAND COUNTY
  COURT, 58
WHAY, Richard, 89
WHEDDON, John, 72
WHEELER, John, 58
WHEY, Richard, 88
WHITE, Griffin, 88, 90; Joseph, 91;
  Mary, 40, 67
WHITE CHAPPEL, 41
WHITEHAVEN, 20, 61
WHITEHEAD, Joseph, 74
WHITEING, Mary, 132
WIAT, Edward, 58
WIATT, Edward, 108, 137
WICCOCOMICO PARISH, 136
WICCOCOMON PARISH, 4
WICCOMICO PARISH, 11
WICCOMOCCO PARISH, 11
WICCOMOCO PARISH, 22
WICCOMOCO RIVER, 16
WICKER, Henry, 3
WICOCOMICO PARISH, 125, 127
WICOCOMO PARISH, 21
WICOCOMOCO, 110
WICOCOMOCO PARISH, 20, 24,
  32, 33, 35, 36, 41, 44, 49, 50, 54,
  58, 59, 65, 68, 71, 74, 86, 92, 98,
  104, 110, 117, 118, 128
WICOCOMOCO RIVER, 128, 140
WIDDOW WATTS, 42
WIGGINS, John, 72
WILDEY, Joseph, 17, 18; William,
  50
WILDY, Joseph, 45, 48, 88, 134;
  Motly, 87, 88, 96, 113; William,
  3, 4, 10, 29, 33, 38, 46, 88, 111,
  119; Winifred, 3; Winifrid, 108,
  112
WILKINS, Catherine, 97; Charles,
  71, 74, 89, 90, 97, 103; Jane, 97,
  107, 110, 113; Janey, 103; John,
97, 106; Sarah, 119; Thomas, 55;
  William, 113
WILLDY, Hannah, 108; Jane, 108;
  Joseph, 134; Leanna, 108; Sinah,
  108; William, 108
WILLIAMS, Absolom, 56, 110, 113;
  Aron, 43, 67, 88, 90; Benjamin,
  67; David, 11, 42, 95; George,
  25; Jane, 42, 134; Jean, 134;
  John, 25; Joseph, 77; Lazarus,
  77; Moses, 77, 88, 90; Owen, 72;
  Samuel, 42; Thomas, 42, 83, 134
WILLIAMSBURG, 52
WILSON, John, 72; Sarah, 72
WINDER, Elizabeth, 15, 57, 133
WINSTED, Samuel, 126
WINTER, Roger, 14, 25, 47, 63, 81,
  89, 90; Thomas, 14, 17, 18, 43,
  47, 51, 63, 69, 70, 85, 91, 102,
  105, 109, 142
WISESTEAD, Samuel, 88
WOMOUR, Thomas, 38
WOOD, John, 29, 31, 128
WOODWARD, Josia, 106
WOOLRIDGE, Massey, 136
WORMUM, Samuell, 9
WORNAM, Thomas, 16; Winfride,
  15; Winifride, 16
WORNHAM, Thomas, 123
WORNOM, Jean, 120, 126; Thomas,
  33, 50, 120, 125, 134
WORNUM, Thomas, 9, 48, 56, 77,
  88
WRAUGHAN, Thomas, 89
WRIGHT, Winifield, 40, 142
WRITONS NECK, 133
WROUT, Richard, 89; Thomas, 89
WYAT, Elenor, 53, 54; Elizabeth, 53;
  John, 53
WYATT, Edward, 53, 54; John, 53;
  William, 72
YARRAT, William, 10

YARRET, Adam, 9, 30, 118;
   William, 9
YATES, Richard, 90
YEOCOMICO, 46
YERBY, Thomas, 110

YOCOMOCO RIVER, 26, 110
YORK, 122, 136
YOUNG, Henry, 122; Mary, 6, 7
ZEISLTH, Matthew, 9

Heritage Books by Mary Marshall Brewer:

Abstracts of Administrations of Montgomery County, Pennsylvania, 1822–1850

Abstracts of Land Records of King George County, Virginia, 1752–1783

Abstracts of Land Records of Richmond County, Virginia, 1692–1704

Abstracts of the Wills of Montgomery County, Pennsylvania, 1824–1850

Early Union County, New Jersey Church Records, 1750–1800

Essex County, Virginia Land Records, 1752–1761

Essex County, Virginia Land Records 1761–1772

Essex County, Virginia Land Records 1772–1786

Kent County, Delaware Guardian Accounts: Aaron to Carty, 1752–1849

Kent County, Delaware Guardian Accounts: Caton to Edinfield, 1753–1849

Kent County, Delaware Guardian Accounts: Edmondson to Hopkins, 1744–1855

Kent County, Delaware Guardian Accounts: Houston to McBride, 1739–1856

Kent County, Delaware Guardian Accounts: McBride to Savin, 1739–1851

Kent County, Delaware Guardian Accounts: Savin to Truax, 1754–1852

Kent County, Delaware Guardian Accounts: Truitt to Young, 1755–1849

Kent County, Delaware Land Records, 1776–1783

Kent County, Delaware Land Records, 1782–1785

Kent County, Delaware Land Records, 1785–1789

Kent County, Delaware Land Records, 1788–1792

King George County, Virginia Court Orders, 1746–1751

King George County, Virginia Court Orders, 1751–1754

Land Records of Sussex County, Delaware, 1681–1725

Land Records of Sussex County, Delaware, 1753–1763

Land Records of Sussex County, Delaware, 1763–1769

Land Records of Sussex County, Delaware: Various Dates: 1693–1698, 1715–1717, 1782–1792, 1802–1805

Land Records of York County, Pennsylvania, Libers A and B, 1746–1764

Land Records of York County, Pennsylvania, Libers C and D, 1764–1771

Land Records of York County, Pennsylvania, Libers E and F, 1771–1775

Land Records of York County, Pennsylvania, Libers G and H, 1775–1793

New Castle County, Delaware Wills, 1800–1813

Northumberland County, Virginia: Deeds, Wills, Inventories, etc., 1737–1743

Northumberland County, Virginia: Deeds, Wills, Inventories, etc., 1743–1749

Probate Records of Kent County, Delaware, Volume 1: 1801–1812

Probate Records of Kent County, Delaware, Volume 2: 1812–1822

Probate Records of Kent County, Delaware, Volume 3: 1822–1833

Quaker Records of Cedar Creek Monthly Meeting: Virginia, 1739–1793

Spotsylvania County, Virginia Deed Books, 1722–1734

Spotsylvania County, Virginia Deed Books, 1734–1751

York County, Virginia Deeds, Orders, Wills, Etc., 1698–1700

York County, Virginia Deeds, Orders, Wills, Etc., 1700–1702

York County, Virginia Deeds, Orders, Wills, Etc., 1705–1706

York County, Virginia Deeds, Orders, Wills, Etc., 1714–1716

York County, Virginia Deeds, Orders, Wills, Etc., 1716–1718

York County, Virginia Deeds, Orders, Wills, Etc., 1718–1720

York County, Virginia Deeds, Orders, Wills, Etc., 1728–1732

York County, Virginia Land Records: 1694–1713

York County, Virginia Land Records:1713–1729

York County, Virginia Land Records: 1729–1763

York County, Virginia Land Records: 1763–1777

York County, Virginia Wills, Inventories and Court Orders, 1702–1704

York County, Virginia Wills, Inventories and Court Orders, 1732–1737

York County, Virginia Wills, Inventories and Court Orders, 1737–1740

York County, Virginia Wills, Inventories and Court Orders, 1740–1743

York County, Virginia Wills, Inventories and Court Orders, 1743–1746

York County, Virginia Wills, Inventories and Court Orders, 1745–1759

www.ingramcontent.com/pod-product-compliance
Lightning Source LLC
Chambersburg PA
CBHW070839300326
41935CB00038B/1153